RACE AND SENTENCING

RACE AND SENTENCING

A STUDY IN THE CROWN COURT

A Report for

THE COMMISSION FOR RACIAL EQUALITY

By

ROGER HOOD

in Collaboration with

GRAÇA CORDOVIL

Centre for Criminological Research
University of Oxford

CLARENDON PRESS · OXFORD
1992

Oxford University Press, Walton Street, Oxford OX2 6DP
Oxford New York Toronto
Delhi Bombay Calcutta Madras Karachi
Kuala Lumpur Singapore Hong Kong Tokyo
Nairobi Dar es Salaam Cape Town
Melbourne Auckland Madrid
and associated companies in
Berlin Ibadan

Oxford is a trade mark of Oxford University Press

Published in the United States
by Oxford University Press, New York

British Library Cataloguing in Publication Data
Data available

Library of Congress Cataloging in Publication Data
Hood, Roger G.
Race and sentencing: a study in the Crown Court: a report for
the Commission for Racial Equality / by Roger Hood in collaboration
with Graça Cordovil at the Centre for Criminological Research,
University of Oxford.
Includes bibliographical references.
1. Sentences (Criminal procedure)—Great Britain—Social aspects.
2. Race discrimination—Great Britain.   3. Race relations—Great
Britain.   4. Discrimination in criminal justice administration—
Great Britain.   I. Cordovil, Graça.   II. University of Oxford.
Centre for Criminological Research.   III. Title.
KD8406.H66 1992 345.41'0772—dc20 [344.105772] 92–2674
ISBN 0–19–825836–4 (cloth)
ISBN 0–19–825840–2 (paper)

Set by Hope Services (Abingdon) Ltd.
Printed in Great Britain by
Biddles Ltd
Guildford & King's Lynn

ACKNOWLEDGEMENTS

My thanks are first due to those officers of the Commission for Racial Equality who responded so enthusiastically to my interest in carrying out a study of the way in which ethnic minorities are dealt with by the criminal justice system. Navnit Dholakia did all in his power to ensure that the project got the financial support it needed and has been a constant source of advice and encouragement. Peter Laing and Cathie Lloyd have also been particularly helpful. Jean Coussins saw the importance of research on this subject and her support for it has been vital. I am most grateful to them all and, of course, to the Commissioners for making the necessary funds available to the Oxford Centre for Criminological Research.

None of this work would have been possible if I had not been able to gain access to the records necessary for such a study. Here I owe a special debt to Raymond Potter, Deputy Under-Secretary of State at the Lord Chancellor's Office, for overcoming several hurdles and ensuring the smooth co-operation of the Crown Courts. He has taken a close interest in the work throughout all its stages. Robin Holmes, the Circuit Administrator for the West Midlands and his staff, in particular Georgina Johnson, arranged for the help we received to extract the relevant documents from court files. This was done most expeditiously by Andrea Lloyd and George Paddock, to all of whom—many thanks.

Many months were spent abstracting information from the files stored at Birmingham, Wolverhampton, Coventry, Warwick, and Stafford Crown Courts. I would like to acknowledge the gracious way in which we were welcomed at each of these courts and considerable help given by the Chief Clerks and their staff, too many to mention all of them individually.

But thanks are due, in particular, to Peter Barton and Vivienne Hayes, Chief Clerks at Birmingham and Wolverhampton Crown Courts respectively, where the bulk of the fieldwork was carried out.

But court records were not the only ones studied. We would have been unable to trace the ethnic origin of prisoners without the assistance of the West Midlands' Police and the West Midlands' Probation Service. An enormous amount of help was given to us by the police. With the support of Mr. Geoffrey Dear, then the Chief Constable, and Mr. Roger Wardle, Assistant Chief Constable in charge of support services, we were given every assistance by Chief Superintendent David Stokes and his staff, in particular, Detective Sergeant Peter Bushell. And at every sub-divisional police station we visited we got the same immediate and vital assistance. The response from the Probation Service was no less helpful. Eric Morrell, the Chief Probation Officer, Keith Harris, the Race Relations Officer, John Hill, then the service's Research Officer, and Mike Madders, the computer services manager, all contributed to make it easy for us to obtain the information required. In addition, the Clerks at nearly all the Magistrates' Courts in the region took time to help me to check information in their records.

A statistical study of sentencing practices, based on records, does of course have certain limitations. While it can show correlations and connections, and can estimate aggregate effects, it ideally needs to be supplemented by interviews with those who make the decisions. Indeed, it was originally hoped that, after the data had been analysed, it would be possible to gain further insights which would help in interpreting the findings through interviews with judges. After having had the opportunity to discuss the research with a number of judges over lunch I sought to interview those who had dealt with a substantial number of cases in my sample. Three judges had said they would see me when, unfortunately, I was informed that the judges whom I had approached had been instructed by 'the powers that be' in the judiciary that my request should not be granted. At a later date, however, I was invited to discuss with several judges my preliminary unpublished summary of findings. This gave me an opportunity to clear up a number of misunderstandings and to correct some potentially misleading passages.

A study based on the collection of data from voluminous files requires a team of dedicated Research Assistants. I would like to pay tribute to all of them for their hard and dedicated work. Roy Heath was my full time helper for a year, and an excellent leader of the team which comprised: Amanda Jackson, Alan Kirby, Jill Mogford, David Dingley and Ruth Trenbirth. At the Centre for Criminological Research, Sylvia Littlejohns administered the grant most efficiently. The long and arduous job of entering the data on to the computer, begun by Susan Standiford, was completed with exemplary efficiency by Sarah Frost, who has continued to be of enormous help in the task of compiling such a vast amount of data and in preparing the graphics and text of the report.

I have been most fortunate to have had as my collaborator Graça Cordovil Espada, whose skills in computing and statistics have made it possible to examine the data from many different angles. I am much indebted to her for her dedication and many contributions. Both of us are very grateful for statistical advice received from Roy Carr-Hill, Clive Payne and Monica Walker. Thanks are due also to my colleague Ros Burnett for commenting most helpfully on several drafts of this report, to Marian Fitzgerald who, as might be expected, made many constructive suggestions, to Shlomo Shoham for several insightful points and to Diego Gambetta for some stimulating discussions. Andrew Ashworth made most helpful comments on the penultimate version. Oxford University Press deserve praise for the speed and efficiency with which they have produced this work.

CONTENTS

FOREWORD

An issue of concern shared by organisations campaigning on criminal justice and race issues and those responsible for administering the system has been the disproportionate number of Afro-Caribbeans appearing before the courts. That is also reflected in the prison population. Accusations that this is the result of racial discrimination have been met by assertions that there is no evidence to support this and that justice is colour-blind.

Broadly speaking, two explanations have been suggested for the over-representation of Afro-Caribbeans in prison. The first is that they are more likely to be guilty of criminal behaviour. The second is that they suffer discrimination at various stages of the criminal justice process—from the excessive attention given to them by the police to the heavier sentences passed on them by the judiciary. Both explanations are simplistic, and detailed research is needed on each stage of the process to find out exactly what is happening.

This important research so ably carried out for the Commission by Dr Roger Hood and his team at the Oxford University Centre for Criminological Research is confined to the point of sentencing in the Crown Courts. It shows that in some courts at least there are significant differences between the treatment of Afro-Caribbean and other offenders, and that these differences cannot always be accounted for by non-discriminatory factors. In these circumstances it is reasonable to infer that discrimination is taking place. There is also evidence of significant differences between courts in their treatment of Afro-Caribbean, as well as other, offenders.

I hope that the support given to Dr Hood in carrying out this work by the Lord Chancellor's Department and the Courts themselves will mean that the findings have real influence and be the basis for serious and constructive action to eliminate the bias which has been identified.

It is common ground that the authority of the judiciary rests upon confidence and respect from all sections of society. As far as ethnic minority communities are concerned, and Afro-Caribbeans in particular, there will rightly be an expectation of a positive response to this study, which, alongside the implementation of section 95 of the Criminal Justice Act 1991, should help to build that confidence.

If sentencing by the courts had been within the scope of the Race Relations Act the discrimination uncovered by Dr Hood's rigorous statistical analysis would have been unlawful. But regardless of this Courts have a clear obligation to ensure that they address any evidence of unfairness in their practice. Priority attention must be given to three conclusions:

- The practice of not making a 'discount' to the length of custodial sentences when a plea of not guilty has been entered should be thoroughly reviewed as it appears to operate in a way consistent with indirect discrimination;

- The circumstances in which pre-sentence reports (formerly known as Social Inquiry Reports) are not required should be urgently reviewed, as their absence indicates potential discrimination; and

- The courts need to introduce a system of ethnic monitoring of sentencing disposals, taking into account the principal variables established by the study together with regular reviews of the data and, where necessary, modifications to sentencing practices. This should be part of a wider policy of monitoring cases as they proceed through all stages of the criminal justice system.

This research is confined to sentencing in the Crown Courts and we are confident that it will lead to effective change at that stage of the criminal justice process. But it should also encourage further research into other stages of the system so that we can reach the fullest possible understanding of why it is that Afro-Caribbeans are so heavily over-represented in custody.

Sir Michael Day
Chair, Commission for Racial Equality

1

THE NEED FOR RESEARCH

1. Race and the Prison Population

Although the Race Relations Act 1976 expressly makes racial discrimination unlawful in the provision of goods, facilities or services to the public, the legislation does not apply to the sentencing of offenders by the Courts. This is because a judge enjoys a general immunity from suit when acting in his judicial capacity. It has also been held that officials who exercise powers to exclude or punish are not providing goods, facilities or services, and, as persons acting on behalf of the Crown, they are excluded from the provisions of the Act.[1] There have been calls for this restrictive interpretation to be removed by legislation[2] and there was pressure to include in the 1991 Criminal Justice Act a general clause obliging a court to act in a non-discriminatory manner.[3] For it is now widely accepted that a pre-requisite for racial equality is that agencies of law enforcement in making decisions, especially those which deprive citizens of their liberty, should act utterly impartially in respect of the racial origins, ethnic membership, colour or creed of the

[1] See, *Halsbury's Laws of England*, 4th edition (1989), vol. 1, paras 212–218: 'Persons exercising judicial functions in a court are exempt from civil liability whatsoever for anything done or said by them in their judicial capacity', at p 324. Also, John Gardner, 'Section 20 of the Race Relations Act 1976: "Facilities" and "Services"', *Modern Law Review*, (1987), Vol. 50, pp 345–353 and *Amin v Entry Clearance Officer, Bombay*, (1983), 2 A.C. 818, which is concerned with analogous problems in the Sex Discrimination Act 1975.

[2] Commission for Racial Equality, *Review of the Race Relations Act*, [1991], pp 20–21.

[3] See, *The Times*, 19 November and 6 December 1990, and *Parl. Debates* (Commons), Vol. 154, cols 318–337, 20 February 1991, and Vol. 193, col 950, 25 June 1991.

defendant.[4] This is not only to ensure justice for the accused but also to give ethnic minorities confidence that they will be afforded equal consideration and protection by legal institutions in general. This has been recently affirmed by the Judicial Studies Board, the body responsible for providing information and training to the judiciary:

It is axiomatic that no court should treat a defendant differently from any other simply because of his race or ethnic origin. Any court that exhibited prejudice against a defendant from an ethnic minority would be failing in its basic duty to treat all defendants before it equally.[5]

Indeed, the clause eventually introduced into the 1991 Act (S.95), although not explicitly making racial discrimination by judges unlawful, obliges the Secretary of State to publish information which will help persons engaged in any aspect of the criminal justice system in 'their duty to avoid discrimination against any persons on the grounds of race or sex or any other improper ground'.[6]

One of the major factors giving rise to the concern that jus-

---

[4] It is, of course, recognized that the concept of Race is a contentious one, but this study, in common with many others, has used the terms Race or Racial as a general way of describing the variable which distinguishes people by their skin colour. Where particular people, for example, those of Afro-Caribbean, Indo-Asian or European origin, are mentioned, the terms 'ethnic group' or ethnic minority (in the case of the former two categories) have been used to identify those who share common characteristics of ethnicity but are, in addition, identified by their colour. The terms, black, Asian and white are, as is common, used to classify people broadly into these ethnic groups. Where other authers have used a different terminology, such as 'West Indian', that has been left in its original form. For a very useful discussion of these problems of definition and their implications see Susan Smith, *The Politics of 'Race' and Residence* (1989), Chapter 1.

[5] *Judicial Studies Board Report for 1987–1991*, H.M.S.O. 1992, at p 18.

[6] Criminal Justice Act 1991, S.95 (1)(b). However, the Minister of State at the Home Office, Mr John Patten, had 'no doubt that any unfair discrimination by those working in the criminal justice system would be unlawful' and, for that reason, he said the Government saw 'no merit in a provision that puts a duty on sentencers and others not to discriminate. That would add nothing to the present legal position'. *Parl. Debates* (Commons), Vol. 154, col 337, 20 February 1991.

tice may not always be administered even-handedly as far as the race of the defendant is concerned has been the growing numbers of men and women of Afro-Caribbean origin serving sentences in the prisons and young offender institutions of England and Wales. When, a few years ago, the Home Office began to publish information identifying the ethnic origin of inmates it became tangibly apparent how great the over-representation of black people of West Indian, Guyanese and African[7] origin was in relation to their number in the population as a whole. And it also became clear, as successive annual statistics appeared, that this disparate ratio was growing ever larger.[8]

By mid-1989, just as the field-work for this research was getting under way, there were 3,672 males and 276 females of West Indian, Guyanese or African origin undergoing a sentence of imprisonment or detention in a young offender institution. In the case of males, this was equivalent to ten per cent of the sentenced prison population, between eight and nine times their proportion in the population at large. In women's prisons black people are even more evident, comprising nearly a quarter of all those serving a sentence, although it has recently been recognized that a substantial proportion of them are not British citizens but women from Africa and the West Indies who are serving long prison sentences for having imported drugs, apparently often in the role of a so called 'mule'.[9]

---

[7] The category used in the annual *Prison Statistics*.

[8] See, Home Office, *The Ethnic Origin of Prisoners: The Prison Population on June 30 1985 and Persons Received July 1984–March 1985*, Home Office Statistical Bulletin 17/86 (1986). The figures are now published annually in *Prison Statistics: England and Wales*, HMSO.

[9] See, *Prison Statistics England and Wales 1989*, Cm 1212 (1990) H.M.S.O. Ethnic minority prisoners as a whole comprised 15% of the male and 26% of the female sentenced prison population (i.e. excluding remand prisoners). Also, Commission for Racial Equality, *Response to the Home Office White Paper: Crime Justice, and Protecting the Public (1989)* at p 3.

A recent study, based on a 25 per cent sample of the female prison population showed that when the women who were ordinarily resident overseas were excluded, the

It is, of course, not surprising that the number and proportion of prisoners of Afro-Caribbean or Asian background should have increased in recent years. It is one of the best established criminological generalisations that the children of immigrants suffer a degree of culture conflict between the values of their parents and that of the host community which is associated with higher rates of crime than among the first generation of settlers.[10] Furthermore, when this is exacerbated by social disadvantages in education, employment, and housing, and by the slackening of familial networks of control, some delinquent responses to lack of conventional opportunities to achieve economic benefits and status are to be expected. It is obviously also necessary to take into account the age composition of males of West Indian or Guyanese origin, 33 per cent of whom were, in 1990, in the age-range 16–29 compared with 22 per cent of the total population,[11] for it is, of course, well known that the likelihood of conviction is at its peak amongst those in this age group. Yet age, in itself, cannot solely provide an explanation for their over-representation in penal institutions because 83 per cent of male Afro-Caribbean prisoners and 80 per cent of the females were adults. Also, the proportion of Afro-Caribbeans was higher in adult prisons than in young offender institutions.[12]

There is certainly evidence to show that black people are over-represented amongst those arrested for indictable offences, in a ratio not dissimilar to their ratio in the prison population,

proportion of black women fell to 12.6 per cent. See, A. Maden, M. Swinton and J. Gunn, 'The Ethnic Origin of Women Serving a Prison Sentence', *Brit J Criminol*, Vol. 32, (1992), pp 218–221.

[10] For the standard American works see, Thorsten Sellin, *Culture Conflict and Crime*, (1938), and Marvin E. Wolfgang and Bernard Cohen, *Crime and Race: Conceptions and Misconceptions* (1970). For an early British study, A. E. Bottoms 'Delinquency Among Immigrants', *Race*, (1967), Vol. 8, pp 357–83. See also R. D. Francis, *Migrant Crime in Australia* (1981).

[11] See, *Social Trends*, Vol 20, 1990, p 25 H.M.S.O.

[12] *Prison Statistics 1989*, op. cit.

and that they are disproportionately arrested for some crimes which are more prone to receive a prison sentence, in particular street robberies and offences connected with the sale of cannabis. On the other hand, there is also evidence that this greater probability of being arrested is, to some degree, the result of the police practice of much more frequently stopping and searching black persons.[13] And the suspicion has grown that this influences the way that their cases are dealt with as they progress through the subsequent stages of the criminal justice process.

It is important from the outset to recognize that, in contrast to Afro-Caribbeans, people of Indo-Asian background are only slightly over-represented in the prison population at present, although their number and proportion is also gradually increasing as the age structure of the Asian community begins to include a far higher proportion of young adults in the 'dangerous age' for offending.[14] Nevertheless, the fact that Asians are not so far greatly over-represented in the prisons cannot, by itself, dispel all need for inquiry into whether they suffer any discrimination from the criminal justice system.

[13] Wesley Skogan, *The Police and Public in England and Wales: A British Crime Survey Report*, Home Office Research Study, No. 117, 1990 pp 26–37. See also, David J. Smith and Jeremy Gray, *Police and People in London*, The Policy Studies Institute Report, 1985, pp 20–108 and 278. This study also found that the probability of being arrested was considerably higher for West Indians aged 15–24 than for whites in the same age range, but that there were no differences in the rate of arrests for blacks and whites in London in the age group 25–44, at p 112. For a very useful review of the statistical data and the pitfalls in drawing inferences from it, see Monica A Walker, 'Interpreting Race and Crime Statistics', *J Royal Statistical Society Series A (General)*, (1982), Vol 150 Part 1, pp 39–56.

[14] On 30 June 1989 there were 1,051 males of Indian, Pakistani or Bangladeshi origin serving a sentence of imprisonment or detention in a young offenders' institution, comprising 2.9% of the prison population compared with 2% of the general population. There were, however, only 22 women of Indo-Asian origin. *Prison Statistics 1989*, op. cit.

In 1990, 27% of the population of Indian origin, 25% of Pakistani origin and 21% of Bangladeshi origin were in the age range 16–29, but 31% of Indians, 43% of Pakistanis and 50% of Bangladeshis were aged 0–15, compared with 20% of the white population. *Social Trends*, Vol 20, 1990, p 25, HMSO.

However suggestive they may be, the raw data relating to the proportion of an ethnic group, or any other social category, among the prison population cannot provide proof, one way or another, on the question of different treatment, let alone of discrimination. Indeed, it is especially dangerous to draw inferences from the characteristics of those who are in prison, about the proportion of people in the population at large who are sentenced to imprisonment amongst all those who have these characteristics. Yet it is often done. The fact, for example, that a higher proportion of women than men in prison have no previous convictions does not mean, as some appear to have assumed, that women with no previous convictions are more readily sentenced to custody than are men with no previous convictions (for a further discussion of this inferential fallacy see p 176 below).[15] To find facts consistent with discrimination having occurred it would have to be shown that, when all other variables that are legally relevant to a decision are held constant, a significantly higher proportion of ethnic minority persons receive a custodial sentence and/or a longer sentence, or a different pattern of alternative community based sentences. This may, as already mentioned, be the result of a cumulation of small 'race effects' at different stages of the criminal process.

Even so, there is obviously a necessity to try to discover whether different decisions made at the point at which the sentence is imposed have contributed to the ethnic imbalance of the prison population. To establish whether this is or is not the case it would be necessary to study sentences handed down in the Crown Court, because over nine out of ten of those serving a sentence in a prison or a young offender institution at any one time have been sentenced at these courts rather than at the

---

[15] For example, the fact that the number of black people in prison is, per 100,000 population, at least 8 times that of white people, has sometimes been reported as if it implies that 'in the general population black people are eight times as likely to be imprisoned as their white counterparts' See, *The Times*, April 2 1990.

Magistrates' Courts.[16] The key issue would be whether Afro-Caribbean and Asian people convicted of crime are sentenced according to the same criteria as are whites and whether these criteria are given equal consideration so that those who have committed similar offences and have other similar relevant legal characteristics and criminal histories receive the same range of sentences and are committed in equivalent proportions to custody and for similar lengths of time. The purpose of this study was to investigate whether this was so. But before describing how it was carried out, it is necessary to establish why the inquiry was considered necessary, given that this is not the first attempt to investigate this issue.

2. Discrimination by the Courts: Facts and Beliefs

There is no doubt that a number of politicians, pressure groups and journalists have assumed that discrimination is so rife that people from ethnic minorities are much more severely dealt with at all stages of the criminal justice process, including the sentences they receive at court. For example, an article in *The Guardian*, published while this inquiry was under way, announced that:

Taking comparable circumstances and backgrounds, black offenders are more than twice as likely to be sent to prison as whites convicted of the same offence.[17]

The Society of Black Lawyers, which has campaigned vigorously on the issue, has insisted that 'each and every black

[16] In 1990, 68 per cent of those received into prison service establishments under sentence (excluding in default of payment of a fine) had been sentenced by a Crown Court. They made up a larger proportion of the daily average population than those sentenced by Magistrates' Courts because, of course, the sentences they received were, in aggregate, considerably longer.

[17] David Rose, 'Acts but no real faith', *The Guardian*, 13 June 1990. The same figure was cited in an article by Kate Muir 'Black look at white justice', *The Times*, 15 May 1992.

defendant was more likely to be given a custodial sentence, for longer and with fewer previous convictions than if they were white.'[18]

Various conference reports and working parties have also reached the conclusion that the evidence available shows that:

black people seem to be sent to prison more readily, and for longer, than others, and to be at a disadvantage in other ways—more likely to be remanded in custody, less likely to have S.I.R.s [Social Inquiry Reports] done on them, when they appear before the court.[19]

They are also said to have a lesser chance of receiving a 'community based provision', such as probation or a community service order, and to enter prison at an earlier stage in their criminal careers: a conclusion inferred from the fact that black offenders in custody have, on average, fewer previous convictions than do whites who have been committed for the same broad band of offences.[20]

Yet, more dispassionate academic analysis has viewed such conclusions as premature, a 'distillation of popular professional wisdom that draws selectively on research' rather than confirmation of reliable findings of universal validity.[21] Indeed, Professor Robert Reiner, in a careful review of the 'scanty' evidence so far available from the studies of sentences meted out by the courts came to the conclusion that:

---

[18] See, 'Black People in Custody' *Justice of the Peace*, Vol 153, 26 August 1989, p 549.

[19] Graham Smith, Presentation to NACRO Conference on *Race and Criminal Justice: A Way Forward,* 3 March 1989, *Report,* p. 10. See also the speech by Mr Roy Hattersley, the Shadow Home Secretary, when the issue of racial discrimination was debated during the passage of the Criminal Justice Bill 1991: 'I have no doubt that the operation of the courts is such that black and Asian people are more likely to receive a custodial sentence than their white counterparts convicted of equivalent or identical crimes'. *Parl. Debates* (Commons), Vol 186 at col 327, 20 February 1991.

[20] See Michael Day, 'Naught for our Comfort', *Black People and the Criminal Justice System,* Howard League, May 1989 pp 5–8.

[21] Robert Waters, 'Race and the Criminal Justice Process', *Brit. J. Criminol.* (1988), vol 28, pp 82–94 at p 84

for all the variations in the results, [none of them] establishes a finding of discrimination against blacks at that stage of the criminal justice process.[22]

On the other hand, there undoubtedly appears to be an impression among black people that they do indeed receive disadvantageous treatment at the hands of the courts as well as the police.[23] The Report of the Policy Studies Institute, for example, found a much higher proportion of West Indians believed that the police in London did not treat ethnic minorities fairly.[24] And, in recent years, the proportion of both blacks and whites who think that the police discriminate against black and Asian people has risen sharply. This is true also of their perception of the courts. In 1982, 38 per cent of black people questioned thought that blacks were treated by the courts worse than whites, but, as a recent NOP poll for *The Independent on Sunday* (7 July 1991) revealed, this has now risen to 57 per cent of black people. Over the same period the proportion of whites who share this belief had trebled from 8 to 24 per cent. In comparison, only 19 per cent of Asians expressed such a view.[25] And while Eric Smellie, the author of

---

[22] Robert Reiner, 'Race and Criminal Justice', *New Community* 16, 1989, pp 5–21 at p 15. And for a useful review of American research on the subject, which has also produced varying findings 'without arriving at any definitive answers. . . . Overall, however, research has consistently unearthed subtle, if not overt, bias', see Marjorie S. Katz,'The Changing forms of Racial/Ethnic Biases in Sentencing', *J Research in Crime and Delinq*, Vol. 24, (1987), pp 69–92 at p 86. It is revealing that one of the fullest reviews of the American literature—a Note on 'Race and the Criminal Process' in the *Harvard Law Review* only devoted 15 of its 165 pages to the subject of Race and Non-Capital Sentencing and only two of these discussed empirical studies, concluding that they had yielded 'mixed results', Vol. 101 (1988) pp 1472–1641 at pp 1636–31.

[23] See, *Racial Justice and Criminal Justice: A Submission to the Royal Commission on Criminal Justice*, Runnymede Trust, (1992), pp 20–23.

[24] Smith and Gray, op. cit., pp 222–237. Also, about half the encounters with the police by West Indian men were regarded in a negative light, compared with 18% of the white men. However, of those actually arrested, a higher proportion of West Indians considered that they had been treated fairly. The authors suggest that this was because they already had low expectations. See pp 281 and 285.

[25] It should be noted that the courts were not thought to be so discriminatory as

a small-scale and rather impressionistic survey for NACRO of *Black People's Experiences of Criminal Justice,* found 'no clear evidence that colour was a factor in the sentences people got', he added that:

the perception, nonetheless, persists in the minds of some [29%] of the black group [which was made up of both Afro-Caribbeans and Asians] that if they were white they might have been treated differently by the courts.[26]

There is then, it seems, a disjunction between what people perceive to be discrimination and the findings of the research so far conducted. Thus, despite noting that 'research has so far failed to produce methodologically sound evidence of either the existence or the extent of race influence on sentencing in the courts', Barbara Hudson nevertheless held that:

it is implausible at a common-sense level . . . that there is a segment of the criminal justice system . . . which is totally devoid of discrimination.[27]

And it is not surprising, therefore, that those who, like Dr. Hudson, believe that racial discrimination in the courts is an inevitable reality have concluded that the failure to find it may lie in the conduct of research itself: 'inappropriate . . . tech-

the police: 75% of blacks, 45% of asians and 48% of whites believing that the police treated non-whites less well.

[26] 1991 at pp. 24 and 26. The fact that the proportion—29%—is so much lower than that found in the NOP survey may well be due to treating Afro-Caribbeans and Asians as if they were one 'black group', thus averaging the large difference between them. See p 16 below for a further discussion of this issue.

[27] Barbara Hudson 'Discrimination and Disparity: The Influence of Race on Sentencing' *New Community* (16) No. 1, (1989), pp 23–34 at p 26. A similar point has been made by the Director of NACRO, Vivien Stern, 'We know that all British institutions operate in a racist way and it is no surprise to find that the Criminal Justice does so also. If you examine this context you would immediately see why you have the gross disparity in the number of black people in the prison population and the treatment meted out to them in courts', quoted in Yasmin Alibhai, 'How the Legal System Treats Blacks', *New Statesman and Society*, 8 July 1988, p 34. For an insight into the different attitudes towards and treatment of black and Asian men in prison, see Elaine Genders and Elaine Player, *Race Relations in Prisons*, (1989), Oxford University Press.

niques . . . used, or the wrong questions asked, or misleading definitions [having] been used'.[28] The failure to find a simple, strong and constant linear relationship between race and sentencing has led American researchers to address the more complex question of disentangling 'where and for which types of offenders are we likely to find evidence of race differences in sentencing?'[29] When one subjects the various British research studies to critical analysis there are, indeed, good reasons why they have been so inconclusive, especially on the question of whether racial discrimination occurs in the criminal courts.[30]

3. Problems of Method: the Validity of Current Knowledge

Firstly, the official data obtained by the Home Office has been insufficient to be able to control adequately for the variables which might legitimately account for different sentences for blacks and whites. Thus, a recently published Home Office survey of cases proceeded against in the Metropolitan Police District in 1984 and 1985 revealed that a higher proportion of black than white defendants were tried at the Crown Court and were remanded in custody before trial. At the Crown Court 57% of blacks received a sentence of immediate custody compared with 51% of whites and 50% of Asians. But no detailed comparison could be made of the offences concerned or of the offenders' circumstances and previous record, and, therefore,

---

[28] Ibid. at p 26. See also, Monica Walker, 'Interpreting Race and Crime Statistics', *J Royal Statistical Society Series A (General)*, (1987), Vol. 150, pp 39–56. 'There has been no satisfactory study of sentencing in relation to race in this country', at p 55.

[29] See, for example, Martha A Myers and Susette M Talarico, 'The Social Contexts of Racial Discrimination in Sentencing', *Social Problems*, Vol. 33, (1986), pp 236–251, also Donna M Bishop and Charles E Frazer, 'The Influence of Race in Juvenile Justice Processing', *J Research in Crime and Delinq*, Vol. 25, (1988), pp 242–263 at p 245.

[30] For a useful review of some of these problems in early American studies, see Cassia Spohn, John Gruhl and Susan Welch, 'The Effect of Race on Sentencing: A Re-Examination of an Unsettled Question', *Law & Society Review*, Vol. 16 (1981–82), pp 71–88 at pp 72–74.

the conclusion that these differences in the use of custody 'may
be explained partly in terms of differences in the types of
offences for which they were prosecuted' must remain hypo-
thetical.[31]

Secondly, the relatively small number of ethnic minority
defendants in the samples of cases studied has raised particular
difficulties. Even the major Home Office inquiry by David
Moxon into *Sentencing Practice in the Crown Court,* which
gathered data on over 2,000 sentencing decisions observed in 18
courts came across only 160 cases in which the defendant was
black and 93 in which he or she was Asian. It was not possible,
therefore, to make more than a superficial comparison of cases
in the most common offence category, theft and handling. This
revealed that virtually the same proportion of blacks as whites
(36% and 38%) received an immediate or partly-suspended custodial sentence for an offence of this type and, furthermore,
that a 'simple comparison' of those convicted of supplying
drugs again showed a virtually identical use of custody. On the
other hand, Moxon found that 'blacks were significantly more
likely to have been convicted of offences which attract a higher
proportion of custodial sentences, particularly robbery and drug
offences'. On the basis of this, admittedly limited, evidence that
'overall differences in the use of custody between ethnic groups
could be accounted for by differences in offences and criminal
history',[32] the Lord Chancellor told a conference called by
NACRO that 'These results point clearly to the conclusion that
colour was not an adverse factor in the sentence imposed.[33]

[31] Home Office *Statistical Bulletin* 6/89. Monica walker's interesting study of court
proceedings in the Metropolitan police District in 1983 could not, as she stressed, be
regarded as a study of the sentencing process 'because unfortunately data were not
available on defendants' previous offences . . . not were full details of the pleas or the
seriousness of the offences, except insofar as these were indictable-only or triable-either-
way'. 'The Court Disposal and Remands of White, Afro-Caribbean and South Asian
Men (London 1983)', *Brit J Criminol*, (1983), Vol. 29, pp 353–367 at p 354.
[32] Home Office Research Study No. 103, 1988, H.M.S.O, pp 59–60.
[33] Speech made on 3/3/89 to a conference organised by NACRO.

It seems hard to justify such a bold conclusion on the basis of a very basic comparison of the sentences imposed on a broad band of offences which, in general, has the lowest rate of custody. And it is also questionable to assume that the offences of robbery for which the black and white offenders were convicted were of equal gravity. There is a strong suspicion that some blacks are charged with robbery in circumstances where whites might be charged with theft from the person, and that, in any case, a higher proportion of the robberies of which blacks are convicted arise from street snatches and threats, while a higher proportion of those of which whites are convicted are 'professional' robberies of high value.[34]

Third, even when the sample size appears large, the analyses may not specify the significance of any differences found. Barbara Hudson's pioneering efforts in collecting information on 8,000 sentencing decisions reached at 14 Magistrates and Crown Courts in Greater London, made comparisons between the custody rates of whites, blacks and Asians, taking into account the nature of the offences and previous records as well as several other (unspecified) variables which Moxon's Home Office study had found to be related to the probability of receiving a custodial sentence. She concluded that 'a small amount of 'residual discrimination' remained, especially in relation to the more mundane offences against the person, and minor robbery'.[35] But, unfortunately, no attempt appears to have been made to quantify the size of this difference, to test

---

[34] Hudson, op. cit. , at p 28. See also, P. Stevens and C. F. Willis, who found that 'there is a higher possibility that a coloured attacker will cause no injury than a white attacker', *Race, Crime and Arrests*, Home Office Research Study No. 58, HMSO (1979), at p 37. Ian Crow and Jill Cove also found that among black offenders sentenced at a number of Magistrates and Crown Courts there was 'a lower incidence of any loss or damage', *Ethnic Minorities and the Courts*, Criminal Law Review (1984), pp 413–417 at 417. For an American study which suggest that black defendants may be initially 'over-charged' see M. D. Holmes, H. C. Daudistel and R. A. Farrell, 'Determinants of Charge Reductions and Final Dispositions in Cases of Burglary and Robbery', *J Research in Crime and Delinq*, Vol. 24, (1987), pp 233–254.

[35] Hudson, *ibid*, p 28.

whether it was statistically significant (that is, whether it was large enough not to have occurred by chance), or to calculate the increased odds of a black person with the same characteristics as a white person being sentenced to custody.

A **fourth** problem, which a number of studies have in common, is the difficulty of drawing overall conclusions from samples of cases which have been gathered from both magistrates' and Crown Courts, especially when the number of ethnic minority defendants is small. For example, Iain Crow and Jill Cove's frequently cited study, which concluded that the 'cases [of the different ethnic groups] are handled in similar ways and the sentences they are given are similar' was carried out in nine courts in London, the Midlands and the North at which probation officers completed forms recording various information on 688 offenders, 85 of them black and 24 Asian. Four of these courts were juvenile courts, three adult magistrates' courts and two were Crown Courts. Yet no attempt was made in the reported findings to disaggregate the sample either by age or by type of court. It is therefore not certain whether the same proportion of black people as white were tried in the Crown Court as opposed to being dealt with summarily in a magistrates' court. This may have led to some misleading conclusions. For example, the surprising finding that only 8 per cent of the black group had been convicted of robbery compared to 14 per cent of each of the other groups may have been due to blacks being underrepresented in the samples of cases drawn from the Crown Courts which alone has the power to try a person aged 17 or over for robbery. And if the black sample was drawn disproportionately from the magistrates' courts this might also explain why, in this study, roughly the same proportion of the each group had a Social Inquiry Report prepared on them. Indeed, the overall low rate of custody (10.7% for blacks, 12.1% for whites and 12.8% for others) suggests that only a small proportion of the total had been sentenced at Crown

Court.[36] It is obvious that different findings may have emerged had the practices of different types of court been analysed separately.

To take another example, this time from a study which came to the opposite conclusions as regards racial differences in sentencing: the interesting analysis by the West Yorkshire Probation Service of 663 Social Inquiry Reports prepared for Leeds Crown Court and Bradford Magistrates' Court in 1987 (69 of them relating to Asians and 30 to Afro-Caribbeans) found that the proportion of Afro-Caribbean and Asian males sentenced to custody was 44 and 45 per cent as compared to 32 per cent of the white defendants. It concluded that 'magistrates' (it is not clear whether this included judges) used custody more frequently for black offenders, meaning both Afro-Caribbeans and Asians, than whites 'at all levels of seriousness of offence' and less frequently sentenced Asians to Community Service Orders:

the trend of sentencing is undoubtedly to the disadvantage of the Black offenders, and . . . this cannot be justified in terms of their offences or personal circumstances. The disadvantage is consistent in nearly all aspects of sentencing. Its effect is that more black people find themselves in prison than whites who have committed the same type of offences, and who are likely to have worse criminal records.

However, the figures reveal that a much higher proportion of the Asians than whites or Afro-Caribbeans had been dealt with at the Crown Courts (71 per cent compared with 48 and 43 per cent respectively). Also, that when a number of serious cases involving drugs were excluded from the Asian sample there were no longer any statistically significant differences between the proportion of white, black or Asian males sentenced to immediate custody by the courts. Again, the number of cases was too small to make any further comparisons: altogether

[36] Op. cit., pp 416–17.

there were only 31 Asians, 12 Afro-Caribbeans and 6 persons of mixed race sentenced to custody by both magistrates and Crown Courts.[37]

A **fifth** problem arises when studies categorize all persons from ethnic minorities of non-white skin colour as a single group called 'blacks'. There may be many good reasons for doing this in other circumstances, but in studying sentencing decisions the grouping together of Afro-Caribbean and Asian defendants may well have been a contributing factor to the finding of no racial differences in the use of custody. This is because the use of custody for blacks and Asians may be so different that, when they are combined, the average use of custody may obscure a difference which exists, say between the use of custody for blacks and whites, but not between Asians and whites.[38] In addition, it will, of course, obscure any differences which might occur between the sentences imposed on the different racial groups for particular types of offence. Further-more, it makes it impossible to investigate whether particular circumstances, say unemployment, are given equal weight in the sentencing of black, white and Asian offenders. For example, the widely quoted study by Michael McConville and John Baldwin of Crown Court trials in Birmingham and London, involving separate samples of contested and guilty pleas, found no consistent[39] or statistically significant differences between the proportions of black people sentenced to custody as opposed to whites. It did not, however, distinguish between Afro-Caribbean and Asian defen-

---

[37] Rob Voakes and Quentin Fowler, (1989), *Sentencing, Race and Social Enquiry Reports*, West Yorkshire Probation Service.

[38] For a discussion of a similar necessity in the United States of distinguishing in California between the sentences imposed on 'Chicanos' and Blacks, rather than treating them as a single category of 'non-whites' see, Marjorie S Katz, 'Race, Ethnicity, and Determinate Sentencing', *Criminology*, Vol. 22, (1984), pp 147–171.

[39] For example, after a guilty plea 48.2% of white's were sentenced to custody compared with 46% of blacks, but among those who had pleaded not guilty 65.6% of blacks were committed to custody and 59.2% of whites.

dants, or provide information on their various proportions amongst the 'black' group.[40]

Sixth, there is the problem that any differences found in the proportions of ethnic minority defendants sentenced to custody by various courts has to be seen in the light of the wide disparities in the general level of sentences which have been discovered whenever the sentencing practices of different courts have been compared. Barbara Hudson has suggested, although she did not investigate the possibility herself, that apparent disparities in sentencing might be 'the product of patterns of consistent discrimination against certain types of offenders, and in particular unemployed, male Afro-Caribbeans'.[41] Whether this is the case or not, any attempt to compare the rates of custody for blacks and whites from cases drawn from several courts (as the Home Office and several other studies have done) must allow for the fact that any overall average might conceal substantial variations in the rates of custody for *both* white and ethnic minority defendants between these courts as well as between individual judges sitting at the same court.[42]

As McConville and Baldwin pointed out, their findings could only be taken as evidence relating to the question of whether there was any 'systematic institutional bias'. It was not appropriate as a method for studying whether individual judges exercised any racial bias in their sentencing decisions, that is, whether the similar average custody rate for blacks and whites concealed differences between individual judges, some of whom

[40] Michael McConville and John Baldwin, 'The Influence of Race on Sentencing in England' *Criminal Law Review* (1982) pp 652–658. Similarly, an unpublished study by the West Midlands Probation Service, *Report on the Birmingham Court Social Enquiry Monitoring Exercise* (February 1987) used the term 'black' to refer collectively to people of Afro-Caribbean, Asian and mixed racial origin.

[41] Op. cit. p 23.

[42] The Home Office Study, *Sentencing Practice in the Crown Court*, op. cit., for example, was based on 2,077 cases heard at 18 different Crown Courts, making it impossible, of course, to compare how the relatively small number of ethnic minority defendants were dealt with at each court.

may have been more severe on blacks than whites and some of whom may have exhibited an opposite tendency.[43]

Seventh, and finally, there is the issue of how cases can be compared in order to test the hypothesis that like cases are treated differently according to the racial characteristics of the defendant when all other relevant variables are held constant.[44] In this country, the methodology employed so far has been relatively unsophisticated compared with the attempts in the United States to unravel, through multivariate regression analysis, the extent to which the race of the defendant and/or the victim affects the probability of receiving a death sentence once a substantial number of legitimate variables which aggravate or mitigate the seriousness of the offence have been taken into account.[45] For example, the study by Baldus, Woodworth and Pulaski of death sentences in Georgia used a logistic regression analysis based on 20 to 30 significant legitimate variables (out of 150 used in the initial analysis) in order to produce a 'culpability index' which distinguished between six groups of cases, ranging from those amongst whom less than one in ten received the death penalty to a group in which all were sentenced to death. The cases in each group were not necessarily factually similar but were similarly 'culpable' in the sense that a particular combination of aggravating or mitigating circumstances had

[43] For a useful discussion of the need to 'uncover the subtlety of the processes at work' behind the general trends, see Robert Waters, *Ethnic Minorities and the Criminal Justice System* (1990), p 75. And for an excellent and easily understood analysis of why overall 'no race of defendant effects' may, in fact, conceal disparities and discriminations that 'offset each other in such a way as to give the appearance of perfect or near-perfect equality', see Stuart Nagel and Marian Neef, 'Racial Disparities that Supposedly do not Exist: Some Pitfalls in Analysis of Court Records', *Notre Dame Lawyer*, Vol. 52, (1976), pp 87–94.

[44] In fact, of course, statistics can only be used to test the 'null hypothesis', i.e. that cases are treated equally and that there is *no* difference with respect to the race of the defendant.

[45] See, David C. Baldus, G. W. Woodworth and C. A. Pulaski Jr, *Equal Justice and the Death Penalty: A Legal and Empirical Analysis* (1989) and Roger Hood, *The Death Penalty: A World Wide Perspective,* (1989) Chapter 5.

produced a similar probability—whether low, medium or high—of being sentenced to death. Within each group it was possible to compare whether black defendants had a greater likelihood of being sentenced to death, or whether, as turned out to be the case, the race of the victim (being white) had a substantial effect on the penalty received.

In relation to the question of whether the racial characteristics of defendants in California affected their probability of receiving a sentence of imprisonment or probation, researchers at the Rand Corporation have analysed over 11,500 decisions made in 1980 on offenders convicted of six different types of crime. Using regression analyses (Ordinary Least Squares) to control for the effect of 30 variables, they found that 'the addition of race to the prediction equation for a given crime type did not improve the accuracy of the prediction' as to whether an offender would or would not receive a prison sentence, nor did it affect its length.[46]

Most of the British studies have either simply compared the proportion of each ethnic group sentenced to custody according to the broad legal category of the offence and number of previous convictions, taken separately or in combination, or they have used some form of 'group matching', as in Baldwin and McConville's study. This involved constructing samples by choosing cases so that those each of the racial groups had the same profiles in relation to eight variables (ie each sample had the same number of persons in the various age categories, the same number of males and females, the same number charged with each type of offence etc.). Although superior to simple variable-by-variable comparisons, this method cannot, of

---

[46] Stephen Klein, Joan Petersilia and Susan Turner, 'Race and Imprisonment Decisions in California', *Science*, Vol. 247, (16 February 1990), pp 812–816. It should be noted that the conclusions of this study are contrary to Dr Petersilia's earlier work *Racial Disparities in the Criminal Justice System* (1983), Rand Corporation, which found suggestive evidence of ethnic minorities being treated more harshly than white offenders at the sentencing stage.

course, take account of whether the different racial groups have these variables in the same combinations.[47]

A few studies which have attempted to control for such individual combinations of variables have used an instrument which has been developed by various probation services in order to construct 'risk of custody scores' as a basis for identifying those cases on which the greatest effort needs to be spent if they are to be diverted from custody. This method was originally devised by the Home Office for use in the parole system to provide a prediction of the likelihood of reconviction following a prison sentence. It assigns to each attribute a score which is the percentage difference, plus or minus, by which the percentage sentenced to custody of those who possess that attribute differs from the mean custody rate for the total sample of defendants. Thus, if the mean custody rate is 50% and those with no previous convictions have a rate of custody of 30% all those with this attribute are given a score of −20. If the custody rate for those convicted of rape is 95%, they get a score of +45. Each person's total score is then obtained by summing the scores for each of the attributes they possess.

This approach has the apparent advantage that it takes into account and assigns a separate weight to every attribute collected for the sample, thus giving the impression that everything relevant has been taken into account. It is also simple to calculate and relatively easy to apply. But it has the disadvantage that the score assigned to a particular variable is not affected by the scores assigned to other variables which are highly correlated with it and this may, of course, produce distortions if

---

[47] The fact that they have the same proportion with two or more previous convictions and the same proportion convicted of robbery does not, for instance, guarantee that the proportions convicted of robbery who have two prior convictions will be the same.

racial groups have dissimilar combinations of offence and offender characteristics.[48]

Like all such empirical methods for matching cases, it can only, of course, be descriptive of the probabilities of custody in the sample from which it has been derived. Therefore, those studies, such as the West Yorkshire survey, which appears to have applied the weights given to variables by the so-called 'Cambridge Risk of Custody Scale' to data from courts in another part of the country, may not have matched like with like. If, in that area, the variables were associated with different rates of custody than in Cambridgeshire, the weights given to them would need to be re-calculated before offenders could be compared according to their risk of custody score.[49]

4. Conclusion

It was because of all these problems that grave doubts remained as to the validity of the findings, one way or another, as to whether sentencing practices existed which were, when all relevant factors had been taken into account, to the disadvantage of any ethnic minority defendants. The researchers themselves had come to the conclusion that:

The sensitivity of the subject demands statistical differences at a high level of significance drawn on a large sample of cases. To date, there has not been a large, multi-factorial study which handled all the variables needing to be taken into account if the race effect on sentencing is to be isolated.[50]

---

[48] For a fuller discussion of the drawback of this method for the purposes of comparing sentencing practices, see Appendix 2.

[49] For a useful collection of papers on such Risk of Custody Scales, See George Mair, (ed.), *Risk Prediction and Probation*. Research and Planning Unit Paper 56 (1989), Home Office.

[50] Barbara Hudson, op. cit., p. 32. Monica Walker has also commented: 'There has been no satisfactory study of sentencing in relation to race in this country', in 'Interpreting Race and Crime Statistics', op. cit., at p 55.

It was in the hope of trying to fill this void and to overcome these methodological difficulties that this inquiry was launched. No one can doubt the need for a sound factual basis for determining if the criminal courts do, in any situations, discriminate to the disadvantage of ethnic minorities in the imposition of punishment and, in particular, in the recourse they have to custodial penalties, and the length of such penalties. But it is not only custodial penalties that matter. Other penalties not only differ in their relative severity and in their degree of intervention in the convicted persons life, they can also have an impact on the penalty that may next be imposed if the person is reconvicted. This is obviously true in the case of the suspended sentence of imprisonment, breaches of which were enforced in 1989 in 70 per cent of cases, but breaches of probation orders and community service orders are also associated with a higher probability of receiving a custodial sentence than is a breach of a conditional discharge or failure to pay a fine.[51] The ultimate proportion of people from different ethnic groups in custody may therefore, to some extent, be shaped by the point on the scale (sometimes called a tariff) of alternatives to custody at which their sentences are placed.

Yet another factor of importance is the range and quality of information made available about the offender, including his or her account of the circumstances leading to the offence and any factors which might mitigate culpability or suggest a change of behaviour in future. The most regular source of such information is the Social Inquiry Report prepared by the probation service (renamed the Pre-Sentence Report by the Criminal Justice Act 1991). The extent to which such reports are provided and

---

[51] See *Criminal Statistics, England and Wales 1990*, Cm 1985 (HMSO 1992), Table 7.28. In 1989, 49% of those who breached a probation order received an immediate custodial sentence for the breach, 26% of those who breached a community service order and 20% who breached a conditional discharge. By 1990 the figures had fallen to: suspended sentence 69%, probation order 42%, community service order 21%, conditional discharge 16%.

the recommendations made in them are another vital factor to be taken into account in investigating whether different treatment is given to defendants according to which ethnic group they belong to.

5. Plan of the Report

While this is primarily a study which attempts to disentangle the impact of race on sentencing practices in the Crown Court, it also sheds light on disparities in sentencing practices in general and on the influences of various factors on sentencing other than race. Some of these issues are alluded to in this report, but for the sake of clarity, others have been put aside for publication in other form. The central thrust of the analysis and discussion which follows concentrates on the racial dimension. Chapter Two explains the approach taken and the methods used in the study. This is followed, in Chapter Three, by a comparison of the pattern of sentences imposed on defendants of different ethnic origin in the courts which were studied: providing the data which needs to be explained. Chapter Four raises the question of whether there were differences in the way that cases were processed and in the characteristics of the offences and offenders which might account for the differences in the proportion of each ethnic group sentenced to custody. Chapter Five examines the association between these variables and the use of custody, explains the multivariate analysis used to devise a 'probability of custody' score, and employs this score to see whether the observed race differences in the use of custody are explained when their expected probabilities of custody are taken into account. Chapters Six and Seven use the same method to investigate differences in the use of custody between courts and judges. This is followed in Chapter Eight by an analysis of the length of custodial sentences, while

Chapter Nine describes the use of other non-custodial penalties. Chapter Ten deals with three important factors which may have an effect on the sentence imposed: how the offence came to light and how the offender was identified; whether the defendant appeared for trial already in custody or on bail; and whether he had a social inquiry report and, if so, what it suggested would be an appropriate sentence. Chapter Eleven analyses separately the data relating to women sentenced in the Crown Court and compares their treatment with that accorded to men. In chapter twelve the threads are drawn together and the question of whether the evidence is consistent with racial discrimination in sentencing is discussed. Finally, there is a detailed summary of the main findings of this survey.

2
APPROACH AND METHOD

1. Choosing a Strategy

Undoubtedly, the ideal method for studying the influence, if any, of the racial factor in decisions which might lead to a custodial or any other sentence would be to follow a 'cohort' of cases from arrest through the various processes—police, prosecution, committal for trial, social inquiry reports—to final disposition at the Crown Court. However, it was soon recognized that such a task would need far greater resources than were available for this inquiry and take an enormous amount of time to accomplish. A very large initial sample would have to be selected for a research exercise which hoped to study the outcome of a sufficient number of cases involving black and Asian defendants at a number of Crown Courts. Indeed, it would almost certainly be necessary to organize an officially sanctioned system for monitoring cases as they passed through the criminal justice system in several parts of the country and over a considerable period of time. This is an idea which is discussed further in the concluding chapter. (See pp 179–192 below)

The problems involved in tracing cases through the system became apparent in the experience gained from the ambitious study by Monica Walker and Tony Jefferson of the University of Sheffield who followed through, from arrest to sentence, 1,058 males aged 10 to 35 who had been arrested in six central sub-divisions of Leeds over a six month period in 1987. All cases identified by the police as non-white were included as well as a sample of white cases. Altogether, data was collected on 255 blacks and 126 Asians. However, by the end of the

criminal process only 76 blacks and 25 Asians were sentenced
by the Crown Court. The authors concluded that 'overall,
whites had more given a custodial sentence, at 62% compared
with 56% for Blacks and 52% for Asians' and that there were
no significant differences when offence seriousness and previous
convictions were controlled for[1]. But because of small numbers
the authors were obviously not able to provide convincing evidence that no racial differences in sentencing existed at Leeds
Crown Court. Indeed, it was obvious from this study that it
would be impossible to make more detailed and reliable comparisons between cases dealt with at the Crown Court without
obtaining a much larger sample of cases drawn from a number
of different judges and courts.[2]

It was decided, therefore, to 'work backwards', so to speak,
from the Crown Courts. That is, to identify all persons appearing for trial and subsequently sentenced at several Crown
Courts who were from ethnic minorities and to compare the
sentences they received with those imposed on a sufficiently
large sample of white defendants dealt with at the same courts.

Any study which attempts to isolate the influence of race will
need, of course, to take into account as many other measurable
factors as possible which may have influenced the sentence
imposed. Some of these will be variables which describe the
way in which the case has been processed: choice of venue for
trial, whether it be a charge which can only be dealt with on
indictment or one which is triable either-way; the form of
remand, whether in custody or on bail; the number of indictments and charges preferred and the nature of those charges,
for instance, whether a section 18 wounding with intent or a

---

[1] In these figures suspended sentences were counted as custody and if excluded the
custody rates were whites 53%, blacks 45% and Asians 40%.

[2] Monica Walker, Tony Jefferson and Mary Seneviratne, *Race and Criminal Justice
in the Inner City,* Report to the ESRC 1990. See also, Tony Jefferson and Monica
Walker, 'Ethnic Minorities in the Criminal Justice System', *Criminal Law Review,* 1992,
pp 83–95.

less serious section 20 wounding; the decision of the defendant whether to plead guilty or not guilty and at what stage of the process to make this decision; the availability of a social inquiry report and the nature of its recommendation. It will also need to gather as much information as possible about the nature of the offence(s); such as the degree of violence, injuries caused, weapons used, amount of money stolen, amount and type of drugs involved; about the previous history of court appearances, offences proven and penalties imposed; about social variables which might have an impact on the penalty chosen, ranging from legally relevant considerations such as age to factors the relevance of which are more contentious, such as employment history.

It is obvious, therefore, that the way that a case is 'presented' will have an influence on the way that it is perceived by the judge in deciding on an appropriate sentence. For example, there is evidence that black and Asian defendants less frequently plead guilty—which can earn a 'discount' on the sentence,[3] make the provision of a social inquiry report more probable and give the opportunity to make a plea in mitigation. As a consequence, they could be more at risk of receiving a custodial sentence, and for a longer term as well. Similarly, if weight is given in mitigation of sentence for a steady history of employment this will inevitably be a consideration less often applied to any ethnic group which is more affected by unemployment. It is for this reason that Sentencing Commissions in the United States have removed this variable from consideration, regarding it as producing indirect discrimination against black defendants.[4] It is also obvious that there is room for different interpretations of facts and varying perceptions of circumstances which could lead some judges to give a different

---

[3] This policy and its effects are discussed below on pp 125–126.

[4] See, John Petersilia and Susan Turner, *Guideline—Based Justice: The Implications for Racial Minorities*, (1985), Rand Corporation.

weight to such variables in cases which involve a certain class
of defendant: just as age, sex and criminal history may
influence these evaluations and perceptions so may ethnic characteristics.

In order to hypothesise the existence of a racially discriminatory effect in sentencing one does not need to subscribe to the
view that it is universal or that it affects the decisions of all
judges to the same degree or in the same way. As mentioned
above (page 16), it would be consistent with the existence of
discrimination to find no **overall** differences in the proportions
of whites, Afro-Caribbeans and Asians committed to custody at
a number of courts if it could be shown that this was the product of a balance between internal variations in the sample—
some judges at some courts being more severe with
Afro-Caribbeans or Asians, some being less severe. It was
essential, therefore, to design the research so as to include a
sufficient number of cases and to ensure that they had been
dealt with at a number of courts, ideally courts serving the
same region and police force area so as to control, as far as
possible, for the overall crime problem as perceived by the
courts. This would have the added advantage of controlling
also, to some extent, for those systemic factors which might
affect the way in which cases are processed by the police and
Crown Prosecution Service *en route* to the Crown Court.

Furthermore, a research design which makes it possible to
compare the sentencing practices of courts is essential in any
study which attempts to isolate the effects of a particular variable—in this cases race—on sentencing practice. No study of a
single court's sentencing patterns for different ethnic groups
could satisfactorily demonstrate that every relevant variable
which might account for any observed differences had been
taken into account. However, when two or more courts are
compared the design of the research can 'control for' variables
which explain a substantial amount of the variance in sentenc-

ing in the same way for cases dealt with at each court. Any racial differences in the pattern of sentencing between these courts would, obviously, have to be explained by variables **other** than those which have been controlled for in **all** the courts. This would mean:

either that the race differences in sentencing patterns were due to relevant variables which were unique to the cases which appeared before at least some of the judges at the courts where sentences differed
or that there was, at these courts, a different relationship between race and the variables which largely accounted for sentencing practices at all courts. In other words, that these variables, where ethnic minorities were involved, were perceived and reacted to differently by at least some of the judges passing sentences at these courts: a finding which would be consistent with racial bias or discrimination in sentencing.

It was decided, therefore, to study the outcome of a large number of cases which had been convicted and sentenced at the Crown Courts serving a metropolitan police force area. The West Midlands was chosen because of the relatively high proportion of ethnic minorities resident there. It was assumed (which proved to be correct) that among 5,800 males and 490 females tried during 1989 at the five Crown Courts to which cases emanating from the West Midlands police were committed, there would be a substantial number of persons from these ethnic minorities. These Crown Courts were: Birmingham, Dudley (which at the time sat in court rooms in Dudley, Wolverhampton and Birmingham),[5] Coventry, Warwick and Stafford.

---

[5] In 1990, with the opening of a new Crown Court building, these courts were renamed Wolverhampton Crown Court. But to mark the fact that, at the time of this study, the court system was differently organised, it will be referred to in this study as the Dudley courts.

2. Sources of Information

The Lord Chancellor's Department gave permission to obtain information on cases which had been dealt with at these Crown Courts in 1989. First, a copy was made of the form[6] which gives, for each person appearing for trial, their name and date of birth, the date of committal and from which magistrates' court, whether committed in custody or on bail, whether legally aided, the name of the judge who tried and sentenced the defendant (which was not always the same person), the names of solicitors and counsel, the date of trial and its outcome, whether the case was then further remanded for inquiries to be made, the date of sentence and the penalty(ies) imposed. Unfortunately, however, there was no information on this form which related to the ethnic origin of the defendant except what might be inferred from his or her name. While the names of most Asian defendants were distinctive this was certainly not the case in respect of people of Afro-Caribbean origin. It was necessary, therefore, to ascertain for more than 5,000 cases the ethnic identity of the defendant. For this purpose the attribution given by the police or the probation service was accepted as providing a reasonable approximation as to how the person would have been characterised by the judge in the Crown Court. Although there can be no perfect fit, and such a method of identification is certainly not the same thing as the way the person might define their own ethnic identity, it seemed nevertheless likely that there would have been a high degree of concordance between how the person was perceived by different parties in the criminal justice system. And, in the event, much evidence was found to support this in the records.

The only sources from which it was possible to gain information about racial appearance were police and probation service records. The West Midlands police gave considerable assistance

---

[6] Form 5089.

in helping to trace the files of persons who had been convicted in the Crown Court. In that file was recorded a hand-written description of the defendant taken down at the time he or she was interviewed by a C.I.D. officer. As far as Afro-Caribbean defendants were concerned these physical descriptions usually said 'negroid' or 'West Indian' or 'black' or 'coloured' or sometimes 'half-caste'. To collect information on so many cases was enormously time consuming but would have taken much longer if the police had not helped us to trace cases in a number of ways. The West Midlands probation service also provided, in strictest confidence, a list of cases currently under supervision or for whom a report had been written for a court during 1989. This merely noted whether a person was 'black' or 'white', but as we had already been able to identify people of Asian origin we could be quite confident that 'black' in the remaining cases almost invariably meant Afro-Caribbean. There were also a very small number of people described as Arab, Chinese etc. and these were simply classified as 'Others'. In the discussion which follows 'black' refers therefore to people of Afro-Caribbean, usually West Indian, origin, Asian to people of Indo-Asian origin and 'white' to people of European origin.

This process led to the identification of 1,441 males and 91 females from ethnic minorities who had been convicted and sentenced at the five Crown Courts in 1989. Sufficient information was also recorded on the cases which had been found not guilty so as to examine whether there were racial differences in relation to the offences with which they were charged and whether they had been in custody or bailed while remanded for trial: an issue of importance in its own right.[7]

---

[7] It was decided to exclude from the main analysis the smaller number of cases which had originally been convicted at a magistrates' court and committed for sentence at the Crown Court because the magistrates had concluded that their sentencing powers were insufficient. There were 550 male cases, 86 of them black offenders and 59 Asians, and 68 women, 8 or them black. They were excluded because there were no details available in the Crown Court records of the offences of which they had been convicted.

Table 1 shows the distribution of cases from each ethnic group which were found guilty or not guilty at each of the courts. This data refers to the males only, as does the analysis

Table 1: Number and percentage of males found guilty at West Midlands Crown Court Centres in 1989

Court and ethnic group	Found guilty	Found not guilty	Percentage found guilty	Percentage of each ethnic group of those found guilty
Birmingham				
White	1782	179	90.9	66.6
Black	569	75	88.4	21.3
Asian (& 8 others)	323	55	85.4	12.1
				100.0
Dudley courts				
White	1201	121	90.8	74.7
Black	246	16	93.8	15.3
Asian (& 4 others)	161	31	83.9	10.0
				100.0
Coventry				
White	375	36	95.9	77.3
Black	35	4	87.5	8.0
Asian (& 1 other)	25	10	71.4	5.7
				100.0
Warwick				
White	301	33	90.1	83.1
Black	22	5	81.5	6.1
Asian (& 2 others)	39	3	92.9	10.8
				100.0
Stafford				
White	89	7	92.7	80.9
Black	17	11	60.7	15.5
Asian (& 1 other)	4	12	25.0	3.6
				100.0

which follows in Chapters 3–10. The much smaller number of female cases is considered separately in Chapter 11.

It will be seen that at the courts with the largest number of cases—Birmingham and the Dudley courts—there were no significant differences in the proportions of white and black defendants who were found not guilty, although a higher proportion of Asians were acquitted. But it is interesting to note that, amongst the black defendants found not guilty, a much higher proportion than amongst the whites had been charged with robbery or a serious offence of violence (44% as compared with 17%) and that substantially more of the not guilty findings in cases involving black males resulted from the judge instructing the jury to bring in a not guilty verdict (22% versus 11%).[8] Furthermore, in view of widespread concern that many black defendants who are subsequently found to be not guilty have been remanded in custody, it is important to note that only a small proportion of any of the defendants who were acquitted had been in custody before trial. Despite the fact that more of the blacks had been charged with an offence involving violence only 8 per cent had been remanded in custody, which was not significantly different statistically from the proportion of the whites, (5%) or of the Asians (3.6%).

3. The Sample

The main analyses in this report are based on all the identified male black and Asian defendants who were found guilty and sentenced by these five Crown Courts in 1989 and a random

---

[8] The reader should be warned that because of the way in which court clerks recorded the verdict it was not always clear that they correctly distinguished those cases where the judge 'directed' the jury to return a not guilty verdict, from those where the judge formally 'ordered' that an acquittal be entered on the record because the prosecution had decided not to proceed with the charge. The cases referred to above are those where it was clear from the record that a trial had begun before the judge directed the acquittal. The difference is statistically significant: $\chi^2 = 12.69$, 1 df, p < .005.

sample of male white defendants at each court. The white sample was of an equivalent size to the total number of both ethnic groups found guilty at that court. Thus, at Birmingham, where one third of the defendants was black or Asian, every second white defendant was sampled, giving a total of 875 cases; at the Dudley group of courts, where the ethnic minorities accounted for a quarter of the cases, every third white case was sampled, giving a total of 404. By a similar process, one in five at Coventry and Warwick and one in three at Stafford were sampled—giving totals of 69, 64 and 31 white defendants respectively. This procedure ensured that the sample of white defendants was weighted according to the relative proportion of ethnic minorities appearing at each of these courts.

Nevertheless, such a procedure obviously under-represents white defendants in the sample of cases as a whole in relation to blacks and Asians. In comparing the sentences imposed on the three racial groups at each court individually, the different sampling fractions taken posed no difficulties as long, of course, as the sample of whites was representative of whites dealt with at that court. In order to check whether this was so, all the forms relating to those white cases not included in the sample were analysed in order to calculate the proportion sentenced to custody. It proved to be almost precisely the same as for the sampled cases, leaving no doubt, therefore, that the samples properly reflected the use of custody for white defendants as a whole in the West Midlands.[9]

Even so, the under-representation of whites and the different fraction at each court had to be taken into account in making any over-all comparisons between the treatment of whites and the ethnic minorities or in comparing the custody rates of the five courts. If this had not been done, the overall custody rates

---

[9] This was true for all courts, with the sole exception of Stafford where only 31 white cases were sampled. The proportion in the sample sentenced to custody was 55%, but for all the white cases dealt with at Stafford it was 68%.

for each court and the sample as a whole would have been distorted by the under-representation of white cases. As it turned out, the custody rate for the total male sample of 2,884 cases, which was 48.6 per cent, was remarkably similar to the custody rate of 48.9 per cent obtained after the white samples at each court had been re-weighted by multiplying them by the sampling fraction taken (i.e. times two at Birmingham, times three at the Dudley Courts etc.) This was further evidence that the sampling procedures gave a valid picture of the use of custody at these West Midlands' courts.

It was also decided to make a separate comparative study of the sentencing of females convicted in the same year by these Courts. Because of the relatively small number involved—76 black and only 14 Asian women—all the 343 white women were included, making a total of 433 female cases.

4. Collecting the Data

The next stage was to examine the full Crown Court file of each case—a total of 3,317: 2,884 males and 433 females. A coding frame was devised (see Appendix 1) on which details were recorded. These files contained, besides the form 5089 mentioned above (p 30, fn 6) all the depositions of evidence relating to the circumstances of the offences of which the defendant had been found guilty, a social inquiry report and/or a medical report if one had been prepared, a police statement of antecedents and a list of previous convictions and sentences. All this information made it possible, in comparing the penalties imposed on defendants from different ethnic groups, to take into account the major factors which are known to have an influence in sentencing decisions.[10] This does not mean, of

---

[10] We were not, however, given access to the judge's papers and notes or to any comments he may have made in passing sentence.

course, that the records make it possible to compare every individual facet of each case. No statistical method can do this.
What can be done is to show whether—when those factors
which appear to be most strongly associated with receiving a
custodial sentence or not, or with the length of the sentence or
the relative severity of the penalty are controlled for—there
remains a significantly different *pattern* in the sentences
imposed on black and/or Asian defendants than on whites. In
other words, and this is vital to understand, a study such as
this does not pretend to investigate whether there has been any
racial bias in any *particular* case, only whether there can be
shown to be *in aggregate* a greater *probability* of persons
from ethnic minorities receiving custodial or other sentences
when other relevant factors have been taken into account. The
test is this: if the race of the defendant is, as it should be, irrelevant, there should be no more variation associated with ethnic
origin, once other factors are taken into account, than there
should be variation in sentencing associated with any other random factor, say colour of the offender's shirt.

But if it is shown that there is some residual variation in the
pattern of sentencing associated with race, it becomes necessary
to seek explanations, some of which may, of course, not be
readily deduced from the recorded information. For example,
they may relate to a judge's perception of the seriousness of
offences committed by persons of different ethnic backgrounds,
or to different reactions to the appearance and demeanour of
defendants in court, or to the ability of counsel to present mitigating circumstances as effectively for one ethnic group as for
another. In a statistical study, of the kind undertaken here, it
was not possible to investigate most of these questions: that
would have required interviews with all the parties concerned
and much painstaking observation if evidence on a sufficient
number of cases were to be gathered. Even if it had been possible to obtain permission to interview judges about individual

cases, it would have needed a different kind of study to investigate individual decisions, and one requiring enormous resources.[11] Nevertheless, some insight into whether judges perceived any special problems relating to the sentencing of ethnic minorities would have been valuable in interpreting the findings of the statistical analysis.[12] Unfortunately they were, I was told, instructed 'by the powers that be' in the judiciary not to cooperate with this part of the planned study.

As a first step in the analysis, it was essential to investigate whether there was at these courts any *prima facie* evidence to support the contention that disparities exist in the sentences imposed on defendants of different ethnic backgrounds which do not appear to be explained by differences in the type, seriousness, and number of offences of which they are convicted or of their record of previous convictions and penalties imposed. This is the subject of the next three chapters.

[11] It has already been noted (p 12 above) that in a large sample of 2,000 Crown Court cases studied by the Home Office, in which the information was recorded by probation officers who observed the cases in court, there were only 160 black and 93 Asians. So far nothing has been published to suggest that the observers systematically recorded differences in the way in which these cases were dealt with.

[12] On the other hand, it has to be recognised that it may be very difficult to elicit information relating to race in a formal interview. One American study which included interviews with judges on 11 circuits, noted that these 'proved less informative than originally expected, . . . judges took special pains to appear color-blind', Martha A Myers and Susette M Talarico, 'The Social Contexts of Racial Discrimination in Sentencing', *Social Problems*, Vol. 33, (1986), pp 236–251 at p 247.

3
SOME BASIC COMPARISONS OF SENTENCING PRACTICES

1. The Racial composition of the sample

It will be readily apparent from the proportion of cases in each ethnic group listed in Table 1 (see page 32 above) that black Afro-Caribbean male defendants were heavily over-represented in relation to their number in the population covered by the West Midlands' police and Crown Courts. Altogether, ethnic minorities accounted for 28 per cent of those sentenced during 1989, whereas, according to a recent estimates they made up 12.5 per cent of the total population in the West Midlands metropolitan area.[1]

But male defendants of Afro-Caribbean origin were much more heavily over-represented than were those of Indo-Asian descent. West Indian and Guyanese men made up 3.1 per cent of the total male population aged 16 to 64 in the metropolitan West Midlands' area (1.7 per cent in the West Midlands as a whole), and yet they accounted for 21 per cent of those found guilty at Birmingham Crown Court, and 15 per cent at the Dudley courts and Stafford: a ratio 5 to 7 times greater than their proportion in the population at large. There was, however, a much smaller percentage (6 to 8 per cent) at Coventry and Warwick.[2]

---

[1] See John Haskey, 'The Ethnic minority populations resident in private households—estimates by county and metropolitan district of England and Wales, *Population Trends*, No. 63, Spring 1991, pp 22–35. The estimated proportion of ethnic minority males aged 16–64 in the Labour Force Survey is very similar.

[2] The estimated proportion of people of West Indian and African origin in Birmingham is 3.9%, in Wolverhampton 3.7%, in Dudley 2.2%, in Coventry 1.3% and

Asian males were also over-represented among the convicted at Birmingham and the Dudley courts, but to a much lesser degree. They accounted for some 7 per cent of the relevant metropolitan population compared with 10 to 12 per cent at these courts. It is interesting to note that there was a higher proportion of Asian offenders amongst those aged under 21 (13 per cent) than amongst adults (9 per cent).

2. Variations in the Use of Custody between Courts Irrespective of Race

That there would be variations in the overall proportion of the cases sentenced to custody[3] amongst those dealt with at the five Crown Court centres was to be expected, because Crown Courts have differing powers in relation to the type of cases which are committed to them for trial. Stafford and Warwick are first tier courts which can try the most grave cases, as can Birmingham, although the latter deals with a much wider range of offences. Dudley, as a third tier Crown court, only received those cases in the most serious category which have been released by the presiding High Court Judge and Coventry, also a third tier court, dealt very rarely with such cases. One indicator of the seriousness of cases committed for trial is the proportion which could be tried only on indictment: such as rape, robbery, arson with intent to endanger life, and wounding with intent (s.18 Offences Against the Person Act 1861), as well as

in Solihull, from where most of the Warwick cases emanated, 2.2%. Ibid. See also, *Ethnic Minorities in Britain: Statistical Information on the Pattern of Settlement*, Commission for Racial Equality, 1985. It must, of course be recognised that the age range 16 to 64 is too wide for a proper comparison to be made with that part of the population involved in crime, amongst whom involvement falls off rapidly in their thirties. These figures are therefore perhaps an *over*-estimate of the amount of over-representation of black males in the prison population.

[3] Custody includes imprisonment, a partially suspended sentence of imprisonment, detention in a young offender institution, and, in a few cases, a hospital order.

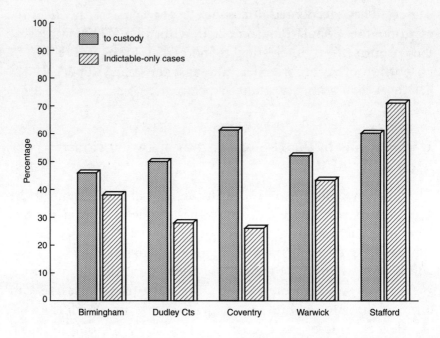

Figure 1 Comparison of the percentage sentenced to custody and the percentage of indictable-only cases at each Crown Court Centre* (males)

*The white sample was weighted approximately for each court. An explanation of the reasons for, and method of, weighting the sample can be found on page 34 above.

as conspiracies to commit offences.[4] And yet, as Figure 1 shows, the proportion sentenced to custody was not related in any consistent way to the proportion of such cases which were sentenced at these courts.

Although there were many fewer indictable-only cases amongst those dealt with at the Dudley Courts than at Birmingham the proportion the judges sentenced to custody was still 4 percentage points higher. Coventry, which had the smallest proportion of the most grave category of offences, sentenced the highest proportion of offenders to custody—at a rate 16 percentage points higher than did judges at Birmingham who dealt with a much higher proportion of the more serious offences.[5] This is equivalent to a rate of using custody at Coventry which is one third higher than for cases at Birmingham. Clearly, any disparities in the proportions of each ethnic group given a custodial sentence must be seen in the light of an apparent considerable variation in practice, irrespective of the ethnic origin of the offender.

3. Racial Disparities in the Use of Custody

Taking the cases dealt with by these courts as a whole, the proportion of black offenders sentenced to custody was 8.2 percentage points higher than the proportion of whites. Asians, on the other hand, were given a custodial sentence less often than either whites or blacks. Without controlling for any of the variables relating to the offences committed or the criminal records

---

[4] Of course, the number of offences which are triable-either-way may be as serious as some of the offences tried only on indictment, notably the most serious offences relating to importing and supply of Class A drugs.

[5] When the National Association of Probation Officers published figures (from the Supplementary Tables of *Criminal Statistics* for 1988) in *Crown Courts and Sentencing* (1990), it too showed that Coventry was the third tier court which made the greatest use of custody: 63 per cent. See also, 'Crown Court Prison Sentences "Resemble a National Lottery"', *The Times*, 23 January 1990.

of the offenders which might have explained these differences, these differences amount to a 17 per cent greater probability that a black defendant would receive a custodial sentence than a white (8.2/48.4) and an 18 per cent lesser probability that an Asian would be sent to custody than a white (8.7/48.4). The effect was that among those found guilty at these five West Midlands Crown Courts, for every 100 whites sentenced to custody there were 117 blacks and 82 Asians who received such a sentence.

The differences between the courts, as Table 2 shows, were even greater.

Table 2: Percentage sentenced to custody by court and ethnic group* (males)

Court	Whites		Blacks		Asians		Total	
	Number	%	Number	%	Number	%	Number	%
Birmingham	875	45	569	52	315	37	1767	46
Dudley Courts	404	48	246	65	157	40	811	50
Coventry	69	62	35	54	24	58	129	61
Warwick	64	52	22	64	37	49	125	52
Stafford	31	55	17	88	3	67	52	60
Total	1443	48.4	889	56.6	536	39.6	2884	48.9

At the Dudley courts the proportion of black offenders who were sentenced to custody was 17 percentage points higher than for white offenders: 65% v 48%. This is equivalent to a 38 per cent higher rate of custody for blacks than whites (17/48). The difference was even greater when black offenders were compared with Asians: 25 percentage points or 66 per cent higher (25/40). There were similar large differences in the black:white 'custody ratio' at Warwick and Stafford, although they were, of course, based on smaller numbers. Only at Coventry were more whites and Asians sent to custody than blacks. As explained above, in the year in which this sample of cases was taken, cases committed to Dudley Crown Court were also heard in court rooms in Wolverhampton and at Birmingham, the Dudley court house being too small to accommodate all the business of the court. Nevertheless, the same large differences between the white and black custody rates were apparent at whichever of these venues the cases were sentenced (See Figure 2).

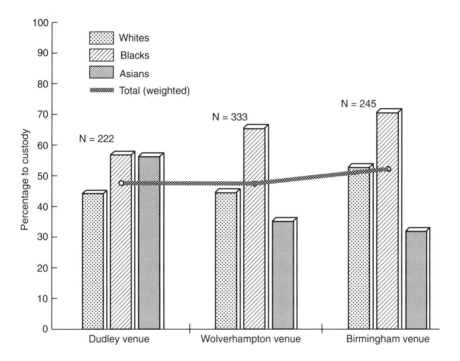

Figure 2 Percentage sentenced to custody at each of the venues of the Dudley Crown Court (males)

As might be expected, there were considerable variations in the proportion of cases which had been dealt with by judges of different status. As Table 3 shows, over 60 per cent of the cases were sentenced by full time Circuit Judges and another quarter

Table 3: Number and percentage of male cases dealt with by judges of different status

Status of Judge	Whites		Blacks		Asians	
	Number	%	Number	%	Number	%
High Court Judges	36	2.5	38	4.3	21	3.9
Circuit Judges	917	63.6	556	62.5	361	67.4
Recorders	348	24.1	222	25.0	115	21.5
Assistant Recorders	141	9.8	73	8.2	39	7.3

by part-time Recorders. Comparatively few had been dealt with by High Court Judges or the relatively inexperienced Assistant Recorders.[6]

There were also considerable variations in the use made of custody by judges of different status. The High Court Judges who were assigned the most serious strata of cases sentenced over 70 per cent of them to custody, while Assistant Recorders did so in less than 40 per cent of their cases. But neither sentenced comparatively more blacks than whites to a penal institution. On the other hand, as Figure 3 shows, both the Circuit Judges and the Recorders did so: and they had dealt between them with 88 per cent of all cases in the sample.

4. Variations between Judges

But, of course, any overall difference in the pattern of sentencing, both within and between courts, may be a product of a good deal of variation between individual judges. It would have

[6] Circuit Judges are full-time judges of the Crown Court. Recorders and Assistant Recorders are barristers or solicitors of at least 10 years' standing appointed as part-time judges. Their duties are specified by the Lord Chancellor. When not sitting they are in private practice. See *Blackstone's Criminal Practice 1991*, pp 866–8.

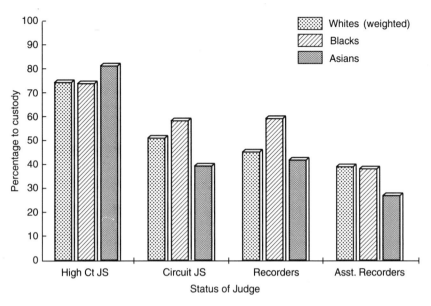

Figure 3 Percentage of males sentenced to custody by judges of different status

been misleading statistically to compare the sentences imposed by each judge, even with a sample of cases as large as that gathered for this study, because the 2,884 sentencing decisions were made by 184 different judges, 147 of whom dealt with less than 20 sampled cases in the course of the year. There were, however, 17 Circuit judges and one Recorder each of whom had sentenced at least 45 of the sampled cases (12 of them 66 or more) and for whom, therefore, it was possible to compare the pattern of their decisions in relation to the use of custody. They had, between them, been responsible for sentencing just over half (54%) of the cases in the sample. It should be borne in mind that even for these judges the numbers they dealt with in each ethnic group were often quite small and the percentage could have been different if a relatively small number of cases had been dealt with differently. It would therefore be inappropriate to compare particular cases dealt with by any individual judge. What this study is seeking to investigate is whether there are any distinctive racial patterns between the judges in the sentences they imposed.

Table 4 shows that any racial differences in the proportions of males sentenced to custody has to be seen in the context of a general pattern of wide variations for offenders taken as a whole. The overall use of custody ranged from 29 per cent to 68.5 per cent, with judges spread right through this wide range. There were more judges who sentenced a higher proportion of blacks to custody than whites and most of the judges sentenced relatively few Asians to a custodial sentence.

Table 4: Number of judges (18) classified by the proportion of male offenders sentenced to custody*

Percentage of cases to custody	Total	Whites	Blacks	Asians
Up to 40	2	5	3	10
41–45	5	4	2	2
46–50	5	3	2	2
51–55	1	1	2	1
56–60	2	2	1	1
61–65	1	0	3	0
66–70	2	2	0	0
71–82	0	0	5	2
Total No. of Judges	18	18	18	18

*Includes only those with 45 cases or more in the sample.

The proportion of each ethnic group sentenced to custody by each judge was compared in order to see whether they appeared consistent, or even-handed in their treatment of ethnic minorities. The following conclusions emerged:

- Not all judges sentenced more black defendants to custody than whites: *three* of them sentenced 10 to 17 percentage points fewer, equivalent to a 26–27 per cent less frequent use.
- Another *eight* were 'relatively even-handed', the difference varying between 6 percentage points fewer to 7 percentage points greater, equivalent to minus 13 per cent to plus 19 per cent greater. One of these, however, had sentenced over 70 per cent of both blacks and whites to custody: so although he was even-handed between his own cases, the probability of either a black or white offender appearing before him being sent to custody was, on the face of it, much higher than if they had come before a different judge.
- The remaining *seven* judges, however, sentenced substantially more blacks to custody than whites. The proportion was between 11 to 42 percentage points higher for blacks than whites.
- *Six* judges sentenced more Asians than whites to custody, but only one of them over 20 percentage points more. *Eleven* sentenced fewer Asians than whites to custody, eight of them at least 20 percentage points fewer.
- This lack of concordance between the level of use of custody for whites, blacks and Asians was evident when the judges were ranked in their order of severity for each ethnic group. A perfect match would have produced, of course, a coefficient of 1.0, but the correlation between the ranking of judges in relation to the proportion of whites and blacks each sentenced to custody was only .32, between whites and Asians .35, and between blacks and Asians only .08.[7]

Thus, one cannot escape the conclusion that if such variations in the use of custody, both on average and for different

[7] The test used was Spearman's Rank Order Correlation. When the Pearson correlation coefficient was computed based on the actual percentage use of custody (rather than their rank order), the results were very similar. Between whites and blacks .29, whites and Asians .39, and between blacks and Asians .09.

ethnic groups, are due to the particular characteristics of the cases appearing before each judge, then the variations in the types of cases they each dealt with would have had to be very substantial indeed.   .

5. Conclusion

Such crude comparisons do, of course, suggest large variations in the use of custody according to the court and before which judge a defendant appeared. They are quite often cited as sufficient evidence of unjustified disparity and unequal treatment. But they will not satisfy the sceptic, particularly the judicial sceptic, who would be likely to claim that they do, in fact, treat like cases alike and that the disparities in the proportions of cases given a custodial sentence are simply due to variability in the nature of the cases dealt with by these judges at the different courts.[8] In other words, disparities are not the same thing as discrimination.[9] And it is to this contention that the analysis now turns.

[8] For a recent example of an analysis based on 'crude' differences in the proportions of cases sentenced to custody by various Crown Courts, see Paul Robertshaw, *Rethinking Legal Need: The Case of Criminal Justice*, 1991, pp 199–201.

[9] For a useful discussion of the difference between the concepts of disparity and discrimination, see, John Petersilia and Susan Turner, *Guideline—Based Justice: the Implications for Racial Minorities*, (1985), Rand Corporation: 'The distinction between **racial discrimination** and **racial disparity** in the sentencing is important . . . Racial **discrimination** occurs if system officials make *ad hoc* decisions based on race rather than clearly defined standards. Racial **disparity** occurs when legitimate standards are applied but have different results for different racial groups', as a result, for example of differential involvements in serious crime, at p v and p ix.

4

DID CASE CHARACTERISTICS VARY ACCORDING TO RACE?

The most obvious question to begin with is whether the case characteristics of the black defendants are worse than those of the whites in respect of those variables which are likely to be related to a higher probability of receiving a custodial sentence, whatever the race of the defendant: thus explaining the higher custody rate for blacks, especially at the Dudley courts and at Warwick and Stafford, and the lower rate for Asians. As explained below (p 65), the proper way to test this hypothesis is through the use of multivariate analysis. Nevertheless, it is first necessary to establish whether there were any differences in the legally relevant and other characteristics of the different ethnic groups.

1. Overall Differences in the Characteristics of White as Compared to Black Defendants

Comparisons were made of white and black defendants in relation to a very wide range of variables which can be grouped into those which described:

a) the legal processing of the case prior to sentence
b) the offence(s) of which convicted
c) previous history of convictions and sentences, and
d) various personal and social characteristics, which might or might not be considered relevant by the court.

The Tables which follow indicate the statistical significance of the comparisons made between the most relevant variables.[1] The data relating to the white sample have, for this purpose, been re-weighted so as to take into account the different sampling fractions of white cases at the five courts.

i) *Legal Process Variables*

As far as those variables connected with the processing of the case were concerned (See Table 5), it was notable that a statistically significant higher proportion of black defendants than whites had been committed for trial in custody rather than on bail and therefore when they appeared for sentence they were already in custody; a considerably higher proportion had initially indicated that they wished to be tried rather than entering a guilty plea and, in fact, had pleaded not guilty on the day of trial. This may indicate that a higher proportion of blacks believed that they had been falsely charged, or that more may have been advised to contest the case in court. But, whatever the reason may have been, it did, of course, remove from them the benefits to be gained from expressions of contrition, and it was therefore not surprising to find fewer definite expressions of remorse or regret recorded in their files. Furthermore, when the defendant intends to plead not guilty it is much less likely that the probation service will prepare a social inquiry report which is designed to provide a better understanding of the circumstances giving rise to the offence and the personal and overall factors influencing its commission. Not only do these reports contain recommendations as to the 'appropriate' sentence—usually non-custodial—but they are also invaluable to defence counsel in making pleas of mitigation. It was therefore

[1] All probability values in Tables 5 to 10 (e.g. p < .01) refer to the chi square test with Yates correction for continuity, with 1 degree of freedom.

Table 5: Percentage of white and black male offenders with characteristics relating to the legal processing of their case†

Attributes	Whites	Blacks
Committed for trial on indictment		
(i.e. not an either-way offence)	27	40
Either-way/Committed by Magistrates	62	51
Either-way/Elected for trial	11	8
Committed for trial (not on bail)	18	22
Appeared for sentenced in custody		
(not on bail)	20	26
Requested trial	39	52
Pleaded **not** guilty at trial	11	23
Had breached bail	9	5
Other offences taken into		
consideration (TIC)	16	9
More than one criminal incident	32	23
Found guilty of 3 or more		
offences of different types	24	17
Had **no** S.I.R.	28	42
Expressed remorse/regret	43	31

†All comparisons are significant *p* <0.01

especially noteworthy that 42 per cent of the black defendants
appeared for sentence without a social inquiry report being
available, compared to 28 per cent of the whites.

Substantially more black offenders had been committed on
indictment i.e. for an offence which could not be tried either-
way, largely due to the higher proportion of them charged with
robbery (see below).[2] Also, of those which could have been

---

[2] Apparently at Leeds Crown Court Jefferson and Walker found that the proportion
of 'indictable only offences was small (about 3 per cent), about the same for each race'.
It is hard to reconcile this with the finding in the West Midlands, See T. Jefferson and
M. A. Walker, 'Ethnic Minorities in the Criminal Justice System', *Criminal Law
Review*, (1992), pp 83–95 at p 89.

tried either-way a higher proportion of blacks had been committed by the magistrates and fewer of them had elected themselves to be tried at Crown Court (8% v 11%), a finding contrary to that of the Runnymede Trust survey in London.[3] On the positive side, significantly fewer blacks than whites had breached their bail (5%) or had other offences taken into consideration, or had committed offences which arose from more than one criminal incident, or were found guilty of 3 or more offences of different types, indicating that they had been less often involved in multiple criminal incidents.

ii) *Variables Relating to the Offence*

There were significant differences in the pattern of the offences for which black and white defendants were originally charged and of which they were finally convicted. They have been grouped into 12 broad offence types in Table 6.

A higher proportion of blacks were convicted of at least one violent offence (whether as the main or a subsidiary charge— 53% v 44%) but there was no evidence to suggest that they were more frequently involved in violence resulting in a conviction for wounding or that the outcome was more serious. Indeed, although a higher proportion of the blacks convicted of serious wounding had used a knife (16% v 8%), the proportion of incidents which resulted in the victim being medically treated or hospitalised for stitches, fractures or internal injuries was no

[3] A. Shalice and P. Gordon, *Black People, White Justice?* (1990). Further, as yet unpublished, research by Monica Walker and Tony Jefferson, relating to cases dealt with at Leeds Crown Court, apparently suggests that a higher proportion of blacks than whites charged with either-way offences in the magistrates' courts had been committed for trial, but that this was equally accounted for by blacks being more likely to elect trial and magistrates more likely to decline jurisdiction and commit to the Crown Court. It is evident that there is a good deal of regional variation in committal of either-way cases. See generally, David Riley and Julie Vennard, *Triable-Either-Way Cases: Crown Court or Magistrates' Court*, 1988, Home Office Research Study No. 98, H.M.S.O.

Table 6: Percentage of white and black male offenders with characteristics relating to the type of offence charged and convicted†

Attributes	Offence charged		Offence convicted	
	Whites	Blacks	Whites	Blacks
Serious violence: S18 GBH				
w/i, Manslaughter	13	14 n.s.	4	6 n.s.
Section 20 GBH	4	5 n.s.	8	8 n.s.
Robbery	6	19	5	15
Blackmail/Kidnap	1	2	1	2
Public Order: Affray,				
Violent Disorder	12	7	13	10*
Minor Violence: S47 Assault	6	6 n.s.	10	10 n.s.
Rape	2	2 n.s.	1	2
Sex offence	3	2*	4	3*
Burglary (household)	14	8	14	8
Burglary (other)	12	7	11	7
Theft	14	8	13	8
Fraud	6	3	6	3
Receiving/Handling	3	2 n.s.	5	4 n.s.
Reckless drive	3	2 n.s.	3	2 n.s.
Supply drugs	1	12	1	11
Others	1	2	1	3

†All comparisons are significant $p < 0.01$, unless indicated; *$p < 0.05$;
n.s. not significant.

higher than in incidents where the perpetrator was white. The
proportion resulting in some continuing impairment, which was
low for both groups, was, in fact, somewhat lower for
blacks(4% v 6%).

As mentioned above, a substantially greater proportion of
blacks (15%) were convicted of robbery than were whites (5%).
But whereas the whites more often threatened with a firearm,
the black offenders more often used their fists or blunt instru-
ments. Even so, there were no differences in the proportion of

victims of blacks or whites who were seriously injured during robberies. Nor were the robberies committed by blacks more serious in their financial consequences: in fact the reverse. More of them left the scene with money or valuables estimated to be worth £100 or less (59% v 46%), and fewer of them got away with a sum of over £1,000 (12% v 16%).[4] The robberies were classified according to whether they could be regarded as an organised or planned attempt to rob a store or security van staff rather than 'muggings' in the street or elsewhere, and whether, if they were 'muggings', harm was caused, or only threats or intimidation used, or the object simply 'snatched'. This revealed that there was a tendency for the white cases to be more often planned robberies (23% v 15%) and the black cases more often to be snatches accompanied by intimidation (20% v 15%). In general, the victim of a black offender was more frequently a female (17% v 11%) or another black or an Asian person (17% v 4%), although less often a child or a person over 65.

A higher proportion of blacks were convicted of offences involving drugs, especially supplying drugs, usually cannabis, yet substantially fewer were convicted of property offences not involving violence, particularly burglary of a household and other burglaries or theft. Fewer were in breach of trust (4% v 13%), perhaps reflecting their employment status (see page 56 below), and fewer, also, had stolen property valued at £1,000 or more (13% v 24%).

Thus, the major difference between the offence patterns of black and white defendants was in their *modus operandi* for achieving financial gain. More of the former had been involved in crimes where the method of acquisition was robbery from the person or in supplying drugs, while more of the latter had

---

[4] The value was not always given, but it was possible to make a rough yet reasonable estimate from the descriptions given.

used household and other burglary, theft and fraud as their means of enrichment.

iii) *Prior Histories of Offending*

There were some significant differences in the distribution of the number of previous convictions of black and white defendants. Slightly fewer blacks had no prior convictions of any kind (18% v 22% See Table 7), but fewer also had eight or more previous court appearances resulting in a conviction. However, significantly more blacks had at least one prior conviction for violence, or for robbery, for carrying an offensive weapon or for a drugs offence. Of those who had been currently convicted of an offence of violence or one involving drugs a significantly higher proportion of blacks had also a prior conviction for an offence of a similar type. Nevertheless, overall, slightly fewer black defendants had a prior conviction for an offence of a similar type to their current conviction.

About two-thirds of both racial groups had previously served a custodial sentence, although significantly fewer blacks than whites had served four or more such sentences, either for any former conviction or for a similar type of offence as the one of which they were currently convicted.

Fewer blacks had previously been on probation but, of those blacks who had been, fewer had breached the order. There was no difference between the proportion of blacks and whites previously given, or who had breached, a community service order. Even so, at the time they appeared for sentencing, a slightly, but significantly, higher proportion of blacks (although only a minority) were currently in breach of a suspended sentence, a community service order or a combination of different sentences.

Thus, looking at the pattern of previous offending as a whole, black offenders might be regarded as having been

Table 7: Percentage of white and black male offenders with various characteristics relating to previous convictions and sentences†

Attributes	Whites	Blacks
No prior convictions	22	18*
8+ previous convictions	24	18
1+ Pre. cons. for violence	28	33
1+ Pre. cons. for robbery	7	20
1+ Pre. cons. for offensive weapon	9	17
1+ Pre. cons. for drugs	5	24
1+ Pre. cons. for burglary	50	46*
Pre. Cons. for offence of similar type to current conviction	46	42*
Previously on probation	35	26
Prev. probation breached	20	12
In breach of a sentence SS/CSO/Prob.	6	9
4+ previous custodial sentences	16	12
One or more previous custodial sentences for offence of similar type to current conviction	28	23

†All comparisons are significant p <0.01, unless indicated; *p <0.05.

slightly more at risk of a custodial sentence, not because they had more prior convictions or custodial sentences, but because if they were convicted of an offence of personal violence, or robbery or drugs, they were rather more likely then whites to have been previously dealt with for such an offence.

iv) *Personal and Social Characteristics*

Rather surprisingly, given the age distribution of the ethnic minority population, slightly fewer of the black defendants were under the age of 21. As regards indices of life-style, a significantly higher proportion of blacks were unemployed or not regularly in employment or, indeed, appeared to have ever had an occupation. As a consequence, more blacks were known to be in receipt of welfare benefits (See Table 8). However, although the black defendants were less often married, significantly fewer were described as having an unsettled or disrupted home life; of having used alcohol prior to the offence; or as being addicted to alcohol or drugs. But, of course, the amount and reliability of information on all these aspects was very much dependent on whether of not a probation officer had compiled a social inquiry report: and they had done so much less often for the black offenders (See Table 5 above).

Table 8: Percentage of white and black male offenders with various known social characteristics†

Attributes	Whites	Blacks
Under 21	35	31*
Unemployed	57	66
No regular employment	70	79
Never employed (but not a student)	12	24
In receipt of Welfare Benefits	47	56
Married	29	19
Unsettled/Disrupted family	32	22
Used alcohol prior to offence	24	11
Addicted to alcohol or drugs	13	6

†All comparisons are significant p <0.01, unless indicated; *p <0.05.

2. Characteristics of Black and White Defendants at Birmingham and the Dudley Courts

Most of the comparative analysis of sentencing which follows will concentrate on the Dudley courts and Birmingham Crown Court where the majority of the cases in the sample had been sentenced and between whom (as shown in Table 2, page 42) there appeared to be substantial differences in the proportion of black male offenders who had been sentenced to custody.

The profiles of white and black defendants were found not to be the same at these courts. At Birmingham Crown Court there were no significant differences between the proportion of blacks and whites who were known to be unemployed, or in receipt of welfare benefits. Similar proportions were convicted of offences against females and of non-household burglary. There were also no differences in the proportion previously convicted of a violent offence; or of those with a current conviction for violence with a prior conviction for that type of crime; or of the number of prior custodial sentences or the length of time previously served in custody. Nevertheless, the difference in the proportion convicted on indictment of robbery (17% v 5%) and drugs offences (16% v 2%) remained substantial.

In contrast, at the Dudley courts a significantly higher proportion of the black offenders had served a prior custodial sentence (55% v 41%), in particular a sentence in a young offender institution (47% v 35%). Furthermore, the employment records of blacks were considerably less favourable than those of the whites (73% of blacks being unemployed compared with 57% of whites, and 84% of blacks not being in regular employment compared with 68% of the whites). On the other hand, black and white offenders at the Dudley courts did not differ in respect of several important characteristics which are known to be related to the use of custody. Similar proportions appeared for trial and sentence in custody; were in breach of bail; were convicted of an offence involving the use of violence (there was also a much smaller difference in the proportion convicted of robbery—11% v 6%—than at Birmingham); were convicted for household burglary or of receiving. They had a similar total number of offences proved at prior court appearances and a similar profile of previous convictions for an offence of the same type as that for which they received their current conviction. And no more blacks than whites had previously served a custodial sentence for the type of offence of which they were currently convicted.

On the face of it, therefore, it would seem unlikely that all of the very substantial difference in the proportion of blacks and whites sentenced to custody at the Dudley courts could be due to blacks having a combination of attributes which would make a higher proportion of their cases deserving of deprivation of liberty.

Nevertheless, it remains to be shown whether, and to what extent, particular combinations of case attributes accounted for the observed differences in the rate at which black and white defendants were sentenced to custody by these courts. In other words: was the custody rate similar for those blacks and whites who had the same characteristics and the difference, therefore, simply due to a higher proportion of blacks having those characteristics which were associated with a higher rate of custody regardless of the race of the defendant?

3. Asian Defendants Compared with White Defendants

In examining the features of those cases which involved Asian defendants there is much to suggest that the lower proportion who were sentenced to custody was largely due to the nature and circumstances of the offences of which they were convicted and their personal characteristics. It is true that a much higher proportion of Asians than whites appeared before the courts charged with an offence which could only be tried on indictment but to a greater extent the charge was reduced at court to a lesser offence which could have been tried either-way.

They were also proportionally much more likely than whites to be convicted of crimes which are legally defined as grave: 35

Table 9: Percentage of white and Asian male offenders with characteristics relating to the processing and character of their case†

Attributes	Whites	Asians
Committed for trial on indictment	27	48
Either-way committed by Magistrates	62	46
Either-way elected trial	11	6
Committed for trial (not on bail)	17	13
Requested trial	39	50
Had breached bail	9	4
In breach of court order	14	8
Other offences TIC	16	7
More than one criminal incident	32	20
Had no SIR	28	43
Pleaded not guilty at trial	11	18
Found guilty of one charge only	50	62
Evidence defendant was provoked	7	14
Charged violent/serious crime	15	20
Convicted of violent/serious crime	5	8
Convicted of blackmail/robbery/ kidnapping	6	11
Convicted of household burglary	14	6
Convicted of other burglary/theft	24	15
Convicted of fraud/handling	11	16
Convicted of public order offence	13	17

†All comparisons are significant p <0.01.

per cent were convicted of serious violence or another serious
crime such as importing drugs, kidnapping, robbery or arson,
compared with only 22 per cent of the whites. Yet, this was
balanced by the fact they had been charged on fewer indictments, were found guilty of fewer charges, and had fewer
offences taken into consideration: all reflecting the fact that
their offences much more often arose from a single incident
rather than being part of a pattern of offending. Many more of
them had had no prior convictions and therefore far fewer had

previously served a custodial sentence. Fewer, also, were in breach of a court order. In relation to social indices, considerably fewer were unemployed, or receiving welfare benefits, or came from obviously unstable backgrounds (See Table 10).

Table 10: Percentage of white and Asian male offenders with various social characteristics, previous convictions and sentences

Attributes	Whites	Asians
Under 21	35	44
Unemployed	57	43
In receipt of welfare	48	32
Married	29	34
Unsettled/Disrupted family	32	19
Unsettled life-style	46	30
Addicted to alcohol or drugs	13	5
First conviction under age 17	50	21
No previous convictions	22	49
8+ previous convictions	24	3
1+ Prev. cons. for violence	28	16
1+ Prev. cons. for robbery	7	4*
1+ Prev. cons. for burglary	50	19
1+ Prev. cons. for drugs	5	3 n.s.
Prev. cons for offence of similar type to current conviction	46	23
One or more prev. custodial sentence for offence of similar type to current conviction	28	9
Previously on probation	35	8

†All comparisons are significant $p < 0.01$, unless indicated; *$p < 0.05$; n.s. = not significant.

Once again, the question which has to be addressed is whether the lower proportionate use of custody for Asians can be explained by the combination of relatively serious offences counterbalanced by relatively good prior histories and not so unfavourable social circumstances as compared with the white defendants. Or whether, indeed, given the profile of their cases their custody rate should have been even lower. In other words, were they being treated more severely than whites despite the favourable balance of their circumstances, of were they, in fact, being treated comparatively leniently?

5

COMPARING CUSTODY RATES

1. Which Variables were Linked to Race Differences in the Use of Custody?

Given similar characteristics was there any evidence to suggest that a higher proportion of black Afro-Caribbean and a lower proportion of Asian offenders were sentenced to custody than whites? A useful, indeed essential, first step to a multivariate analysis is to compare, variable by variable, the proportion of each ethnic group which received a custodial sentence. Tables 1, 3 and 4 of Appendix 3 list all the attributes for which there was a statistically significant difference in the proportions of white and black males sentenced to custody for the sample as a whole and also separately for Birmingham and the Dudley courts.[1] An examination of these comparisons reveals that there were only two instances (one of which involved very few cases) where white offenders were significantly more frequently sentenced to custody than blacks. On the other hand, there were about 100 variables, the possession of which by blacks was associated with a greater use of custody. The number, the size and the significance of these differences associated with a higher custody rate for blacks were much larger at the Dudley courts than at Birmingham Crown Court. This immediately suggests that the greater use of custody for black offenders must be at least in part due to a greater judicial propensity to impose custodial sentences upon them.

Several pointers emerged from this preliminary analysis:

---

[1] Table 2 of Appendix 3 gives similar comparisons for white and Asian offenders.

- Whites who were convicted of robbery were sentenced to custody more often than blacks (78% v 69%), perhaps reflecting the less serious nature of street robberies by black offenders already noted above (see page 53). This difference was not, however, statistically significant.
- The custody rates for whites and blacks were not significantly different for offences of personal violence or any of the measures relating to the motive, the weapons used, or the degree of injury incurred.
- Blacks were sentenced to custody at a significantly higher rate than whites where the offence involved theft of property (53% v 40%), especially where the value of the property taken was below £500 (54% v 46%) and for those convicted of household burglary (73% v 55%).
- The proportion of those sentenced to custody who had no previous convictions was the same for blacks and whites in the sample as a whole and at Birmingham, but was significantly higher (42% v 27%) for those dealt with at the Dudley courts.
- Amongst those with previous convictions but no prior history of custody the proportion of blacks sentenced to custody was significantly higher (53% v 42%). In other words, a higher proportion of blacks were being sent to custody for the first time.
- Blacks with two or more previous convictions were significantly more often frequently given a custodial sentence (66% v 54%).
- The proportion of black offenders given a custodial sentence was significantly higher for those who were unemployed (64% v 55%) and for those in receipt of welfare benefits (62% v 52%). It was also higher, it should be noted, for those blacks for whom there was **no** evidence that they were leading an unsettled life-style or came from disrupted family backgrounds (55% of whom went to custody compared to 45% of the whites).

- Blacks and whites (as well as Asians) were sentenced to custody in much the same proportions when there were strong adverse features in their case: in particular appearing for sentence having already been remanded in custody (86% v 82%); being charged on 3 or more separate indictments (78% v 81%); and being found guilty of three or more charges of different kinds (75% v 00%).

These findings suggest that differences in the use of custody for blacks and whites were not evident when the case characteristics were generally regarded as the most serious and where there was consequently little room to exercise discretion in choosing between custody and an alternative sentence. They do suggest, however, that where there was room to exercise greater discretion, the racial factor was associated with a pattern in the use of custody which was disadvantageous to blacks and that the degree of this disadvantage was much more evident at the Dudley courts than at Birmingham.

2. Devising a Multivariate 'Matching' Method

Yet, however revealing such an item-by-item analysis may appear, it cannot satisfactorily resolve the issue of whether or not black Afro-Caribbean or Asian defendants were treated equally to whites. This, of course, is because it can be argued that it is the combination of factors in a case and the weighting given to them that will have determined the sentence chosen. The task, therefore, was to devise a method which would 'match' cases as closely as possible in terms of those legally relevant variables which can be shown to have had the most significant impact on the decision whether or not to commit an offender to custody. One could, of course, have matched cases by variables which the researcher believes **should** have influenced the use of custody. But this has the drawback that

judges might not agree, and the researcher's choice might turn
out not to have had any impact on what, in practice, actually
did determine the decision to choose a custodial sentence. It
was decided, therefore, to use an empirical method. In other
words, to find out which variables did, in fact, affect whether a
custodial sentence was passed or not, and to use this as the
measuring rod to compare whether whites, blacks and Asians
were treated equally with regard to the weight given to these
variables in the sentencing process. This approach, in effect,
tests whether judges applied their current practice equitably. It
does not, of course, imply that that practice was necessarily
correct.

The matching was done by using standard multivariate statistical techniques (stepwise linear regression, discriminant
analysis and logistic regression analysis). The aim was to calculate—when controlling for that combination of variables which
provided the best model of the probability of a case receiving a
custodial sentence—whether the ethnic origin of the defendant
was still a factor associated with a greater or lesser probability
of receiving a custodial sentence. A detailed description of the
statistical methods employed can be found in Appendix 2.

The advantage of deriving a 'probability of custody score'
through a logistic regression analysis was that it made it possible to assign a weight to all the variables (and their constituent
attributes) which were significantly associated with receiving a
custodial sentence or not: a weight which took into account the
impact of all the other variables included in the analysis.[2]

This method allowed for the fact that in different cases different combinations of attributes, some aggravating and some
mitigating the seriousness of the case, could have been associ-

---

[2] The anti-log of the linear combination of the coefficients obtained for each
attribute was then transformed into an odds ratio for each case. This was further transformed into a probability of receiving custody through the formula: **Probability =
Odds/ 1+Odds.**

ated with a similar probability of receiving a custodial sentence. To take a simple example: offenders who commit one crime of medium gravity, such as burglary of commercial premises and who have no previous convictions, may be sentenced to custody at the same rate as those who commit several less serious thefts and have a previous conviction for theft. Thus, a score derived in this way made it possible to classify all the cases according to the probability of their receiving a custodial sentence. At one end of the scale certain combinations of attributes were associated with a low probability of custody—ten or twenty per cent—at the other end with a very high rate of custody—eighty or ninety per cent. The sample could then be divided into a number of groups each having a different rate of custody, enabling a comparison to be made between the observed rate of custody of white, black and Asian defendants with the expected rate of custody for all offenders who were in the same probability of custody group. And, of course, this method took account of the fact that the distribution of cases between the risk groups could be different for each racial group. If, for example, blacks had more of the attributes associated with being in a high risk of custody group, their overall expected rate of custody would be higher than that for whites.

Therefore, if race had no effect on the sentences imposed there would be no significant differences between the 'observed' and 'expected' proportions of whites, blacks and Asians given a custodial sentence when all legal and social variables significantly associated with the use of custody had been considered. Such a score could also, of course, be used to compare expected and observed rates of custody at different courts and, within courts, to compare the expected and observed proportions of each ethnic group sentenced to custody by different judges.

Another method of checking whether race had a significant impact on the use of custody was to calculate a new logistic regression model which included race as a variable. In effect this showed the extent to which the odds of receiving a custodial sentence increased or decreased according to the ethnic origin of the offender whilst holding constant all the other variables which were considered in calculating the probability of receiving a custodial sentence. Similar models were developed to calculate the changes in the odds of a custodial sentence depending on the court which dealt with the case.

3. The Probability of Custody Scores

The analyses which follow are based on the probability of custody score calculated for the total sample of 2,884 male cases (TPCS), irrespective of the ethnic origin of the defendant. The results obtained have been checked against and compared with those derived from an analysis based solely on the sample of white male cases.

A score based on all cases had the advantage of increasing the statistical significance and reliability of the findings because it took into account, and gave weight to, the whole range of characteristics of cases across all ethnic groups. Thus, for example, if the amount of money or degree or type of violence involved in offences committed by different ethnic groups were substantially different, a score based on the white cases only could give insufficient weight to the influence of some variables on the use of custody for blacks or Asians. But a score based on all cases did have a potential disadvantage in that it compared the expected and observed custody rates for each racial group with the average obtained for all the groups together. This meant, for example, that the black observed custody rate was compared with an average expected rate which might have been affected by a higher custody rate for blacks with the same characteristics as whites. If this were the case it would tend to diminish the size of the ratio between the expected and observed custody rate for black defendants. In other words, this approach tends to minimise rather than maximise differences.

The second score, calculated on the basis of the white cases only (WPCS), had the advantage that it made it possible to apply the weights given to attributes in the white cases to the same attributes in the black and Asian cases. This estimated what the difference between the observed and expected custody rate for blacks or Asians would have been if the factors which explained the varying custody rates of the white sample had been given the same weight in sentencing the black or the Asian samples. It had the disadvantage that it might not give sufficient weight to certain variables which might be specifically associated with black or Asian offenders. It therefore tended to produce a maximum estimate of racial differences.

Separate probability of custody scores were also calculated for black defendants (BPCS) and Asians (APCS) in order to see if different attributes were included in the models which best predicted their rates of custody. This was a way of checking whether cases from different racial groups were given 'equality of consideration'—the same factors receiving the same weight in relation to the decision whether or not to impose a custodial sentence.[3]

In addition, in those instances where there were shown to be apparent racial differences in the custody rate observed compared to the rate expected, further analyses were undertaken in an attempt to discover whether, when the effect of the legal variables was controlled for, any differences remained which could be attributed to non-legal factors other than race, such as unemployment.

The analysis began with linear regression and discriminant analyses of over 80 variables describing all the attributes of the

[3] For a discussion of the idea of equality of consideration see Roger Hood *Sentencing in Magistrates' Courts* (1962) pp 13–16

offence and the offender that could be derived from the files and reliably measured. Several logistic models were constructed and from these the model which had the most significant coefficients and greatest discriminant power was selected. This logistic model for the whole sample (TPCS) was based on 15 variables which described over 50 attributes of the offence and the offender's criminal record. These variables correctly predicted whether a case would receive custody or not in 75 per cent of cases. Given the already noted the fact that a substantial amount of variation appeared to be related to the judge and the court at which cases were sentenced, the discriminatory power of this model was probably as high as one could hope to obtain from a large data-base of this kind.[4] The variables were:

Most Serious Offence of which Convicted:[5]

- Serious Violence and other Grave Crimes: e.g. Aggravated Burglary, Arson, Rape, Manslaughter, S18 Wounding with Intent, Arson with Intent, Threats to Kill, Possessing Arms and Explosives, Importing Dangerous Drugs
- Blackmail, Robbery and Kidnapping
- Supplying Drugs
- Sexual offences (other than Rape)
- S.20 wounding (Grievous Bodily Harm)
- Death by Reckless Driving and Reckless Driving

---

[4] It is interesting to note that Carol Hedderman, in her study based on the Home Office data on Crown Court sentencing decisions, used a discriminant analysis for nine factors which partial correlation had shown to be independently related to the use of custody for property offenders. This successfully predicted the use of custody in 75% of cases. See, 'Custody Decisions for Property Offenders in the Crown Court', *Howard J.*, Vol. 30, (1991), pp 207–217 at p 215.

[5] The crimes grouped into these categories, and the proportions of males and females sentenced to custody for each, are listed in Appendix 4.

- Public Disorder (Affray and Violent Disorder, Criminal Damage and Perverting Course of Justice)
- Household Burglary
- Other Burglaries and Thefts
- Frauds and Handling Stolen Goods
- Minor Violence (S.47 Assaults Occasioning Actual Bodily Harm, Common Assault)
- Other Offences (all with very low rates of custody)

Mode of Trial:

- Main Offence Triable only on Indictment
- Triable-Either-Way

Remand Status:

- Appeared for Sentence on Remand in Custody
- Appeared for Sentence on Bail

Plea:

- Pleaded Guilty to Main Charge Proceeded With
- Pleaded Not Guilty to Main Charge Proceeded With

Number of Charges of Which Convicted:

- One
- Two of same type
- Two of mixed type or 3 of same type
- Three of mixed type or 4 of same type
- Four of mixed type or more

Outstanding Court Orders:

- Not in breach of any previous court order
- In breach of a Conditional Discharge or Probation Order
- In breach of a Suspended Sentence of Imprisonment, a Community Service Order or any combination of Orders

Violence in the Offence(s):

- Violence in Most Serious and/ or Lesser Offences Convicted
- No Evidence of Violence in any Offence

Degree of Injury

- Violence Threatened, no Harm Caused
- Bruises/Grazes/Cuts not Requiring Stitches
- Wounds Requiring Stitches
- Broken Bones/Fractured Limbs/Skull/Severe Internal Injuries

Motive For Violence:

- Violence Arising from Personal Dispute
- Other Motives: Theft/Sexual Gratification/Resisting Arrest/Unprovoked

Effect of Violence:

- Continuing Impairment
- No Lasting Effects

Amount of Financial Loss Involved:

- £Nil–499
- £500–999
- £1,000–9999
- £10,000 plus

Vulnerability of Victim(s):

- Victim a child under 16 or aged adult 65 plus or female
- Other victims

Total Number of Offences Previously Convicted of (which was more significant than the Number of Previous Court Appearances leading to a conviction):[6]

- None
- 1–3
- 4–5
- 6–10
- 11 or more

Previous Custodial History for Similar Type of Offence:

- No Prior Custodial Sentence for Similar Offence
- One or More Prior Custodial Sentence for Similar Offence

---

[6] On the problems of choosing appropriate measures of prior record, see Susan Welch, John Gruhl and Cassia Spohn, 'Sentencing: The Influence of Alternative Measures of Prior Record', *Criminology*, Vol. 22 (1984), pp 215–227.

> **Previous Breach of a Community Service Order:**
>
> • No Previous CSO or Previous CSO without breaching
> • Previous CSO Breached

Although this has been called a 'Probability of Custody Score', it can be seen that all the attributes summarised by the score relate in one way or another to variables which would have been legally relevant in assessing the overall seriousness of the case.[7] It could therefore also properly be considered a 'Seriousness of Case Score'. No one could argue that there would be any justification for applying such variables unequally in the consideration of the appropriate sentence for defendants with different ethnic backgrounds.[8]

The scores derived from the combination of weights assigned to each of these variables for each case were regrouped into 9 intervals each defining cases with a different predicted probability of custody, ranging from those with a probability of

[7] Several other significant variables were not included in the score, either because they related to non-legal factors such as unemployment, or to factors too obviously related to racial differences, which were often dependent on a plea of guilty and the availability of a social inquiry report, such as expressions of remorse or evidence of intent to reform. It should also be noted that probation officer's recommendations were not included in the score. This is because a recommendation was not regarded as a characteristic of the case but as a judgment on it similar to the sentencing decision. Recommendations therefore needed to be considered as a dependent variable and are analysed separately, see below Chapter 10, pp 150–160.

[8] It should be remembered that this study was carried out before the Criminal Justice Act 1991 came into effect. Section 1 of that Act, of course, has changed the law in relation to sentencing; firstly by making the criteria for imposing a custodial sentence (a) 'that the offence, or the combination of the offence and one other offence associated with it, was so serious that only such a [custodial] sentence can be justified for the offence; or (b) where the offence is a violent or sexual offence, that only such a sentence would be adequate to protect the public from serious harm from him'; and secondly, by laying down the principle in Section 29 that 'an offence shall not be regarded as more serious for the purpose of any provision of this [Act] . . . by reason of any previous convictions of the offender or any failure of his to respond to previous sentences'. For a discussion of the 'not entirely clear' meaning of this section, see M Wasik and R D Taylor, *Blackstone's Guide to the Criminal Justice Act 1991*, (1991), pp 27–29.

between .10 and 19.9 per cent to those with a probability of 95 to 100 per cent. The average proportion sentenced to custody in the sample as a whole, irrespective of race, varied between those levels from .10 (10.4 per cent) to .97 (96.9 per cent). The overall average custody rate for offenders, irrespective of race was, at each level:

Predicted Probability of Custody	Average Custody Rate for Whole Sample
Level 1 (0–19.9%)	.10
Level 2 (20–24.9%)	.26
Level 3 (25–39.9%)	.34
Level 4 (40–44.9%)	.42
Level 5 (45–54.9%)	.54
Level 6 (55–69.9%)	.59
Level 7 (70–79.9%)	.76
Level 8 (80–94.9%)	.88
Level 9 (95–100%)	.97

The slope of this score is illustrated in Figure 4.

4. Comparing the 'Custody Rates' of White, Black and Asian Defendants in the West Midlands Crown Courts as a whole.

Figure 5 (below) reveals that when the white, black and Asian cases were classified according to the seriousness of their case profiles, as reflected in the Probability of Custody Score, a higher proportion of black offenders, compared with whites, fell into the highest risk category and fewer into the least serious category. Asian offenders, on the other hand, were much less likely to be in the highest risk category and were much more frequently in the lowest.[9]

---

[9] The differences in this distribution are statistically significant $\chi^2 = 64.5$, 4 df, p < .0000.

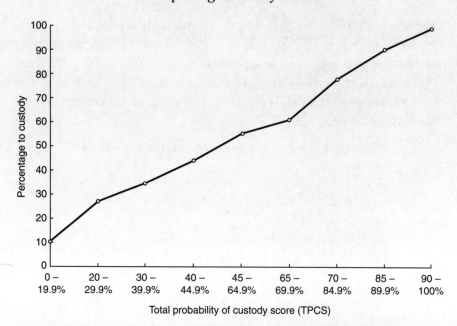

Figure 4 Percentage sentenced to custody according to probability of custody score based on all cases (TPCS, males)

To what extent did this account for the differences in the observed custody rates for whites (48%), blacks (57%) and Asians (40%)? Figure 6, below, shows the percentages of each racial group who were sentenced to custody at each of the 9 predicted custody score levels. And Table 11 shows the difference between the overall proportion of each group which was observed compared with the rate expected after taking into account the distribution of the cases relating to each ethnic group between the various levels of seriousness.

Taking, as the point of comparison, the average custody rate for the male sample as a whole, blacks were committed at a rate of around 2 percentage points higher than would be expected from the profiles of their offences, whites at the rate expected, and Asians 2 percentage points lower. The expected

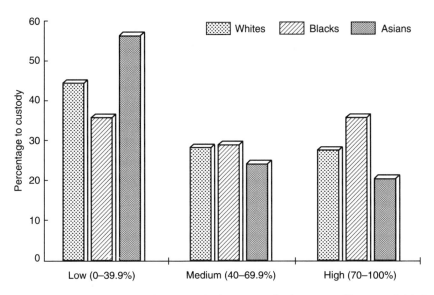

Figure 5 Percentage of each ethnic group in low, medium and high risk of custody groups (males)

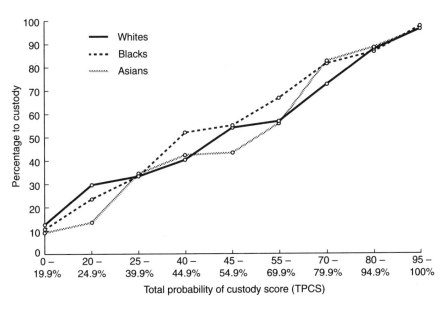

Figure 6 Percentage of each ethnic group sentenced to custody by risk of custody score (TPCS, males)

Table 11: Observed rates of custody compared with expected rates (total male sample)

	Whites	Blacks	Asians
Number observed	1813	503	213
Number expected	1822	484	224
Per cent observed	48.4	56.6	39.7
Per cent expected	48.7	54.4	41.8
Ratio Obs.–Exp. (Percentage points)	−0.3	+2.2	−2.1
Obs.–Exp./Exp. (Percentage difference)	−0.6	+4.0	−5.0

difference between whites and blacks was 5.7 percentage points (54.4−48.7) not the observed 8.2 points (56.6−48.4). Thus, there was a 2.5 percentage points difference which was not explained by the types of cases for which blacks appeared in court.

It should be noted that a difference of 2.5 per cent as a fraction of an expected white custody rate of 48.7 per cent amounts to an increased probability of receiving a custodial sentence of just over 5 per cent (.051). This finding was confirmed by the logistic regression analysis which showed that, when all the variables used to construct the score were held constant, a black offender was about 5 per cent more likely to be sentenced to custody than a white. This is the equivalent of 105 blacks for every 100 whites. This difference was liable to be due to error in less than one in ten samples (p < .08).[10]

It is also apparent that the observed comparatively low custody rate for Asian defendants was almost entirely accounted for by the factors which predict custodial sentences for the

[10] This is the significance of the coefficient for black offenders obtained from the logistic regression model (TPCS), adding race (being black). See Table 1a of Appendix 8.

sample as a whole. In other words, by the fact that Asians had fewer of the attributes which, when taken together, are associated with a high risk of custody. Even so, their probability of getting a custodial sentence was 5 per cent lower than expected.

5. Comparing Blacks and Asians as if they had been Treated Like Whites

A score based on the same combination of variables was calculated which best modelled the variability in the custody rate of the white defendants only (The White Probability of Custody Score: WPCS).[11] This was then used to calculate the observed/expected differences in the custody rates of the black and Asian defendants when the variables in their cases were given the weights which best explained the custody rate when defendants were white. The difference between the white and black rates of custody were the same as when the total score was used and disaggregated, but compared with whites only Asians had an even lower custody rate than expected:

The five per cent greater probability of blacks receiving custody than would be expected if their attributes had been given the same weight as for whites, could have occurred by chance less than one in ten samples ($p < .07$). Thus, a 'raw difference' between white and black custody rates equivalent to 117 blacks for every 100 whites (see p above) was reduced to 105 blacks to custody for every 100 whites. In other words, seventy per cent of the 'raw difference' was accounted for by the type of offences and other characteristics of the cases of which blacks were convicted. But thirty per cent of the black-white difference remained unexplained. Although a five per cent greater probability of getting a custodial sentence is not nearly as great a

---

[11] For the model for the 'White Score' see Table 3A Appendix 8. This model successfully predicted the outcome for whites in 75% of cases, and for all cases in 74%.

Table 12: Ratios of observed compared with expected rates of custody (WPCS, males)

	Whites	Blacks	Asians
Ratio Obs.–Exp. (Percentage points)	baseline	+2.7	–3.7
Obs.–Exp./Exp. (Percentage difference)	baseline	+5.0	–8.5

difference as many have feared (See pp 7–8 above), it is not trivial in human terms. On the basis of these comparisons it is estimated that in this sample 479 black defendants would have been expected to get a custodial sentence at a Crown Court in the West Midlands in 1989, rather than the 503 who did in fact get such a sentence. It is important to understand that, in a statistical study, it is not possible to be absolutely certain that all of this difference is due to race rather than some other unmeasured factors and that this estimate does not refer to any *particular cases*, only to the *aggregate difference* between the observed and expected *probability* of receiving a custodial sentence.

Of course, it might be questioned whether a 5 per cent greater probability is of importance, given that it could be attributable to chance once in 14 times (.07). As Nagel and Neef pointed out, 'statisticians generally demand that before the null hypothesis of no discrimination can be rejected, the probability of the difference observed between blacks and whites must be less than a 0.5 probability'. But they go on to stress that this may be a much too demanding test when seeking to demonstrate whether there is evidence of discrimination or not:

One is in effect saying that it is about 19 times as bad to make the mistake of accepting the hypothesis that discrimination exists when the hypothesis is false (a type-1 error) than it is to make the mistake of rejecting the hypothesis that discrimination exists when the hypothesis is true (a type-2 error). Although the 19 to 1 error costs may be conventional, it would be difficult to justify that ratio with this subject matter since it seems to be at least as harmful to make the mistake of thinking there is no discrimination when there really is as it is to make the mistake of thinking there is discrimination when there really is not. By demanding that the disparities observed be almost totally unattributable to chance, one is in effect demanding that (1) the differences be proved beyond a reasonable doubt and that (2) a strong presumption prevail in favour of ignoring real disparities'.[12]

In this context, therefore, it seems reasonable to accept that a difference between the white and black custody rates which is significant at the 0.7 level should not be lightly dismissed.

Furthermore, when a Probability of Custody Score was calculated solely for the black offenders (BPCS), it was found that the difference between the custody rates for whites and blacks was somewhat larger: The proportion of whites sentenced to custody was 4 percentage points lower than would have been expected if they had been treated like black offenders. This was equivalent to a probability of receiving custody if the offender was white which was 7.6 per cent lower than if he were black.[13] The proportions of black and white offenders sentenced to custody at various points of the black offender scale is shown in Figure 7.

[12] Stuart Nagel and Marian Neef, 'Racial Disparities that Supposedly do not Exist: Some Pitfalls in Analysis of Court Records', *Notre Dame Lawyer*, Vol. 52 (1986), pp 89–94 at p 93. Similarly, Spohn and her colleagues concluded; 'Even though race accounts for 'only' four per cent of the variation in our study in the decision to incarcerate, the tremendous difference between being confined and being free makes it a difference which is both substantial and disturbing'. Cassia Spohn et. al., 'The Effect of Race on Sentencing: A Re-Examination of an Unsettled Question', *Law & Society Review*, Vol. 16 (1981–82), pp 71–88 at p 86.

[13] For the model for the 'Black Score' see Table 4A Appendix 8. This model successfully predicted the outcome for black offenders in 80% of cases, and for all offenders in 72%.

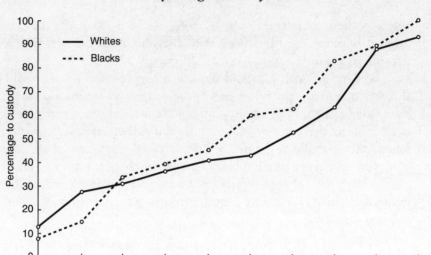

Figure 7 Percentage of black and of white offenders sentenced to custody by black risk of custody score (BPCS, males)

A Probability of Custody score was also calculated solely for Asian offenders (APCS). It was found that, when whites and blacks were judged by the same criteria that affected the use of custody for Asians, there was no significant difference between the custody rates of whites and Asians. However, black offenders were significantly more likely to be incarcerated than Asians.[14]

Thus, all these models, as well as others devised in course of their preparation (with fewer and different combinations of variables), produced roughly similar racial differences in the use

---

[14] The observed custody rate for black offenders was 56.6%. Their expected rate calculated from the Asian score was 50.8% (Obs-Exp +5.8, Obs-Exp/Exp +11.4%). The Asian model successfully predicted the sentence for Asian offenders in 83% of cases, and for all offenders in 71%.

of custody. This can be regarded as a re-assurance that these findings are valid.

6. Attempting to Locate Where Racial Differences Occurred

The figures so far presented relate solely to the overall probabilities of the different ethnic groups receiving a custodial sentence. It is possible of course that these averages masked substantial variations which were related to particular types of offence or offender characteristics or concealed differences of a much greater degree between courts and judges.

There is a wealth of research on sentencing which shows that variations in practice are much more common amongst cases of medium seriousness, which are neither obvious cases for custody or for a non-custodial penalty. In these cases judicial views on the seriousness of the offence, the weight that should be applied to previous convictions and other characteristics of the offender, the balance struck between competing aims of punishment, as well as knowledge and opinions on the effectiveness of the penalties available, will all affect the way in which they choose to exercise the considerable amount of discretion available to them.[15] In the context of this research this obviously raises the question whether the ethnic characteristics of the defendant have a greater impact in such cases. Figures 6 and 7 showed that the line for the black custody rate was consistently above that for whites in the middle to high range of scores (see above). The cases were therefore grouped into three risk bands: low(0–44.9%), medium to high(45–79.9%), very

[15] See, Roger Hood and Richard Sparks, *Key Issues in Criminology*, (1970), Chapter 5, 'Understanding the Sentencing Process', at p 147; also James D. Unnever and Larry A. Hembroff, 'The Prediction of Racial/Ethnic Sentencing Disparities: An Expectation States Approach', *J. Research in Crime & Delinq.*, Vol. 25 (1988), pp 53–82.

high(80–100%). This analysis, which is illustrated in Figure 8, showed that:

- Where the probability of custody was very high (80% or over) or comparatively low (less than 45%) there were no overall differences which could be attributed to race.
- But where the probability was in the medium to high range of the Probability of Custody Score (45%–79%) the black custody rate of 68.0% was significantly higher than the white rate of 60.0%: A difference which amounts to a 13 per cent (8/60) greater probability of a black than a white male receiving a custodial sentence in this range of cases. This confirmed the hypothesis that race appeared as an influential variable where the courts had greater room to use their discretion in sentencing.

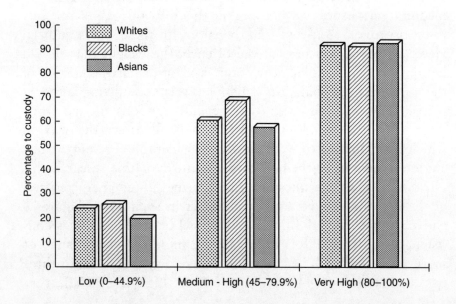

Figure 8 Percentage of each ethnic group sentence to custody in low, medium and high risk of custody groups (TPCS, males)

An entirely separate analysis was made of those offenders who had been convicted of three groups of offences: burglary of a household, theft, and supplying cannabis and Figure 9 shows the substantial differences in the rate at which whites, blacks and Asians were sentenced to custody for them. Each of these offences was analysed so as to distinguish those with the most and least serious circumstances from those of medium gravity and each of these groups was further sub-divided according to whether the offender had no previous convictions or just one, or two or more, previous convictions for the same broad category of offence.

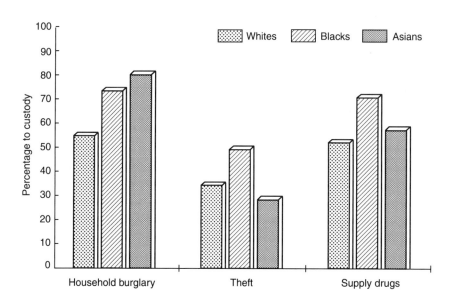

Figure 9 Specific offence categories showing the proportion of each ethnic group sentenced to custody (males)

Whether the crime was housebreaking, theft, or involved the supply of drugs, there were no racial differences in the proportions sentenced to custody who had committed the most serious and the least serious offences in each category. But there were significant differences for each offence amongst those whose crimes were of middling gravity. For example, in housebreakings involving loss of property of less than £1,000 and where the offender had no or only one prior conviction for burglary, 70.6% of blacks got sentenced to custody but only 46.4% of the whites. Twice as many blacks as whites (82.4% v 40.2%) who were convicted of a theft of less (usually far less) value than £10,000 and who had been convicted at the same time of another property offence and had more than one prior conviction for theft, received a custodial sentence.[16] This evidence, although relating relatively to small numbers, re-inforces the view that race differences were located in the middle range of the cases being dealt with at the Crown Courts.

Two other variables which were related to racial differences in the use of custody were age and employment. It was found that there was no difference between the observed and expected proportions of young adult blacks—those aged 20 or less -who were sentenced to custody, all of the race difference occurring amongst those aged 21 or over. The same pattern was found in relation to employment: the differences between the observed and expected rate being entirely confined to those black offenders who were unemployed. This was confirmed when the black probability of custody score was calculated. Being unemployed was a factor significantly correlated with receiving a custodial sentence if the defendant was black but not if he was white or Asian.

Finally, something must be said about the effect of pleading

[16] $\chi^2 = 9.06$, 1 df, p < .0026. The number of whites with no prior convictions involved in offences relating to cannabis was too small to be able to make a meaningful comparison with the black offenders.

not guilty on the probability of receiving a custodial sentence. Andrew Ashworth had noted that 'there is some evidence for the proposition that a guilty plea may make the difference between a custodial and non-custodial sentence . . . and the Court of Appeal has not clearly disallowed the practice'.[17] Further evidence emerged from this study. Holding all the variables constant, a not guilty plea was associated, over the whole range of cases, with an increased odds of receiving a custodial sentence, on average, of 1.7, and it was much the same whether the defendant was white or black. To put this in more graphical terms, an offender whose characteristics (other than plea) would predict a 50% probability of a custodial sentence would, if he pleaded not guilty, have this predicted probability raised to 62 per cent. If the probability were 75% it would be increased to 84%.[18] On the face of it, this would seem likely to have disadvantaged more black offenders, 23 per cent of whom pleaded not guilty compared with only 11 per cent of whites. However, because of the way that the cases involving blacks were distributed across the spectrum of seriousness, it was estimated that if the same proportion of blacks as whites had pleaded not guilty, the expected custody rate for the black offenders as a whole would have been very little changed. This was not, therefore, a factor which could account for racial differences in the use of custody.

7. Conclusion

This overall view of the use of custody at these five West Midlands' courts has revealed that a considerable amount of the variance in the 'raw' custody rates observed for white,

---

[17] Andrew Ashworth, *Sentencing and Criminal Justice*, (1992), at p 312. For an analysis of the effect of guilty pleas on sentence length see pp 125–126 below.

[18] For an explanation of how percentage probabilities are derived from the odds multiplier see Appendix 2, section 4ii.

black and Asian defendants was explained by the fact that a higher proportion of cases involving blacks and a lower proportion involving Asians were of the kind which would have resulted in a custodial sentence irrespective of the race of the defendant. Nevertheless, some moderate yet significant and unexplained differences relating to the race of the defendant remained:

- a *five to eight* per cent higher than expected custody rate for black offenders was found (whether in relation to the risk of custody for all cases, or when blacks were judged by the same criteria that most affected the use of custody for whites, or when the whites were judged by the criteria affecting custody for black offenders)
- a greater use of custody for blacks in the 'middling' range of offence and offender characteristics.

But, of course, the 'raw' comparisons made in Chapter 3 suggested that there might be large variations between the extent to which custodial sentences were used at the various Crown Courts to which cases were committed in the West Midlands and between the sentencing practices of different judges at these courts. The aggregate averages for the sample as a whole could mask such variations. To what extent, for example, could the much larger observed difference between the use of custody for whites and blacks who were committed to the Dudley courts as compared with those committed to Birmingham Crown Court be explained by the characteristics of the cases appearing before them?

6

RACE AND VARYING COURT PRACTICES

1. Comparing the Use of Custody at each of the Five Courts by Race of the Defendant

An obvious hypothesis to explain the much higher proportion of black than white defendants who were sentenced to custody at the Dudley courts and at Warwick and Stafford Crown Courts is that a higher proportion of the Afro-Caribbean defendants dealt with there had those characteristics which were strongly associated with receiving a custodial sentence irrespective of race and, furthermore, that they were a much 'worse' cohort of offenders in this sense than black males sentenced at Birmingham. Also, although it would seem very unlikely, given that Coventry is a third tier court, it could be that the overall much higher use of custody at Coventry, for all three ethnic groups, could be associated with a court case-load that contained a disproportionate number of such custody-prone offenders. It could similarly be argued that the variations in the use of custody for Asians reflects a different distribution of cases between the five courts.[1]

Table 13 shows that, although the proportion of black offenders who were in the worst risk group for custody was indeed higher than the proportion of whites at both Birmingham and the Dudley courts, this could not explain the large

---

[1] When the probability of custody score was based on white cases, there were no differences between the distribution of white and Asian cases between risk groups, which suggests that in the score based on the total sample Asian cases had a significant impact on the score at the bottom end of the scale.

Table 13: Comparison of the proportion of cases by risk of custody groups at Birmingham and the Dudley courts (males)

Risk group (TPCS)	Whites	Blacks	Asians
Low risk (0–44.9):			
Birmingham	49.9	40.8	61.0
Dudley courts	53.2	41.5	65.6
Medium risk (45–79.9):			
Birmingham	30.4	32.0	23.8
Dudley courts	26.2	35.4	20.9
High risk (80–100):			
Birmingham	19.7	27.2	15.2
Dudley courts	20.5	23.2	14.0

difference in the use of custody for the black people who had been committed to the Dudley courts as compared with those dealt with by Birmingham Crown Court. This is because the proportions of whites, blacks and Asians in the low, medium and high risk of custody groups were virtually the same at these two courts.

It was not surprising to find, therefore, as Figure 10 shows, that differences in the use of custody of quite a substantial degree persisted even when the seriousness of cases was controlled for.[2]

It has already been mentioned (see page 29 above) that at the time the samples for this research were drawn cases committed to Dudley Crown Court were heard in court rooms either at Dudley or at Wolverhampton or in the court rooms of Birmingham Crown Court. The Dudley courts sample was therefore analysed separately as shown in Figure 11, in order to see if the

---

[2] The Observed percentage use of custody and the Expected rate, calculated from the TPC Score, for cases dealt with at each of the Crown Courts (Warwick and Stafford combined) is set out in Table 1 of Appendix 5.

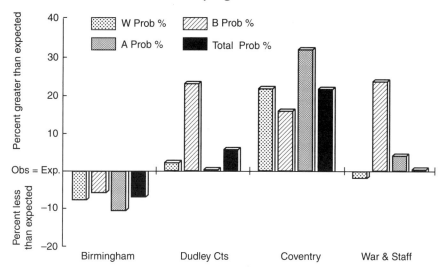

Figure 10 Percentage use of custody greater or less than expected (Obs–Exp/Exp) by race and court (males)

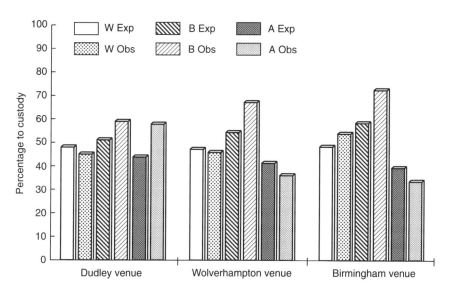

Figure 11 Observed and expected percentages sentenced to custody by race at each venue of the Dudley Crown Court (TPCS, males)

differences between the black observed and expected rate of custody for black defendants was evident wherever the judges assigned to hear cases committed to the Dudley Crown Court sat.

The following conclusions can be drawn from these Figures:

- The custody rates for whites, blacks and Asians sentenced at Birmingham Crown Court were uniformly below the average level of expectation for the West Midlands courts as a whole. And there were no significant differences between the observed and expected rates for any of the ethnic groups.
- The overall (i.e. the total) observed proportion of cases sentenced to custody at the Dudley courts and at Warwick and Stafford was only slightly greater than what would have been expected. At these courts, the observed rates for whites were quite close to the rates expected.
- The proportion of black offenders sentenced to custody by these courts was, however, considerably greater then expected. At the Dudley courts the rate for blacks was 12.3 percentage points higher than expectation and for whites 1 percentage point higher. The expected difference between the use of custody for blacks and whites should have been 6.6 percentage points not the 17.9 percentage points 'raw difference'. The remaining 11.3 percentage points difference is equivalent to an increased probability of custody for black offenders in relation to the rate expected for whites of 24 per cent (See Appendix 5 Table 1 for these calculations). In real terms it meant that instead of an expected 131 out of 246 black offenders getting a custodial sentence, 161 did. The substantial difference between black observed and expected rates was found at whichever of the three venues (Dudley, Wolverhampton or Birmingham) at which the Dudley Crown Court sat at the time this research was carried out.[3]

---

[3] The logistic regression analysis showed, after controlling for the risk of custody,

- Although the number of black defendants who had been sentenced at Warwick and Stafford was much smaller (n=39), only 7 of the 'raw' 22 percentage points difference between the proportion of blacks and whites sentenced to custody could be accounted for by the profile of black cases: the increased probability for blacks in relation to expectation being 28 per cent.
- The custody rate for all sentenced at Coventry Crown Court was much higher than expected, given the profile of cases dealt with. It was even somewhat higher for whites and Asians than for blacks. Overall, the probability of receiving a custodial sentence at Coventry was about 28 per cent higher than at Birmingham: in other words, for every 100 'sent down' at Birmingham, 128 were at Coventry. The reason for this different practice appeared to be the much greater use of custody at Coventry for offenders who were unemployed as well as for the smaller number who had previously breached a community service order. When those two variables were controlled for, in addition to the risk of custody score, the differences between Coventry and the average use of custody disappeared.
- When these calculations were made on the basis of the Probability of Custody Score derived for white cases, the observed custody rate for the black offenders sentenced by the Dudley courts was even greater than that expected: 14 percentage points or a 37 per cent greater probability. And yet no more whites than would be expected were sentenced to custody at these courts, and also rather fewer Asians.
- It is apparent from all these comparisons that the reason why the differences in the proportions of whites, blacks and Asians who were sentenced to custody in the sample as a whole were relatively small was largely due to the lack of any

that the odds multiplier for a black offender receiving custody compared with a white offender at the Dudley courts was, on average, 1.96, p < .0001 (Wald statistical test).

overall racial effect in the use of custody at Birmingham where half the total number of cases had been sentenced.

Finally, a probability of custody score was calculated on the basis of the cases tried and sentenced at Birmingham. This was done so as to estimate what the expected rates of custody would have been at other courts if the cases had been dealt with as they had been at Birmingham. As Figure 12 shows, this produced the same pattern of results, although the difference between the observed and expected use of custody at Coventry was even greater: 140 committed to custody for every 100 at Birmingham. Also, compared with Birmingham the differences for black offenders sentenced by a Dudley court or at Warwick and Stafford even more pronounced.

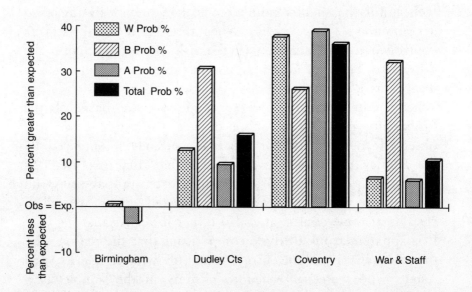

Figure 12 Percentage use of custody greater or less than expected (Obs–Exp/Exp) by race and court (Birm PCS, males)

Thus, whichever of the scores is used as a means of controlling for the seriousness of the cases dealt with, the differences between the observed and expected proportion of blacks sentenced to custody by the Dudley and by the Warwick and Stafford Crown Courts remain at a very statistically significant level.

2. Seeking to Locate the Race Difference amongst cases sentenced by the Dudley courts.

The analysis so far has revealed that, compared with their expected rates of receiving a custodial sentences, whites were dealt with in a very similar way at the Dudley courts as they were at Birmingham. Black offenders, on the other hand, had a considerably greater probability of being sentenced to custody if they had been committed to Dudley Crown Court.[4] Was this pattern common to offences at all levels of seriousness?

To test this, the cases were divided in a variety of ways into different levels of seriousness. This revealed that the large difference between the treatment of blacks at the Dudley courts as compared with Birmingham occurred mainly amongst those who had, for the sample as a whole, a relatively low predicted probability (less than 45%) of receiving a custodial sentence. Although almost the same proportion (41–42%) of black offenders dealt with by these courts fell into this category, only 17% of those dealt with at Birmingham were given a custodial sentence compared with 44% at the Dudley courts. On the other hand, as Table 14 shows, the proportions in the risk group of over 45 per cent were much more similar, and indeed

---

[4] The odds multiplier for a black offender receiving a custodial sentence at the Dudley courts compared with a black offender dealt with at Birmingham was, on average, 2.62, p < .0000. Translating this into actual percentages, this means that a black offender with a 30% probability of custody at Birmingham would have a 53% probability if he had been dealt with at the Dudley courts.

Table 14: Use of custody for blacks and whites at Birmingham and the Dudley courts by risk of custody group* (males)

Risk group (TPCS)	Whites				Blacks			
	Birmingham		Dudley Cts		Birmingham		DudleyCts	
	Number	%	Number	%	Number	%	Number	%
Prob. custody								
0–44.9	437	21.1	215	24.2	232	16.8	102	44.1
45.0–100	438	69.2	189	74.1	337	75.7	144	80.6

* The difference between Blacks at the Dudley courts and Birmingham in the risk group 0–44.9 was highly significant χ^2=26.6, 1 df, p <0.000; in the risk group 45–100 it was not significant. The difference between Black and White offenders at Dudley was significant, χ^2=12.0, 1 df, p <0.0005. In the risk group 45–100 the difference between Blacks and Whites in Dudley was not significant, but it was nearly significant at Birmingham: χ^2=3.7 1 df, p <0.06.

was not statistically significantly different. Thus, while for the sample as a whole, small race effects were found in the medium to high risk group only, the differences evident at the Dudley courts were located amongst those cases which were, in general, the least likely to be thought deserving of a custodial sentence. Figures 13 and 14 compare the proportions of black and white offenders sentenced to custody at each point of the risk of custody scale at the Dudley Courts and at Birmingham.

Were there any factors which might explain why there was at the Dudley courts a very large difference in the treatment of blacks in the lower risk group compared with whites? And why were the blacks dealt with apparently so much more severely

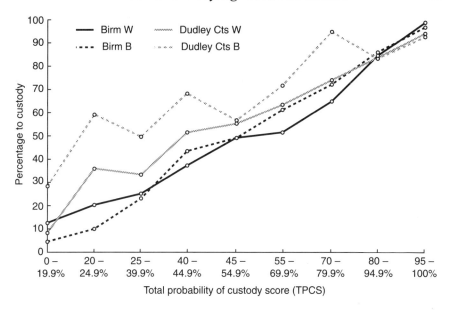

Figure 13 Percentage of black and white offenders sentenced to custody at Dudley courts and at Birmingham by risk of custody (TPCS, males)

than blacks and whites sentenced by Birmingham Crown Court?

Table 15 compares for a large number of variables the proportion of blacks at the Dudley courts who were sentenced to custody with the proportion of whites at that court and of blacks sentenced at Birmingham. One simple pattern stands out. The proportion of blacks at Dudley sent to custody was much higher even when attributes which would normally be associated with mitigation of sentence are considered: attributes such as being a young adult under 21; appearing for sentence already on bail; on a single charge, pleading guilty; having no other offences to take into consideration; being not in breach of any court order; having done no physical harm; stolen a relatively small amount of money; being in employment; not

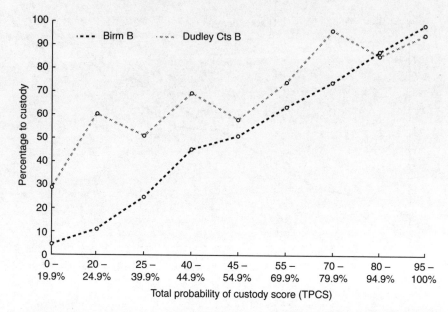

Figure 14 Percentage of black offenders sentenced to custody at Dudley courts and at Birmingham by risk of custody (TPCS, males)

having been previously in custody etc. In other words, amongst this less serious group of cases, blacks sentenced by the Dudley courts appeared much less likely than whites or blacks dealt with at Birmingham to receive the benefits of mitigation. As a consequence, blacks at Dudley Courts, unlike blacks in the sample as a whole (See p 86 above), were just as likely to go to custody whether they were young adults or adults, employed or unemployed.

Nor was the high use of custody for blacks sentenced by the Dudley courts due to differences in the numbers of those with more previous convictions. At Birmingham 53 per cent of the blacks had 2 or more prior convictions and 25 per cent of them were given a custodial sentence. At the Dudley courts 54% of the blacks had 2 or more prior convictions and 53%, more

Table 15: Percentage of white and black male offenders with various mitigating factors at the Dudley courts and at Birmingham, in the risk category (0–44.9% TPCS), who were sentenced to custody

Attributes	Birmingham		Dudley		Comparison Whites/Blacks Dudley courts
	Whites	Blacks	Whites	Blacks	p<
Aged 14–20	22.7	16.9	24.4	45.2	0.06
Appeared for sentence on bail	20.9	15.3	24.3	43.0	0.001
Charged 1 or 2 offences only	21.0	13.7	25.2	43.4	0.007
Plead guilty to main charge	22.2	21.5	23.1	54.7	0.0001
Not in breach of court order	21.0	16.1	24.0	43.5	0.001
Not in breach of bail	21.0	16.2	24.5	44.3	0.0008
No offences TIC	21.0	15.5	23.8	42.4	0.002
No breach of trust involved	21.1	17.1	24.6	43.0	0.002
Not unemployed	13.3	9.7	20.4	39.5	0.04
Married	17.6	15.2	23.9	53.3	0.05
No evidence of unsettled, irresponsible, unstable	18.6	16.0	25.0	42.9	0.003
Expressed remorse/regret	21.1	18.0	20.4	45.5	0.01
Evidence of unsettled/disrupted domestic life	23.1	22.2	16.7	44.4	0.04
No evidence of unsettled/disrupted domestic life	20.6	15.8	26.3	44.0	0.007
No prior convictions for violence	20.4	13.7	22.1	40.3	0.007
No previous detention centre	20.1	16.2	21.8	39.8	0.004

Table 15: *cont.*

Attributes	Birmingham		Dudley		Comparison Whites/Blacks Dudley courts
	Whites	Blacks	Whites	Blacks	p<
No previous borstal	20.3	15.8	24.6	43.2	0.002
No previous youth custody	20.3	14.4	22.7	44.3	0.0006
No previous prison sentence	20.9	16.1	23.8	41.5	0.005
No previous custodial sentence of any kind	20.5	16.5	22.3	46.0	0.0001
Most serious previous sentence a discharge	22.9	17.4	25.1	43.8	0.0046
Value of property stolen £0–499	19.8	16.4	25.1	39.3	0.03
Previous convictions but no previous custody	21.1	21.1	23.0	48.6	0.01
Previously on probation and not breached	21.1	17.4	24.3	53.7	0.0001
No previous CSO	19.8	14.2	22.0	39.5	0.006

than twice as many of them, got sentenced to custody: a difference which was highly statistically significant.[5]

Stepwise regression analyses were therefore undertaken to identify which variables were most significantly correlated with receiving a custodial sentence amongst blacks dealt with in the Dudley courts as compared with whites at the same court and blacks at Birmingham. This produced a very interesting finding. The variable which had (after taking into account the seriousness of cases as measured by the TPCS) the greatest impact on

[5] $\chi^2 = 12.27$, 1 df, p < .0005.

the use of custody for blacks sentenced at the Dudley courts was having been charged with a co-defendant or co-defendants of the same ethnic background.[6] This variable was not significantly related to custody for whites with white co-defendant(s), nor was it associated with custody among blacks who had a black co-defendant(s) at Birmingham. Furthermore, in the more serious cases with a probability of custody of .45 or greater, the custody rate for blacks and whites was unaffected by whether or not there were co-defendants or by the ethnic group to which they belonged.

A comparison was therefore made of the rate of custody where the offender was a) the sole person convicted; b) where he had been charged with others of the same race; c) where he had been charged with co-defendants who were not all of the same race. The results, set out in Table 16, suggest that a substantial amount of the greater than expected proportion of black offenders sentenced to custody by Dudley courts might be explained by the very much greater recourse to penal institutions for blacks who were involved in crime solely with other blacks. It should be noted, however, that this could not be the sole explanation, because in all three categories the blacks sentenced by Dudley courts were sentenced to custody more frequently than were blacks at Birmingham.

Could this be attributed to the fact that amongst the cases dealt with by the Dudley courts there were many more cases involving blacks where the co-defendant was of the same race, perhaps giving rise to some apprehension that black people were more often acting in concert to commit crime? There was no evidence for this at all. In fact, there were more whites than blacks who had been convicted with co-defendants of the same race.

---

[6] This did not, of course, include every case where the defendant had committed the offence with others, only those where a co-defendant was charged and convicted. There were very few cases where the co-defendant had not been charged at the Dudley courts: only 6 white and 7 black offenders and in most cases it was not possible to identify the race of the other person involved.

Table 16: Percentage use of custody for blacks and whites at Dudley courts and Birmingham, by race of co-defendant (risk of custody 0–44.9% TPCS, males)

| | Dudley courts | | | | Birmingham | | | |
| | Blacks | | Whites | | Blacks | | Whites | |
	Number	%	Number	%	Number	%	Number	%
Co-defendant(s)								
None	57	31.6	93	21.5	136	18.4	215	20.0
Same race	31	71.0	103	25.2	56	8.9	195	22.1
Other race(s)	14	35.7	19	31.6	40	22.5	27	22.2
Total	102		215		232		437	
Per cent same race		30.4		47.9		24.1		44.6

*No Co-defendant: no significant differences;

Co-defendants other race(s): no significant difference—Dudley Blacks : Birmingham Blacks χ^2=1.04, 1 df, p<0.31;

Co-defendants same race: Dudley Blacks : Dudley Whites χ^2=21.2, 1 df, p<0.0000; Dudley Blacks : Birmingham Blacks χ^2=41.4, 1 df, p<0.0000.

It should be noted that Asians who had solely Asian co-defendants were sentenced to custody at Dudley courts less frequently than either Blacks or Whites: 18.8%.

To what extent could these differences be explained by the type and seriousness of the cases involving blacks who had only black co-defendants appearing before the Dudley courts? Were they, by virtue of their characteristics more liable to custody irrespective of having co-defendants? After all, the risk band 0–44.9% encompassed a wide range of probabilities and included 47% of all the cases of all the cases involving both whites and blacks at Dudley and Birmingham. This risk band was therefore divided into four levels (the first four levels of the Probability of Custody Score, see above p. 75) and, as can be

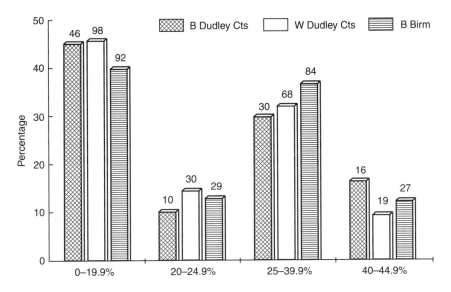

Figure 15 Cases involving co-defendants of the same race: comparisons of the proportions in four risk of custody groups (TPCS) at Dudley courts and Birmingham (males)

seen in Figure 15, there appeared to be very few differences between the distribution of the black and white cases.[7]

The expected custody rates were therefore calculated, controlling for the number of cases appearing at each of these four score levels. Table 17 shows that there were very small differences in the *expected* custody rates for cases which had co-defendants of the same race, whether they were blacks or whites at the Dudley courts or blacks at Birmingham. Yet the *observed* rate at the Dudley courts was 50.4 percentage points higher than expected, which is equivalent to 234 per cent or more than twice as high. At Birmingham, on the other hand, a

[7] The distributions were not significantly different. Comparing white/black at the Dudley courts p < .26; black at Dudley cts/black at B'ham p < .42; white/black at B'ham p < .57. When a similar comparison was made for the cases which only involved defendants of the same race, the distribution of cases was again remarkably similar.

Table 17: Observed vs. Expected Custody Rates at Dudley courts and Birmingham for offenders in risk of custody band 0–44.9% (TPCS) with co-defendants of the same race (males)

Race/Court	Percentage observed	Percentage expected	Percentage obs.–exp.
Blacks/Dudley courts	71.0	21.5	+50.4
Whites/Dudley courts	25.2	22.3	+2.9
Blacks/Birmingham	8.9	23.6	−14.5
Whites/Birmingham	22.1	22.9	+0.8
Asians/Dudley courts	18.8	18.3	+0.5
Asians/Birmingham	11.5	22.0	−10.5

lot fewer blacks than expected got a custodial sentence. Furthermore, the larger than expected use of custody for black offenders with black co-defendants was not found for Asians with Asian co-defendants.

These findings were confirmed by an analysis of variance which included all the other variables which the regression analysis had found to be significantly associated with custody for black offenders. Having a co-defendant of the same race was, for blacks sentenced at the Dudley courts, the most significant variable affecting the use of custody once the probability of custody score for each case had been taken into account.[8]

It could, of course, still be that the black cases at Dudley were worse in some respects, not identified by the Probability of Custody Score, than the white cases at that court or the black cases at Birmingham. One way of exploring this was to see if probation officers who had prepared reports with recommendations as to the appropriate sentence differed in their

[8] p < .032.

judgements of black and white co-defendant cases at Dudley courts (For the method and fuller details of the analysis of Social Inquiry Reports see below pp 150–160). This revealed that although the black males sentenced at Dudley were more likely than whites at Dudley or black offenders at Birmingham to have had the benefit of a Social Inquiry Report (71% v 60% v 52%), they were much more likely to have received a sentence which was more severe than that recommended in the Report (67% v 47% v 47%).[9]

Next, a comparison was made of the proportions sentenced to custody for each type of crime of which the blacks and whites were convicted. This showed that, whatever the offence, a greater proportion of blacks with black co-defendants at the Dudley courts got a custodial sentence than either the whites or the blacks at Birmingham. For example:

Violent Disorder
Dudley 10 blacks: 8 to custody (80%)
Dudley 4 whites: 1 to custody (25%)
Birm. 10 blacks: 0 to custody (0%)

Household Burglary
Dudley 5 blacks: 4 to custody (80%)
Dudley 13 whites: 3 to custody (23%)
Birm. 2 blacks: 0 to custody (0%)

Handling
Dudley 7 blacks: 3 to custody (43%)
Dudley 8 whites: 0 to custody (0%)

Theft
Dudley 2 blacks: 2 to custody (100%)
Dudley 14 whites: 5 to custody (36%)
Birm. 11 blacks: 0 to custody (0%)

[9] For those cases with co-defendants of the same race, 91% of the blacks at the Dudley courts got a sentence greater than that recommended compared with 44% of the whites at Wolverhampton, and 60% of the blacks at Birmingham.

Although the numbers in each category are small, there is a consistency in this pattern which would be very unlikely to occur by chance. As a final check, the cases of violent disorder were compared through an analysis of variance. All relevant variables describing the nature and degree of the violence as well as the defendant's previous convictions and the precise probability of custody score were considered. Other than the custody score, only two other variables were statistically significant: being a black male with a black co-defendant dealt with at the Dudley courts[10] and the degree of violence.[11] And, being black and appearing for sentence at a Dudley court explained six times more of the variance in whether or not a custodial sentence was passed than did the degree of violence. Moreover there was no significant interaction between these variables: in other words, no evidence that degree of violence had a significant impact on the high rate of custody for the blacks with black co-defendants at Dudley.

It is possible to make an estimate of the degree to which this variable explained the difference of 12.3 percentage points between the observed proportion of blacks sentenced to custody by a Dudley court (65.4%) and the expected rate (53.1%) after taking into account the probability of custody score for these cases (see p 92 above). If the blacks with black co-defendants with probability scores of 0–44.9% had been sentenced at the rate expected, which was 21.5%, rather than at the rate observed 71% (See Table 17, p 104 above), 7 of the 31, not 22, would have received a custodial sentence. This would have meant that the observed number of black offenders sentenced to custody at the Dudley courts would have fallen from 161 (see p 92 above) to 146 or from 65.4% to 59.3%: a difference

---

[10] $p < .0000$.

[11] $p < .01$. A degree of violence scale of 1–4 was composed, depending on the number of the following 4 characteristics the offender had: violence plus another offence; violence used for sexual gratification, theft, or to resist arrest; violence using a firearm or a knife; violence leading to hospitalisation or continuing impairment.

of 6.1 percentage points, rather than the 12.2 percentage points gap between the observed and expected rates. Thus, it seems that the different treatment accorded a relatively small number of cases involving black defendants who had only black co-defendants may have accounted for a half of the higher than to be expected custody rate for black males as a whole at the Dudley courts.

These findings go some considerable way towards explaining the disproportionate use of custody for blacks at Dudley courts. It may be, in this less serious category of cases, that perceptions of black crime are heightened when black offenders appear for sentence with others of their race and this was one reason why less weight was given to mitigating factors. If so, it would be the result of discriminatory stereotyping because white offenders who appeared with white co-defendants were not treated with such severity.[12]

3. Conclusion

This chapter has shown that there are, indeed, substantial variations in court practices in relation to the proportion of blacks as compared with whites who receive a custodial sentence. While at Birmingham Crown Court the judges as a whole are, by all these measurements, acting in an even-handed way, it does not appear that this can be said of at least some of those who sit and pass judgement in the Dudley Crown Court. The next chapter, therefore, aims to show whether, when the probability of custody score is taken into account, there were variations between the patterns of sentences imposed by individual judges who had dealt with cases committed to the Dudley courts and the Birmingham Crown Court.

---

[12] For a discussion of stereotyping see B. Hudson, op. cit., pp 32–33.

7

VARIATIONS BETWEEN JUDGES

As already explained in chapter 3 (see pp 45–46 above), in a study of this kind, which is concerned with the *aggregate* effect of race on the pattern of penalties imposed, it is hazardous to compare the sentences given by individual judges many of whom only dealt with a relatively small number of defendants each year. Any differences observed, even when cases characteristics are controlled for by the probability of custody score, could, in a small sample of decisions, be subject to a degree of error. The analysis which follows does not seek, therefore, to compare the details of each case dealt with by every judge, but rather to establish whether the pattern of variations between judges in the proportions of defendants they each sentenced to custody, described in Chapter 3, still remains when the case characteristics have been taken into account.

1. The Status of the Judge

It will be recalled (see p 44 above) that High Court Judges sent the highest proportion of defendants of all ethnic groups to custody and Assistant Recorders the lowest. To what extent did this reflect the seriousness of the cases, as measured by their expected custody scores, which the different categories of judge dealt with?

It was not surprising to find that the High Court Judges dealt with the most serious of the crimes. Nevertheless, as Figure 16 shows, they committed slightly more blacks and Asians to custody than was to be expected. However, the number dealt with by these High Court Judges was too small to be confident that these racial differences were statistically significant.

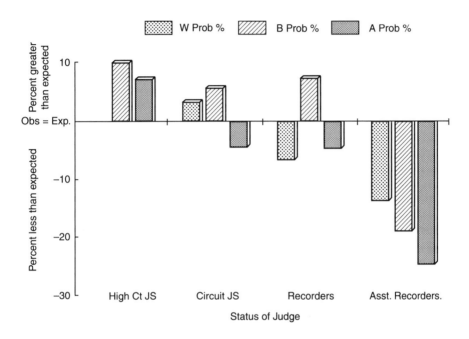

Figure 16 Percentage use of custody greater or less than expected (Obs–Exp/Exp) by race and status of the judge (TPCS, males)

Circuit Judges and Recorders also made slightly greater use of custody for blacks than could be explained by the characteristics of the cases: the difference being three and four percentage points higher respectively, which is equivalent to an increased probability of 5.5 to 7 per cent. On the other hand, the part-time Assistant Recorders were relatively lenient. Overall, their observed rate of use of custody was 37% compared with an expected rate of 43%. And they were most lenient in respect of black defendants, of whom only 37% got a custodial sentence when the expected rate for cases of the kind they dealt with was 46%. This greater reluctance to use custody may, of course, reflect their lesser experience but it may also indicate a different attitude towards the use of custody in general and perhaps, in a younger age group, a greater awareness of the problem of racial discrimination in particular.

2. Variations Between Individual Judges

But, of course, it has already been shown that there were striking variations in the proportion of cases sentenced to custody by 18 judges (17 Circuit Judges and 1 Recorder) for whom there were at least 45 cases in the sample (See Table 4 p 46 above). Again, the question is whether these 'raw' or 'unadjusted' differences remained once the characteristics of the cases they dealt with, measured by the probability of custody score, had been taken into account.

For each of these 18 judges, therefore, a calculation was made of the percentage of each ethnic group expected to be sentenced to custody after taking into account the average risk of a custodial sentence being imposed for the type of cases they each dealt with.[1] This made it possible to calculate for each judge the 'adjusted' difference between the percentage use of custody for blacks and whites.[2] As already mentioned, the numbers in each ethnic group were inevitably quite small, even for those judges who had dealt with as many as a hundred

---

[1] The expected rate for each judge was calculated by multiplying, in each of nine risk categories, the number of cases by the average percentage of cases sentenced to custody in that category (eg. in category one n was multiplied by 10.4% to give the expected rate). The expected numbers at each level were added together to give the total number expected to receive a custodial sentence. This was then compared with the number observed.

[2] For example. If a judge sentenced 40% of whites to custody but the proportion expected was 49% (O–E = –9%) and sentenced 62% of blacks to custody but the proportion expected was 52% (O–E = +10%), the difference between the black and white custody rate would be 19% (–9%+10%).

cases. Yet, it is possible to perceive several distinctive patterns in the variations between judges in their sentencing 'profiles'.

First, the judges were ranked according to their relative severity in the 'unadjusted' percentage of each ethnic group they sentenced to custody. They were then ranked according to their relative severity based on the 'adjusted' size of the difference between their observed and expected percentage use of custody. A perfect matching of these rankings would of course produce a correlation coefficient of 1.0. And, in fact, the size of the correlation was very high: being .81 for the ranking of judges by their 'unadjusted' and 'adjusted' severity for white offenders, .88 for black offenders and .89 for Asians. This obviously means that the mix of cases each judge dealt with made little difference to their comparative ranking in terms of the proportionate use they each made of custody. The differences remained substantial and can be summarised as follows:

- *Seven* judges had appeared to be relatively severe on black offenders and for *five* of them the difference between their 'adjusted' use of custody for blacks and whites remained high—by 27, 25, 20, 12 and 11 percentage points respectively: equivalent to between 50% and 19% greater than the average expected for the type of cases they dealt with. On the other hand, the 'unadjusted' high proportion of black defendants sentenced to custody by *two* of the judges was entirely explained by the nature of the cases they had dealt with.
- Of the *eight* judges who had, on their 'unadjusted' data appeared relatively even-handed, *two* were, in fact, relatively severe on blacks, three remained even-handed, and *three* were less severe on blacks than whites.
- The *three* judges whose observed 'unadjusted' custody rates were relatively low for blacks compared with whites, proved, when their expected rate was taken into account, still to use custody considerably less than expected.

- This suggests, therefore, that, if differences between the observed 'unadjusted' rates of individual judges are very substantial they usually reflect, although not invariably, good approximations to real differences in sentencing patterns.

To what extent, therefore, was the disparity between the proportion of black defendants sentenced to custody at the Dudley courts and at Birmingham accounted for by the different sentencing practices of the judges who happened to sit there?

In order to make this comparison the 18 judges were grouped into four categories (See Figure 17):[3]

1. The *seven* judges who were relatively severe on the black defendants, meaning that their 'adjusted' rate of use of custody was 10 or more percentage points higher for blacks than for whites;
2. The *five* judges who were relatively evenhanded, meaning that the 'adjusted' proportion of blacks sentenced to custody was in the range of plus 7 to minus 4 percentage points of the custody rate for whites
3. The *six* judges who were relatively more severe on white than on black defendants, the 'adjusted' difference in the proportion sentenced to custody being ten or more percentage points lower for blacks than for whites.
4. The remaining judges who dealt with fewer than 35 cases each, sometimes only a handful. There were 31 such judges who sentenced cases at the Dudley courts and 88 at Birmingham Crown Court.

At both the Dudley courts and at Birmingham there were four judges who appeared to be relatively severe on black

---

[3] Charts showing the Observed compared with the Expected percentage sentenced to custody by each of these judges can be found in Appendix 5, Figure 1.

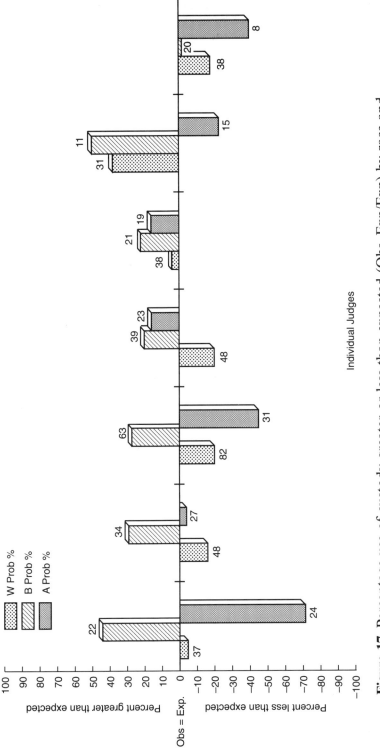

Figure 17 Percentage use of custody greater or less than expected (Obs–Exp/Exp) by race and relative severity of judge (males). Number of cases shown at end of each bar I. Judges relatively severe on black offenders (10 or more percentage points higher): 7 judges

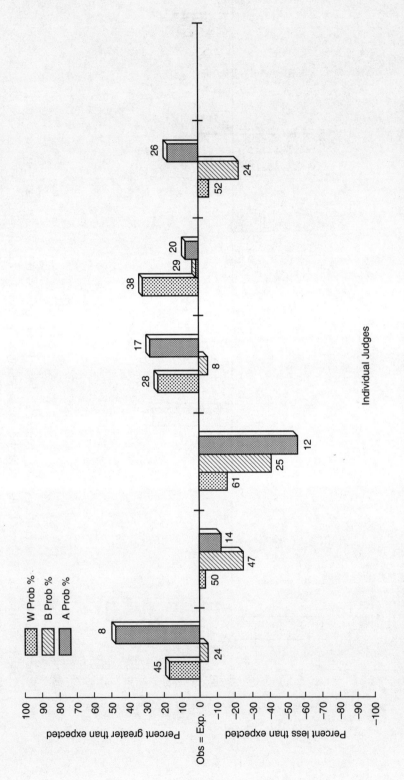

II. Judges relatively lenient on black offenders (10 or more percentage points lower): 6 judges

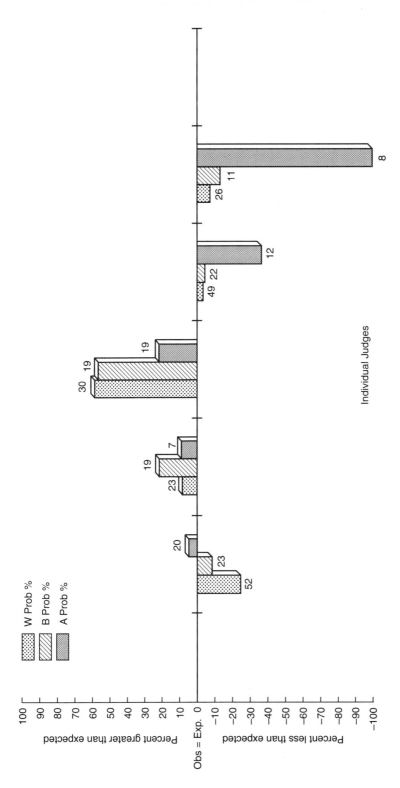

III. Judges relatively even-handed with black and white offenders (1between 7 percentage points higher and 4 percentage points lower): 5 judges

defendants.[4] On the other hand, at Birmingham there were four judges who sentenced considerably fewer blacks to custody than whites, but only one judge who did this amongst those who sat in the Dudley courts.

The sentencing practices of the judges sitting in the Dudley courts were compared with those sitting at Birmingham Crown Court and, for this purpose, the 'even-handed' and `relatively lenient' judges were grouped together.

Table 18[5] shows that the greater number of black offenders sentenced to custody at the Dudley courts was not due only to the four judges who were relatively severe on blacks: they sentenced only a slightly higher proportion than expected than the four relatively severe judges at Birmingham. Rather, the difference between these courts was due to the practices of the other judges, both those who were relatively even handed and those who dealt with a relatively small number of cases. At Birmingham, these two 'categories' of judges sentenced between them 28 fewer blacks than expected, equivalent to 11 per cent fewer (28/250). In contrast, these 'categories' of judges at the Dudley courts sentenced between them 19 more blacks than expected, 24 per cent higher (19/179) than expected.[6]

These findings indicate that:

- At both the Dudley courts and the Birmingham Crown Court there is considerable variation in the extent to which judges resort to a custodial sentence. There are some judges who are

[4] One of those judges heard cases at both the Dudley courts and Birmingham, and had therefore, for this purpose, been counted twice. Two of the 18 judges were excluded from this comparison. One dealt with cases entirely at another court, and the other heard too few cases at either one of the Dudley courts or Birmingham.

[5] Similar tables for the white offenders sentenced at these courts are reproduced in Appendix 5 Table 2.

[6] The fact that judges at the Dudley courts who sentenced an equal or lesser number of blacks to custody than whites, still sentenced more blacks than would be expected in the sample as a whole was largely due to one judge who sentenced a much higher proportion (27 percentage points) of both blacks and whites to custody than expected.

Table 18: Comparison of the proportionate use of custody for black offenders compared with the expected rate by judges sitting at Birmingham and the Dudley courts (males)

Black Offenders Sentenced at Birmingham Crown Court

	Percentage of cases dealt with	Percentage to custody	Number to custody	Number expected	Number Obs.–Exp.
Judges (4) higher Black/White	19.0	66.7	72	63	+9
Judges (6) equal (2) or lower (4) Black/White	29.2	45.2	75	93	−18
Judges (88) less than 35 cases each	51.8	49.8	147	157	−10
Total		52	294	313	−19

Black Offenders Sentenced at the Dudley Courts

	Percentage of cases dealt with	Percentage to custody	Number to custody	Number expected	Number Obs.–Exp.
Judges (4) higher Black/White	39.0	65.6	63	52	+11
Judges (3) equal (2) or lower (1) Black/White	24.8	60.7	37	31	+6
Judges (31) less than 31 cases each	36.2	68.5	61	48	+13
Total		65	161	131	+30

relatively severe on black defendants at both courts. However, it should be noted that their impact on the probability of a black person receiving custody was greater at the Dudley courts because, between them, these relatively severe judges dealt with 39 per cent of the sentenced black cases compared with only 19 per cent dealt with by the relatively severe judges at Birmingham.

- In addition, the combined effect of the sentencing practices of all the **other** judges at the Dudley courts was very different from that of the other judges at Birmingham. At the former these judges sentenced between them considerably more blacks to custody than expected, at the latter court considerably fewer.

A multivariate analysis of variance in the use of custody was computed for the cases dealt with by the 7 judges at the Dudley courts and the 10 at Birmingham who had sentenced 45 cases or more. It was found that, for the cases dealt with by the Dudley judges, the race of the defendant (being black) had—after the Possibility of Custody Score—the largest and most significant effect on custody.[7] It had a much bigger effect than the particular judge who dealt with the case.[8] In other words, the judges were relatively consistent as regards the effect of race on their sentences. At Birmingham, however, where race did not have an overall effect on the use made of custody,[9] there was evidence that judges did vary to some degree according to the race of the defendant.[10] In other words, differences in the 'race effect' at Birmingham between individual judges balanced each other to produce no effect on the cases taken as a whole.

---

[7] The significance of F is $p < .001$. The analysis controlled for the probability of custody score and several other variables: unemployment, indicators of efforts to reform, groups of the same race, whether the offence was planned, age and social stability.

[8] $p < .07$. [9] $p < .17$. [10] $p < .002$.

It is important to recognise that these findings are the outcome of the *aggregate* of sentences passed by a large number of judges. They do *not* imply that all judges sentenced more blacks to custody than whites. Nor can they be used to identify any *individual case* in which there was a clear racial bias in deciding on the sentence. What they do imply, however, is that race does not appear to be, in all instances, as it should be, a factor which is entirely irrelevant in affecting the *probability* of receiving a custodial sentence. And it seems to show that the judges whose decisions were influenced either by the race of the defendant, or by some unmeasured factors associated with race; were not randomly distributed between the Crown Courts of the West Midlands.

However one looks at it, a black male committed to the Dudley Crown Court in 1989 had a greater probability of receiving a custodial sentence than if he had been committed to Birmingham Crown Court. The last chapter suggested that this was because, in aggregate, the judges who sentenced the cases at the Dudley courts gave less weight to mitigating factors in cases involving blacks and appeared to have a propensity more often to sentence blacks to custody when they appeared in court with black co-defendants. It was suspected that it might be due to the development of shared perceptions and attitudes amongst the judges sitting at Dudley Crown Court, in much the same way as 'court sentencing cultures' have been identified by previous research on magistrates' courts.[11] However, I was

---

[11] On bench sentencing cultures see, Roger Hood, *Sentencing in Magistrates' Courts*, (1962), pp 64–85 and *Sentencing the Motoring Offender* (1972), pp 143–8, and Roger Tarling, *Sentencing Practice in Magistrates' Courts*, Home Office Research Study, No 56, (1979), p 28. The Oxford pilot study by A. Ashworth, E. Genders, G. Mansfield, J. Peay and E. Player, suggested that the degree of consistency among judges and knowledge of other judges' sentencing patterns may be linked to the size of the court centre. Those at very small or large courts might have little chance to share information, whereas at a medium-sized court centre 'judges would meet more frequently and were better informed about each other's sentencing practices', see *Sentencing in the Crown Court: Report of an Exploratory Study*, (1984), University of Oxford, Centre for Criminological Research, Occasional Paper No. 10, p 36.

informed that the judges assigned to the Dudley Crown Court had little, if any, opportunity to meet to discuss aspects of their work because they were, as already explained, sitting in court rooms spread between Dudley, Wolverhampton and Birmingham. How such a pattern could emerge in these circumstances is a question which a study which had no access to the judges themselves was unable to investigate.

8
LENGTH AND SEVERITY OF SENTENCES

Prison populations are, of course, determined not just by the inflow of cases, but also by their length. A relatively small proportion of persons sentenced to long terms of imprisonment can become a very sizeable proportion of the prison population. For example, defendants sentenced to life imprisonment only account for 0.2% of all those received into custody under sentence, yet they make up 7.6% of the daily average male prison population. Therefore, if black defendants were considerably more likely to receive long prison terms this would account in part for their over-representation in the prison population.

The data relating to length of custody were analyzed in a number of ways, but always separately for adults and young people under the age of 21 because the sentencing powers of the courts in relation to the latter are much more restricted, especially for those under the age of 17 for whom the maximum period of custody that could be imposed was twelve months detention in a young offender institution.

1. Length of Sentences

i) *Adult Males*

The first step was to make a simple comparison between the lengths of the prison sentences passed on the three ethnic groups. This showed (See Table 19) that there were statistically significant differences in the distribution of sentences between

Length and Severity of Sentences

Table 19: Total length of imprisonment: adult males*

	Whites		Blacks		Asians	
	Number	%	Number	%	Number	%
1–6 months	261	22.1	57	16.3	22	19.1
7–12 months	291	24.7	82	23.4	30	26.1
13–18 months	205	17.4	58	16.6	23	20.0
19–36 months	298	25.2	92	26.3	18	15.7
37 months +	125	10.6	61	17.4	22	19.1

*White/Black comparison χ^2=15.24, 4 df, p<0.004: white/Asian χ^2=11.61, 4 df, p<0.021. Whites weighted.

both whites and blacks and between whites and Asians. In particular, a greater proportion of blacks and Asians received sentences of over 3 years' imprisonment and a smaller proportion of blacks than whites got short sentences of six months or less.[1]

It was also, of course, possible to compute the mean length and the size of the variance of imprisonment for the sample as a whole as well as for the two courts which dealt with the bulk of the cases, Birmingham and the Dudley courts. Figure 18 shows the mean lengths for the main offence of which the defendant had been found guilty as well as the total length imposed for all the offences of which he had been convicted.

The average (mean) length of the prison sentences imposed on black and Asian adult males in the West Midlands' Crown Courts as a whole was substantially longer than those for whites. These differences were also highly statistically significant. At both Birmingham and the Dudley courts, the only courts where there were a sufficient number of cases to make this analysis possible, the mean level of custody for

[1] The small number of cases where a partially suspended sentence of imprisonment was imposed were included, counting the part to be served immediately in prison as the length of imprisonment.

blacks was between four and five months longer than for whites, and for Asians even longer.[2]

An analysis of variance showed that the factors which had the greatest impact on sentence length were the seriousness of the case (as measured by the Probability of Custody Score) and whether the defendant pleaded not guilty. The mean lengths of imprisonment and standard deviations were therefore compared (See Table 20), controlling for whether the case fell into the low, medium or high risk of custody group and whether the defendant pleaded guilty, and thus earned a 'discount' on sentence length for doing so,[3] or pleaded not guilty at trial.

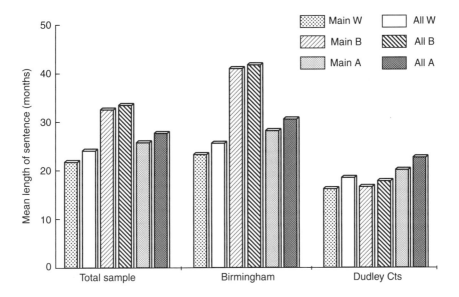

Figure 18 Adult males. Mean length of prison sentences for main offence and all offences by race for total sample, Birmingham and Dudley courts

[2] However, because the numbers were smaller and the range of penalties for blacks and Asians wider, these differences were not statistically significant.

[3] For a discussion of the Court of Appeal policy on giving credit to defendants for pleading guilty—in effect a 'discount' on the sentence which would have been imposed

Table 20: Adult males: mean lengths of sentences for all offences controlled by plea and risk of custody (TPCS)

Risk Group (TPCS)	Whites			Blacks			Asians		
	Number	mean	sd	Number	mean	sd	Number	mean	sd
Pleaded Not Guilty									
Low 0–39.9%	8	10.1	5.8	8	12.8	8.2	6	22.3	30.7
Med. 40–69.9%	16	11.2	5.6	28	17.4	16.4	4	21.0	18.5
High 70–100%	40	33.7	31.9	64	43.4	41.4	18	70.8	63.6
Pleaded Guilty									
Low	81	8.5	5.9	36	8.1	5.9	28	9.8	6.2
Med.	128	14.2	10.3	88	17.3	12.7	24	15.9	14.9
High	176	30.6	23.7	126	31.2	30.0	33	36.2	36.1

Numbers not weighted

The following conclusions can be drawn:

- When seriousness and guilty plea were controlled for, none of the white/black/Asian racial differences were large.
- The mean lengths of sentences of those who pleaded not guilty were, however, longer for blacks and Asians, particularly in the highest risk of custody group. This was particularly disadvantageous to the ethnic minorities: of those blacks

had he or she been found guilty after a trial, see, Andrew Ashworth, *Sentencing and Penal Policy*, (1983), pp. 310–314, and D A Thomas, *Current Sentencing Practice*, (1983, continuing), Section A 8.2.

and Asian defendants who were in the highest risk of custody group, 34 and 35 per cent respectively pleaded not guilty compared with only 19 per cent of the whites who were in this high risk group. Thus, not only did the black and Asian offenders more often forego the benefits of a 'discount' given for a guilty plea and the potential advantage of having a social inquiry report, they also, on average, were sentenced to longer terms of imprisonment than the whites.[4]

A stepwise regression analysis was used to examine the influence of all relevant variables on the actual length of the prison sentence, measured in months, for each case. This showed that, when the impact of all other variables had been taken into account, there was a significant difference between the length of sentences imposed on those who pleaded not guilty rather than guilty: the former receiving, on average, prison sentences 3.1 months longer than the latter.[5]

Amongst those who pleaded not guilty, the Asians, on average, got the longest sentences: 51.2 months, compared with an average length of 33.7 months received by blacks and 25.6 months by whites. This, of course, could have been due to a few exceptional cases which distorted the distribution of cases, and unduly affected the average, for Asians and blacks. In order to allow for this, all offenders who got a sentence of over 8 years were excluded. Even so, as can be seen from Table 21, the average remained considerably longer for Asians and blacks than for whites.

This could, of course, still have been due to differences in the

---

[4] See, Moxon, *Sentencing Practice in the Crown Court*, op.cit., p 33.

[5] See Table 3, Appendix 10. Moxon found, without controlling for relevant variables or for age, that 'the average sentence length for those pleading not guilty was 23.2 months; for those who pleaded guilty it was 18.2 months—an average reduction of 22%', ibid., p 32. Making a similar comparison for male adults in the West Midlands Courts, the average sentence for those pleading not guilty was 30.4 months and for those pleading guilty 21.0 months—an average reduction of 31%. There was virtually no difference for male offenders under the age of 21.

Table 21: Adult males: length of prison sentences imposed on those who pleaded not guilty (excluding sentences of over 8 years)

	Number	Mean	Standard deviation
Whites	62	20.6	16.6
Blacks	96	27.7	20.2
Asians	26	31.8	27.2

nature of the cases. When this was controlled for by the regression model which predicted length of sentence for adult males, the average length of sentence imposed on Asians who pleaded not guilty was still 9 months longer than the average sentence given to whites who pleaded not guilty.[6] And blacks got 3.4 months longer than did whites.[7]

ii) *Males Under the Age of 21*

As far as young males were concerned, Figure 19 shows that the mean length of sentence in the sample as a whole and at Birmingham was greater for blacks, but not at the Dudley courts. However, none of these differences was significant at the 5 per cent level of confidence.[8] Nor did the analysis of variance reveal any significant differences when the seriousness of the cases were taken into account.[9]

2. Accounting for the Over-representation of Black Males in the Prison Population

To what extent did the cumulative effect of race differences—in the proportion of cases sentenced to custody; in the proportions

---

[6] $p < .002$.   [7] $p < .06$.   [8] See Table 4 Appendix 10.
[9] For an explanation of this analysis on the adult cases see above p 123.

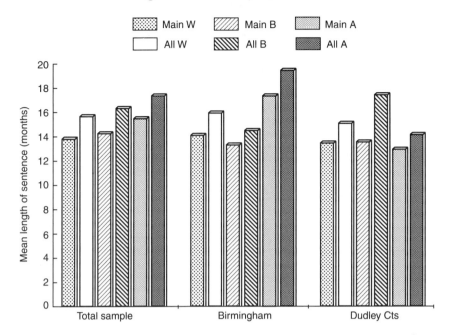

Figure 19 Males under 21. Mean length of custodial sentences for main offences and all offences by race for total sample, Birmingham and Dudley courts

pleading not guilty; and in the average length of sentences imposed—account for the substantial over-representation of black males in the prison population? It is impossible to assess this accurately. Nevertheless, one indicator is the changing ratio of whites to blacks and Asians as cases progressed into the court and on to prison.

Among the adult males who were sentenced at the West Midlands Crown Courts in 1989, the ethnic groups were distributed as follows:

Whites   72.7%
Blacks   18.3%
Asians   8.9%

The proportion amongst those sentenced who were **expected** to receive a custodial sentence, after controlling for the probability of custody score, was:

Whites   72.1%
Blacks   20.4%
Asians   7.4%

The actual proportion who were **observed** to get a custodial sentence was:

Whites   71.2%
Blacks   21.8%
Asians   7.0%

By multiplying the number of each ethnic group sentenced to custody who had pleaded guilty or not guilty by the average length of sentence for guilty and not guilty plea cases, it was possible to obtain a rough estimate of the total number of months to be served by each ethnic group sentenced in the West Midlands in 1989. This can be used as a proxy for the proportion of those sentenced in that year to be found in the prison population.[10] Because more blacks and Asians pleaded not guilty—and when they pleaded not guilty they got on average longer sentences than whites—they accounted for a higher proportion of the total amount of prison time to be served by the sample as a whole. It can be seen that the increase in the black : white ratio is entirely amongst those who pleaded not guilty:

	Months to be Served	Per cent of Total Time Served	Per cent for Plea Guilty	Per cent for Plea Not Guilty
Whites	24,807	66.5	73.3	44.45
Blacks	9,122	24.4	20.2	38.1
Asians	3,387	9.1	6.5	17.4

[10] It is, of course, recognized that this can only be a rough approximation because the averages conceals any skewness in the distribution of sentence lengths. Also, this measure cannot take into account any differences in the proportions of the sentence actually served by offenders from different ethnic groups.

Thus, due to the combination of a higher proportion sentenced to custody, a higher proportion who decided to plead not guilty and who therefore received, on average, longer sentences, the ratio of blacks to whites increased:

from

     18.3 : 72.5 amongst those sentenced

to

     24.4 : 66.5 of the total amount of prison time to be served (i.e. of the prison population).

The ratio of Asians to whites was virtually unchanged: 8.9% of the total sentenced and 9.1% of the time served.

It can therefore be roughly estimated that the over-representation of black males occurred through the following sequence:

Baseline	3.8 per cent of the male population served by the courts[11]
Per cent Sentenced	18.3 per cent
Per cent Expected to go to Custody	20.4 per cent
Per cent Observed to go to Custody	21.8 per cent
Per cent of Total Time to be Served	24.4 per cent

Thus, the proportion of blacks in the prison population was 20.6 percentage points higher than in the population at large (24.4–3.8%). Of this:

- 70 per cent (14.5 percentage points) was accounted for by the **number** appearing for sentence. This would reflect, of course, all the stages leading up to appearance at Crown Court: not only the crimes committed, but those reported and recorded; persons arrested, charged and prosecuted; as well as the

---

[11] This can also only be a rough approximation, taking into account the areas covered by the courts at which most of the cases were sentenced.

nature of the charges laid (whether indictable only or triable-either-way); decisions of magistrates and defendants on the mode of trial; and finally on a finding of guilt. Decisions at all these stages, of course, might be affected by racial factors.

- 10 per cent (2.1 points) by the more serious nature of the offences and other legally relevant characteristics of the charges on which black defendants were convicted;
- 7 per cent (1.4 points) by a greater use of custody than expected and;
- 13 per cent (2.6 points) by lengthier sentences, which appears to be entirely due to a greater propensity to plead not guilty, and to the lengthier sentences for those who did so.

While these estimates, of course, must be regarded with a degree of caution, they give a clearer picture than hitherto available of how the racial imbalance between the proportion of adult black males in the population and their proportion in the prison system may be accounted for. It seems that about:

- 80 per cent can be accounted for by the **number** appearing at the Crown Court for sentence and the **nature** of the characteristics of the cases they were convicted of, and
- 20 per cent can be attributed to subsequent different treatment.[12]

It is interesting and important to note that, when the same calculations were made for offenders under the age of 21, as much as 92 per cent of the over-representation of black offenders was accounted for by the number appearing for sentence

---

[12] Reviewing American studies, Professor Norval Morris regarded as 'fair' the conclusion that 'about 80 per cent of the black over-representation in prison can be explained by differential involvement in crime and about 20 per cent by subsequent racially discriminatory processes', although he believed more of this occurred at the police, prosecution and bargaining stages than at the punishment stage. 'Race and Crime: What Evidence is there that Race Influences Results in the Criminal Justice System?', *Judicature*, Vol. 72, No. 2, Aug–Sept 1988, pp 111–113 at p 112.

and the seriousness of their cases. The remaining 8 per cent was due to longer sentences, particularly for those who pleaded not guilty, but, as already noted above, this was largely accounted for by the more serious characteristics of the cases in which black offenders were involved.[13]

This finding, that it is among adult rather than younger black offenders that a significant proportion of this over-representation appears to be due to differential treatment in the courts, will be a corrective to the commonly held assumption that the opposite is the case.

[13] Amongst those appearing for sentence the proportions were: whites 71.6%, blacks 15.0%, Asians 13.0%. The proportions expected to receive custody was: whites 71.7%, blacks 16.4%, Asians 11.6%; the proportions observed to get custody: whites 72.3%, blacks 16.2%, Asians 11.1%. The proportion of total time to be served: whites 70.9%, blacks 17.6%, Asians 11.5%.

9
THE RANGE OF SENTENCES AND THE USE OF NON-CUSTODIAL ALTERNATIVES

The length of a custodial sentence is, of course, only one measure of severity. It also matters to a defendant what kind of non-custodial penalty he receives, not only because it may intrude more or less into his daily life but also because it may have a strong impact on the likelihood of him receiving a custodial sentence should he re-offend. It has been claimed that black offenders who escape the fate of a custodial sentence more frequently receive a 'high tariff' alternative such as a suspended prison sentence or a community service order.[1] There is certainly evidence that blacks and Asians are less likely than whites to be placed on probation, and this may in part be due to the fact that fewer of them have had the benefits of a Social Inquiry Report into their background, circumstances, attitudes and prospects (See below page 151).[2]

Two complementary analyses were carried out. First, a calculation was made for whites, blacks and Asians separately (and again separately for those under 21 and for adults) of the distribution of sentences along a continuum of severity: from imprisonment of over three years at one end to a discharge at the other. The scale is shown at the bottom of Figure 20.[3] Second,

[1] See, Barbara Hudson, 'Discrimination and Disparity: the Influence of Race on Sentencing' New Community, Vol. 16(1), (1989) pp. 23–34 at pp 32–33.

[2] See, for example, David Moxon, Sentencing Practice in the Crown Court, 1988, Home Office Research Study No. 103, p.60. Also, George Mair. 'Ethnic Minorities, Probation and Magistrates' Courts', Brit J Criminol, (1986), Vol. 26, pp 147–155. For a discussion of the influence of Social Inquiry Reports see below pp 150–160.

[3] 'Severity scales' are always open to the criticism that penalties do not fall into a

a comparison was made, controlling for the level of seriousness of the case, of the sentences imposed on those who were *not* sentenced to custody.

1. Adults

It is clear from Figures 20 and 21 that the major differences between the range of penalties imposed on blacks and whites, other than in the lengths of imprisonment they received, was that the former were more often given a suspended sentence of imprisonment and were less often placed on probation or given a community service order.[4] Asians were also less often made subject to a probation order, but they were more likely to have been fined or conditionally discharged.[5]

These different sentencing patterns were, as Table 22 shows, related to the seriousness of the case as measured by the probability of receiving a custodial sentence—whether relatively low, medium or high:

simple linear scale. Is a suspended sentence of imprisonment always regarded by the judge and/or the defendant as more severe than a community service order? And is the latter always more severe than a fine? A suspended sentence has been regarded as more severe than a community service order for two reasons: first it can only be imposed when the court has already decided that a sentence of imprisonment is the appropriate penalty, and secondly, the consequences of a breach are much more serious, leading far more often to the imposition of an immediate custodial sentence. Thus, a pragmatic approach has been taken which is in line with the distinctions made in the Criminal Justice Act 1991 between custody, suspended custody, community sentences, fines and discharges. The scale originally devised, distinguished between lengths of suspended sentences, community service and probation orders and the amount of the fine and/or compensation. This was collapsed in order to provide sufficient numbers for comparative analysis. The full scale is referred to in Appendix 10.

[4] $\chi^2 = 12.0$, 4 df, p < .017. Amongst those placed on probation there were no statistically significant differences between the proportion of whites and blacks with a condition attached to the order, or in the length of the probation order.

[5] $\chi^2 = 47.0$, 4 df, p < .0000. There were no statistically significant differences in the proportion given a probation order with conditions or in the length of the order. There was a tendency for the fines imposed on Asians to be lower than those on whites, but the difference was not statistically significant.

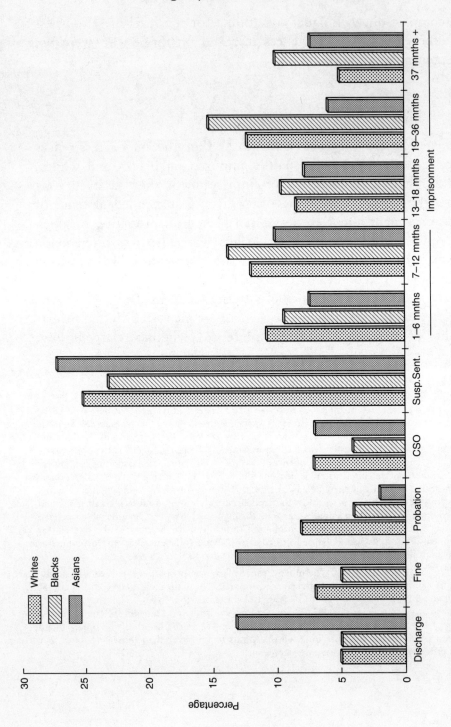

Figure 20 Adult males. Percentage receiving various penalties: scaled in order of severity

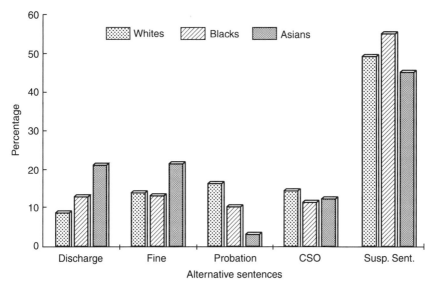

Figure 21 Adult males. Percentage of those *not* sentenced to imprisonment receiving alternative penalties

Table 22: Adult males not sentenced to custody: percentage given alternative sentences controlled by risk of custody (TPCS)

	Low Risk (0–39.9%)			Medium Risk (40–69.9%)			High Risk (70–100%)		
	Whites	Blacks	Asians	Whites	Blacks	Asians	Whites	Blacks	Asians
SS	46	49	44	53	64	40	49	59	100 (n=3)
CSO	14	12	10	15	6	20	12	18	—
Prob.	12	7	2	20	14	5	32	24	—
Fine	17	17	24	10	6	13	3	—	—
Disch.	12	15	20	3	11	23	3	—	—

- Black defendants with low probabilities of custody did not receive significantly more severe alternatives to custody than did whites.[6]
- Significantly more Asians in the lowest risk group for custody were discharged and fined and fewer given a C.S.O. or placed on probation than whites.[7]
- In the medium risk group for custody, the pattern of penalties given was significantly different for blacks than whites.[8] More blacks got a suspended sentence of imprisonment and less often a probation order, a CSO or a fine, although slightly more were conditionally discharged.
- Many fewer Asians in the medium risk group received a probation order and they were much more frequently discharged. In general, therefore, they suffered less intrusive alternative penalties than either whites or blacks.[9]
- There were no significant differences in the pattern of alternative sentences for any of the ethnic groups when it came to those who had a high likelihood of being imprisoned.[10]

But, of course, the variables which best predicted the likelihood of receiving a custodial sentence, did not necessarily include all those which could explain these differences in the range of sentences imposed on whites, blacks and Asians. A step-wise regression analysis was therefore carried out which included 80 variables,[11] 29 of which were found to be significantly related to the severity scale.[12] Using this model, the race of the defendant was then included in order to test

---

[6] White/black low risk: $\chi^2 = 5.41$, 4 df, p < .25.
[7] White/Asian low risk $\chi^2 = 23.02$, 4 df, p < .0001.
[8] White/black medium risk (40.0-69.9): $\chi^2 = 17.31$, 4 df, p < .002.
[9] White/Asian medium risk: $\chi^2 = 35.6$, 4 df, p < .0000.
[10] The number of Asians in the high risk group was too small for analysis (3 cases).
[11] Excluding race, the type of judge sentencing the case, and whether or not a Social Inquiry Report was made.
[12] See Table 1 Appendix 10 which lists these variables, their co-efficients and levels of significance.

whether, when all other explanatory variables were controlled for, it added, at a statistically significant level, to the explanation of severity of sentence. This analysis revealed that:

- If the defendant was Asian this did not add significantly to the explanation of severity.
- If the offender was black, the severity of sentence was significantly higher than expected in the adult sample as a whole.[13]
- When the court at which the case was dealt with was controlled for, being a black defendant was not related to severity at Birmingham but was significant at a very high level at the Dudley courts. The size of this difference was such that adult black offenders at the Dudley courts are almost one step up the severity scale in relation to whites, when 29 variables have been controlled for.[14] In part, this finding was, of course, a reflection of the greater likelihood of a black offender receiving a custodial sentence, but it was also due to the fact that blacks who were not sentenced to imprisonment more frequently received a fully suspended sentence and less frequently a community service or a probation order. And once again it was found that these differences were located in the band of cases with a medium risk of custody.
- Thus, again, there was strong evidence of a large overall 'court effect' in relation to the sentencing of adult black defendants, with a marked contrast between the Dudley courts and Birmingham Crown Court.

2. Males Under the Age of 21

The range of sentences imposed on young male persons, which is set out in Figures 22 and 23, shows large statistically

---

[13] The co-efficient was .42, p < .009.   [14] The co-efficient was .73, p < .005.

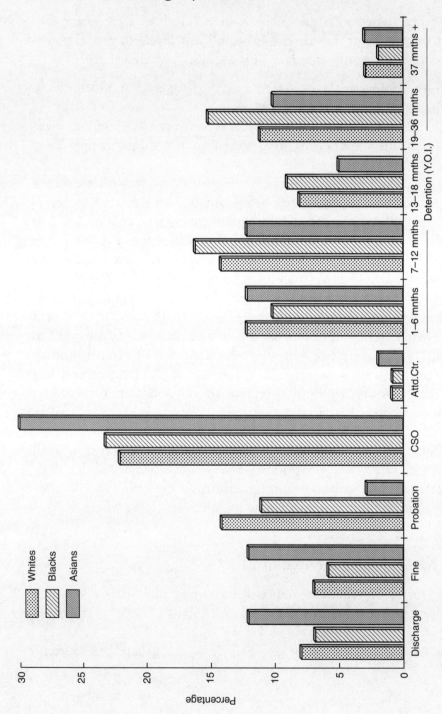

Figure 22 Males under 21. Percentage receiving various penalties: scaled in order of severity

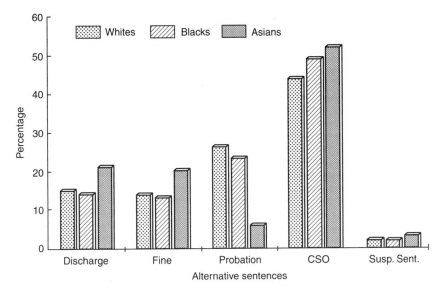

Figure 23 Males under 21. Percentage of those *not* sentenced to custody receiving alternative penalties

significant differences in the pattern for white offenders as compared with Asians[15] but the differences between blacks and whites were not significant.

When comparisons were made (see Table 23) controlling for the probability of custody, the only statistical differences were again found in the medium risk of custody group, where more blacks received a CSO or an Attendance Centre Order, fewer were placed on probation (or a supervision order) and more were given a discharge rather than fined.[16] Asians, on the other hand, were treated significantly differently from whites in both low and medium risk groups,[17] being much less likely to be

[15] Total Scale (Figure 20) χ^2 = 37.2, 9 df, p < .0000. Non-custodial Scale (Figure 21) χ^2 = 28.6, 4 df, p < .0000.

[16] χ^2 = 12.07, 4 df, p < .017. The results of the regression analysis are presented in Table 2 of Appendix 10. There were no significant differences for black or for Asian offenders.

[17] Low Risk: White/Asian χ^2 = 13.67, 4 df, p < .008;
Medium Risk: White/Asian χ^2 = 12.88, 4 df, p < .01;
The number of Asians in the high risk group was too small for analysis.

placed on probation and more often fined or discharged when they had a low risk of custody, and much more prone to receive a CSO when they were in the medium risk of custody group.

Table 23: Males under 21 not sentenced to custody: percentage receiving alternative penalties controlled by risk of custody (TPCS)

	Low Risk (0–39.9%)			Medium Risk (40–69.9%)			High Risk (70–100%)		
	Whites	Blacks	Asians	Whites	Blacks	Asians	Whites	Blacks	Asians
Att. Ctr.	2	—	4	1	10	—	—	—	—
CSO	44	47	43	47	52	76	31	47	75 (n=6)
Prob.	19	16	6	35	24	4	69	53	13 (n=1)
Fine/ Comp.	17	21	25	9	—	4	—	—	—
Discharges	19	17	23	8	14	16	—	—	13 (n=1)

3. Conclusion

In conclusion it can be said that there is, indeed, evidence that, where the range of discretion is widest for judges, they were more likely to choose a 'high tariff' alternative for blacks than for whites. On the whole black adults fared worse than did black young offenders in comparison with their white contemporaries. On the other hand, Asians in both age bands fared rather better. Once again, it appeared that, in respect of the severity of sentences imposed, black adult males were dealt with, on average, at a higher point in the scale of punishments than were whites, and especially so at the Dudley Courts

It is particularly noticeable that neither Afro-Caribbean nor Asian defendants were being placed on probation as readily as whites. Black adults, in particular, were more likely to receive a suspended sentence of imprisonment and young adults, if in the median risk group for custody, a community service order. Was this due to probation officers themselves less frequently recommending probation for blacks and Asians? This certainly appeared to be the case, for they did so for 26% of whites, but only for 16% of blacks and 9% of Asians. And this was no doubt exacerbated by the much larger proportion of ethnic minority defendants on whom no Social Inquiry Report had been prepared. But, in addition, as Table 24 reveals, those black adults who were recommended for probation were still less likely to receive it than whites and more likely, if they did not go to prison, to get instead a more severe sentence: either a CSO or a suspended term of imprisonment. The same was true

Table 24: Adult males: percentage receiving alternative sentences*
Recommended Probation†

	Number	Probation	CSO	Susp. Sent.	Cond. Dis.	Fine
Whites	247	70.5	3.6	25.9	—	—
Blacks	29	58.6	6.9	31.0	3.4	—

Recommended CSO‡

	Number	Probation	CSO	Susp. Sent.	Cond. Dis.	Fine
Whites	252	0.8	50.6	36.8	5.2	6.7
Blacks	45	2.2	31.1	60.0	2.2	4.4

*Although only 7 Asians were recommended for probation only 2 of them (28.6%) received it. Three (43%) got a Suspended Sentence. This was significantly different from the treatment of whites. $\chi^2=12.2$, 2 df, $p<0.002$.

†$\chi^2=9.98$, 3 df, $p<0.019$.

‡$\chi^2=9.91$, 4 df, $p<0.04$. There was no significant difference between white and Asian adults or young adults.

(Whites weighted)

for recommendations to a community service order: substantially more blacks got, instead, a suspended sentence.

It is widely feared that this 'up-tariffing', as it has been commonly and crudely called, is a factor which puts blacks at more risk for receiving a custodial sentence should they re-appear on fresh charges.

10

PRE-SENTENCE FACTORS

This study was concerned with whether judges in the Crown Court were even-handed in respect of cases as they appeared before them. But, of course, decisions made earlier in the process may affect the way in which a case is presented. It was possible to shed some light on three areas which may have such an impact, all of which have given cause for concern in relation to differential treatment of ethnic minorities. These were:

1. Whether the incident from which the conviction had ensued had come to light as a result of a 'stop-and-search', or some other action initiated by the police.
2. Whether the defendant had been remanded in custody or on bail by the magistrates' court from which he was committed while awaiting trial and sentence.
3. Whether a social inquiry report was prepared and, if so, what sentence was recommended to the court.

1. How the Incident Came to Light

As mentioned above (see p. 5), it is now well established that black people are much more likely to be stopped and questioned by the police. It has therefore quite naturally been suggested that this begins a process which leads to a higher proportion of them being sent to prison. But, of course, many stop-and-searches relate to relatively petty, if irritating, matters. Whether they have a large impact on the number of persons from ethnic minorities who are sentenced to custody will depend, of course, on whether a disproportionate number of the crimes for which black and Asian offenders are convicted at the Crown Courts were the result of such action by the police.

Although it was not always easy to be sure of the precise sequence of events which had led to the arrest of the offenders, it was possible in most cases to assess:

- Whether the case had come to the notice of the police through being reported to the police by the aggrieved person, or by some other party, or whether it had been discovered by the police themselves.
- How the defendant came to be arrested: whether at the scene of the crime, after identification by the victim or other witnesses or from other clues; whether he was known already to the police and arrested on suspicion; whether he was previously unknown but arrested on suspicion; or whether he surrendered himself to the police.

Not surprisingly, almost all the offences involving drugs had come to light through the activities of the police or, very occasionally, by the customs authorities. And they accounted for a much larger proportion of the Crown Court cases which involved blacks: 14.5 per cent as against 3.4 per cent of the Asian cases and 1.7 per cent of the whites.

Leaving aside the drugs cases, it was interesting to note that 27 per cent of the offences by black males who were convicted of non-domestic burglary or theft were 'discovered' by the police in comparison with only 15 per cent of the white and 6 per cent of the Asians convicted of these offences. These offences were discovered either at the scene of the crime, or while making enquiries, or through stops and searches.

When the ethnic groups were compared, according to how the police came to gather the information on which the arrest had been made, there was evidence that black offenders had been more often arrested 'on suspicion' than the white offenders, but only amongst those blacks already 'known to the police'. Even so, the relatively small proportion of such cases (6% of the total) could not have accounted for much of the large over-representation of black offenders sentenced at the Crown Court.

Table 25: How the offender was apprehended (percentage)* (males)

	All Offences			Excluding Drugs		
	Whites	Blacks	Asians	Whites	Blacks	Asians
Arrested at scene	27.5	27.9	25.4	27.1	22.2	24.9
Identified by witnesses/clues	56.3	53.9	60.3	56.8	59.7	60.6
Known to police: arrested on suspicion	3.4	6.0	2.4	3.5	5.0	2.3
Not previously known: arrested on suspicion	1.9	2.1	3.4	1.8	1.6	3.5
Surrendered to police	3.0	2.4	3.2	3.1	2.8	3.3
No information	7.8	7.8	5.4	7.7	8.7	5.4

Comparing all offences: White/Black χ^2=13.71, 5 df, $p<0.018$; White/Asian χ^2=12.16, 5 df, $p<0.033$.

Comparing offences excluding those arrested for drugs as main charge: White/Black χ^2=11.43, 5 df, $p<0.043$; White/Asian χ^2=13.55, 5 df, $p<0.019$, but note that if the two categories of arrested, previously known and not previously known, are combined the differences are not significant.

Whites weighted

As far as could be gathered from the depositions, the black defendants appeared more often to have had legal advice at the police station. In at least 73 per cent of cases white defendants made their statement without a lawyer being present compared with 59% of the blacks and 58% of the Asians.[1] This, of course, might be a factor which explains, to some degree, the higher proportion of blacks and Asians who maintained their innocence and pleaded not guilty at their trial.[2]

2. The Effect of Having Been Remanded in Custody

One of the variables most powerfully associated with receiving a custodial sentence, even after all other variables significantly associated with the custody decision had been taken into account, was appearing for sentence already in custody, having failed to obtain bail at an earlier hearing. This is not to imply that this proves that there is a causal relationship between being on remand and subsequently being sentenced to custody. It may be that some factors (for example, unmeasured aspects of the seriousness of the offence or of the offender's prior history) influenced both the decision to remand and the decision to impose a custodial sentence. They would, however, need to be very potent to explain all the 'remand in custody effect'[3] which Figure 24 shows to be very strong for all ethnic groups:[4]

However, as can be seen from Figure 25, a significantly higher proportion of blacks had appeared for sentence already in custody: 26% of them, compared with 20% of the whites

---

[1] It was not possible to tell whether or not a lawyer had been present in 2.3% of white cases, 8.5% of black and 18.7% of Asian.

[2] Carol Hedderman and David Moxon's study, *Magistrates' Court or Crown Court? Mode of Trial Decisions and Sentencing*, (1992), Home Office Research Study No. 125, found that 'only two per cent of those who elected trial said they had made their decision without seeking legal advice', at p 19.

[3] This finding that remand in custody is a highly significant predictor of being sentenced to custody has recently been supported by a similar finding by Carol Hedderman, 'Custody Decisions for Property Offenders in the Crown Court', *Howard J.*, Vol. 30, (1991), pp 207–217 at p 215.

[4] The white/black (p < .20) and white/Asian differences (p < .09) were not statistically significant.

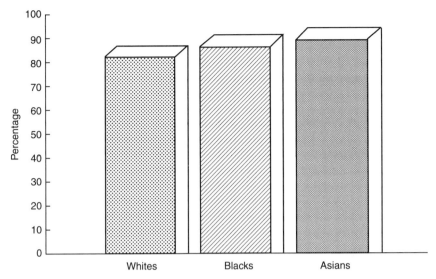

Figure 24 Percentage of each ethnic group sentenced to custody among those who appeared for sentence having been remanded in custody (males)

and 18% of the Asians.[5] Was this the result of an unequal application of the criteria which should determine the custody/bail decision?

In order to investigate this another logistic regression analysis was undertaken, the purpose of which was to model the factors significantly associated with whether or not a defendant was already remanded in custody when he appeared for sentence. Unlike the probability of custody score, which was empirically based, the variables used to model the decision to remand in custody were chosen *a priori*, as those which were known to be

[5] Comparing whites and blacks $\chi^2 = 13.7$, 1 df, p < .0002 and whites with Asians p < .17 n.s.

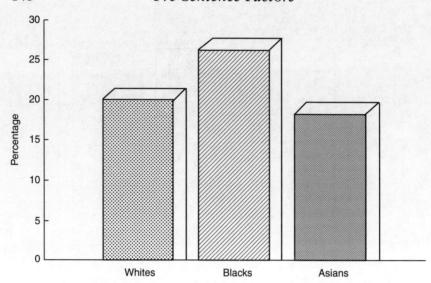

Figure 25 Percentage of cases appearing for sentence on remand in custody (males)

legally relevant to the bail/custody decision. They may not, of course, be those which would best explain the actual use of remand in custody. They were:

- The seriousness of the offence charged, ranked in 8 categories (see Table 1, Appendix 9)
- Whether the defendant was already in breach of a court order
- Whether he had previously served a custodial sentence
- Whether there was evidence that he had an unsettled lifestyle
- Whether there was evidence that he was of no fixed abode or living in privately rented accommodation
- Whether his employment status was 'marginal', meaning that he was currently unemployed or not regularly in employment.
- Whether he intended to contest the case at trial.

The co-efficients for these variables were weighted to give a score which was named the **Custody Remand Score**.[6] As before, scores calculated on the basis of the sample as a whole and on the white cases only were used to calculate the expected rate of custodial remand for each ethnic group, controlling for the influence of variables listed above. The results were very similar, whichever of the two scores was used, as can be seen from Table 26:

Table 26: Observed rates of remand in custody at appearance for sentence compared with expected rates: controlled by custody remand scores (PRCS, males)

Whites				Blacks				Asians			
Obs.	Exp.	O–E	O–E/E	Obs.	Exp.	O–E	O–E/E	Obs.	Exp.	O–E	O–E/E
Total PRCS:											
20.2	21.0	–0.8	–3.8	25.9	22.4	+3.5	+15.6	17.5	17.0	+0.5	+2.9
White PRCS:											
20.2	21.1	–0.9	–4.3	25.9	22.1	+3.8	+17.2	17.5	17.6	–0.1	–0.6

This provides evidence that, even when the cases were 'matched' according to the weight given to variables which might be expected to have some effect on the decision whether to remand in custody, black offenders still had a greater likelihood of being remanded in custody and thus, appearing before the court already with a disadvantage linked to an increased likelihood of getting a custodial sentence. However, this disadvantage was found amongst the black males sentenced at Birmingham Crown Court, where the probability of remand was more than 5 percentage points higher than expected (a

[6] See Appendix 9, which presents the Probability of Remand in Custody Score (PRCS) based on the total male sample.

23% greater probability), but not amongst those sentenced by
the Dudley Courts, where slightly fewer blacks had been
remanded in custody than expected. Therefore, the large difference between the custody rates of blacks and whites amongst
the cases sentenced at the Dudley courts might have been even
larger if the black offenders had been remanded in custody as
readily as whites.

In order to assess the impact of a prior remand in custody on
the overall race difference in the proportion sentenced to custody, the prediction of custody score was recalculated excluding
'remand in custody' as a variable. This showed that the difference between the observed and expected rates for black and
white offenders increased from 2.5 to 3.7 percentage points or
from a 5 per cent to 7.6 per cent greater probability (See Table
2, Appendix 8). The difference was not only greater but also
more statistically significant. This shows, in other words, that
the 'race effect' for the sample as a whole would have been
greater and more statistically significant had black offenders
been remanded in custody before sentence in the same proportion as were whites.

3. The Influence of Social Inquiry Reports

Another major influence on the sentence passed may be the
amount and quality of information made known to the court
about the offender. And, of course, this will depend upon
whether a Social Inquiry Report has been prepared by the probation service. Not only do these reports contain recommendations as to the 'appropriate'—usually non-custodial—sentence,
but they are also invaluable to defence counsel in making pleas
of mitigation. This was another area where ethnic minorities
appearing before the West Midlands Crown Courts appeared to
be at a disadvantage. A significantly higher proportion of both

blacks and Asians had had no Social Inquiry Report prepared on them:[7]

Whites	28%
Blacks	42%
Asians	43%

This, as mentioned earlier, was in part due to the fact that a considerably higher proportion of blacks and Asians had indicated that they intended to contest the charges against them, although it should be noted that amongst those offenders who did plea not guilty at trial there were no statistically significant differences in the proportion of white and black offenders who had no report. But a higher proportion pleading not guilty was not the only reason why fewer ethnic minorities were sentenced without a report being available. Both blacks and Asians who had pleaded guilty were significantly less likely than the whites to have an S.I.R., both young offenders and adults, as Figure 26 shows.[8]

And, of those with no SIR a significantly higher proportion of black offenders received a custodial sentence whether they pleaded guilty of not guilty (see Figure 27):

The effect of this was that, amongst those sentenced to custody, a significantly higher proportion of black and Asian offenders had been incarcerated without the benefit of a social inquiry report being available for the court to consider. Amongst those under 21, for whom there is a statutory duty to consider a report before sentencing to custody unless 'in the circumstances of the case the court is of the opinion that it is

[7] White/black χ^2 = 43.2, 2 df, p <.0000; white/Asian χ^2 = 49.9, 1 df, p < .0000. It is interesting to note that this is a different finding from that reported by George Mair from his study of persons sentenced a Leeds and Bradford Magistrates' Courts, where 35% of whites, 52% of blacks and 31% of Asians were referred for a Social Inquiry Report, 'Ethnic Minorities, Probation and Magistrates' Courts', *Brit J Criminol,* (1986), Vol. 26, pp 147–155 at p 152.

[8] Moxon also noted 'that substantial differences remain in the extent to which reports were provided for different racial groups after allowing for plea' op. cit., p 60.

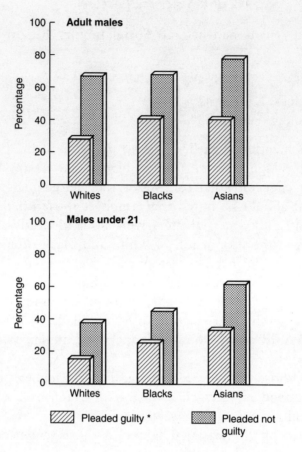

Figure 26 Percentage of male offenders with no Social Inquiry Report controlled by plea

* Pleaded guilty includes: entered guilty plea, no trial arranged; went for trial but pleaded guilty to a lesser charge; went for trial but changed plea to guilty at Court. Appendix 6 gives full details for each of these categories. For those who pleaded guilty the difference betyween whites and blacks and whites and Asians with no SIR's are all statistically significant: 14–20 w/b χ^2 = 9.88, 1 df, p < .002; w/A χ^2 = 31.89, 1 df, p < .0000; 21+ w/b χ^2 =24.23, 1 df, p < .0000 w/A χ^2 = 11.72, 1 df, p < .0006. For those who pleaded not guilty the only statistical difference was between whites and Asians aged 14–20, χ^2 = 4.43, 1 df, p < .04.

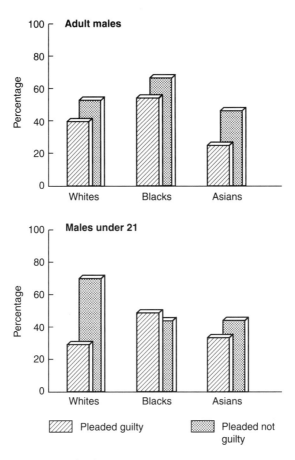

Figure 27 Percentage of adult and young adult males with no Social Inquiry Report sentenced to custody*

* Pleaded guilty : 14–20 w/b χ^2 = 7.40, 1 df, p < .007;
      21 plus w/b χ^2 = 10.59, 1 df, p < .001;
      14–20 w/A ns; 21 plus χ^2 = 7.28, 1 df, p < .007.

Pleaded not guilty : 14–20 w/b χ^2 = 2.32, 1 df, p < .13 ns;
       21 plus w/b χ^2 = 4.80, 1 df, p < .028;
       14–20 w/A ns; 21 plus ns.

unnecessary', as many as 26% of young black and 31% of young Asian offenders had no report prepared about them.[9] This compares with only 13% of the young white offenders. And among adults there were similarly sized differences: 47% of the black and 40% of the Asian men sentenced to prison had no SIR, but only 30% of the white offenders. The differences for both young offenders and adults were found among those who pleaded guilty but **not** among those who had pleaded not guilty.[10] There appears therefore to be a difference in practice as regards the ordering and preparation of social inquiry reports for black and white males which cannot be explained solely by the greater propensity of Afro-Caribbean men to contest the case in court.

To what extent was this due to a higher proportion of the cases involving blacks being more likely to receive a custodial sentence (irrespective of whether or not there was a Social Inquiry Report) because of the seriousness of the charges made against them? Figure 28 shows that, indeed, a much higher proportion of the black defendants without an SIR were at a higher risk of receiving a custodial sentence.[11]

When this different distribution of cases was taken into consideration (see Table 27), the following conclusions emerged:

[9] Criminal Justice Act 1982 S 2(2) and 2(3). In some cases 'stand down' reports may have been prepared but no records could be traced of them.

[10] Aged under 21: plead guilty white:black χ^2 = 16.5 1 df p < .0000; white:Asian χ^2 = 19.4 1 df p < .0000. Adults: plead guilty white:black χ^2 = 19.5 1 df p < .0000; white:Asian n.s.

[11] This finding is at variance with Moxon's conclusion that it was 'the more difficult cases which were targeted for reports—those where there is a real risk of custody'. But the fact that more of the blacks with no SIR were in the highest risk of custody group perhaps illustrates Moxon's point that 'The interactions between probation reports, plea and ethnicity illustrate how complex are the factors which may contribute to apparent differences in the treatment accorded by the courts by members of different ethnic groups' op. cit. at p. 60 and 61. There were no significant differences in the distribution of Asian and white cases with no S.I.R. between the low, medium and high risk of custody groups.

Table 27: Percentage observed and expected custody rates for those with no social inquiry reports (SIR): controlled by risk of custody (TPCS, males)

	Observed	Expected	O–E (%)
Whites	41.5	42.3	−0.8
Blacks	56.4	52.8	+3.6
Asians	33.5	40.6	−7.1

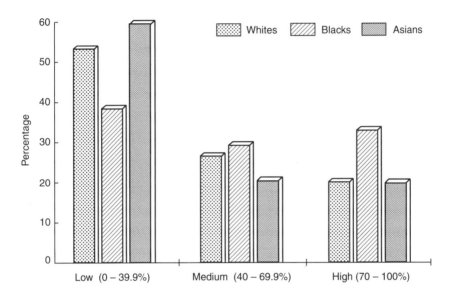

Figure 28 Percentage of cases with no Social Inquiry Report in low, medium and high risk of to custody groups* (males)

* Comparing white/black $\chi^2 = 32.2$, 2 df, p < .0000; white/Asian $\chi^2 = 3.74$, 2 df, p < .15.

- The 15 percentage points difference between the observed proportion of blacks and whites with no SIRs who were sent to custody was largely accounted for by the fact that the black cases were generally of a more serious kind. Even so, a 4.4 (3.6 + 0.8) percentage points difference still remained.
- Asians were less likely to go to custody than would be expected, even after taking into account the fact that nearly two thirds of the cases for which no SIRs were prepared were in the low risk category for custody.
- When the cases were examined separately for each of the Crown Courts the findings mirrored the differences in sentencing practice already presented. Among those sentenced at Birmingham Crown Court about the same number of black offenders with no Social Inquiry Report went to custody as would have been expected given the seriousness of the cases. Amongst those sentenced at the Dudley courts, however, the proportion of blacks given custody was 13.2 percentage points higher than expected (64.1% compared with an expected rate of 50.9%): equivalent to 26 per cent greater.

Among those for whom a Social Inquiry Report had been prepared (which contained explicit or implied recommendations as to the appropriate penalty) the proportion of blacks and whites sentenced to custody was almost identical. But at the Dudley courts a significantly higher proportion of blacks (49%) than whites (24%), were given a custodial sentence amongst those who had a probability of custody of 44.9% or less.[12] And comparing blacks in this risk group at Dudley courts with those sentenced at Birmingham the difference was even greater: 49% v 21%.[13] This finding is closely in line with other findings of the comparatively severe treatment of black offenders in this lower risk group amongst those sentenced at the Dudley courts (See pp 95–107 above).

[12] $\chi^2 = 11.05$, 1 df, $p < .0009$.   [13] $\chi^2 = 14.59$, 1 df, $p < .0001$.

Of course, it was possible that these sentencing variations reflected variations in the recommendations made by the probation officers serving those courts. In order to test this hypothesis the sentence imposed in each case was compared with that which had been recommended,[14] according to whether it was more severe, the same, or less severe. This revealed that the penalty had been more severe for 60% of the whites, 66% of the blacks and 59% of the Asians.[15] However, yet again, as Table 28 reveals, there were substantial variations between the courts.

Table 28: Percentage receiving sentences, greater, the same, or lesser than recommended in SIR (males)

Court	Whites			Blacks			Asians		
	Greater	Same	Lesser	Greater	Same	Lesser	Greater	Same	Lesser
Birmingham	54.4	41.4	4.6	58.7	38.3	3.0	55.5	38.4	6.2
Dudley									
courts	60.9	35.7	3.4	78.9	19.0	2.1	60.0	33.0	7.0
Coventry	77.6	22.4	0.0	52.4	38.1	9.5	73.7	26.3	0.0
Warwick &									
Stafford	60.7	33.5	5.8	73.9	26.1	0.0	64.7	35.3	0.0

[14] In this analysis only those cases where that was an explicit or clearly implied recommendation were included.

[15] In view of the finding (see p. 44 above) that Assistant Recorders were comparatively the least likely to impose a custodial sentence on black offenders, it should be noted that 44% of them gave a sentence greater than that recommended in the SIR, compared with 67% of the Circuit Judges and 69% of the Recorders. Furthermore, the Assistant Recorders gave the same sentence for black offenders as that recommended in 41% of cases, but Circuit Judges and Recorders only accepted the recommendations in 36 and 37% of cases respectively. For a comparison (although Recorders and Assistant Recorders are joined in one category), see Moxon, *op.cit.*, p. 52.

It will be apparent that there is a remarkable concordance between the pattern of these findings and the variations in the custody rates between whites, blacks and Asians at these courts. The proportion of blacks receiving a sentence more severe than that recommended[16] was considerably higher than for whites at both the Dudley courts and at Warwick and Stafford Crown Courts. It is also notable that the proportion of whites and Asians receiving a more severe sentence is highest at Coventry, the Court which sentenced the greatest proportion of whites and Asians to custody in the region.

One explanation in relation to the Dudley courts could be that the black offenders received sentences more severe than those recommended because probation officers, in their desire to keep black defendants out of custody, recommended a non-custodial penalty for a higher proportion of those black defendants who had characteristics associated with a high probability of custody. But no evidence was found to support this 'bending over backwards' hypothesis. Indeed, when recommendations were divided into those which suggested a non-custodial penalty as opposed to custody (usually implicitly) or a suspended sentence, or, refrained from making any proposal (which was associated with a high use of custody), the distribution of white and black offenders between the low, medium and high risk groups was remarkably similar (see Table 29).

Although the black defendants dealt with at Dudley courts were significantly more likely than whites to be recommended for a Community Service Order, which is generally regarded as higher up the 'tariff' of penalties than a Probation Order (see Table 30), significantly fewer of the black offenders than at Birmingham had reports which implicitly recommended a custodial or a suspended sentence or made no recommendation at all: only 18 compared with 31 per cent.[17]

---

[16] Which was in 78% of both white and black cases and in 69% of Asian cases a custodial sentence   [17] $\chi^2 = 8.58$, 1 df, p < .003.

Table 29: Percentage of whites and blacks in each risk group at the Dudley courts who were explicitly or implicitly recommended for a non-custodial sentence (males)

Risk group	Whites		Blacks	
	Number with recommen-dations	Percentage rec. non-custodial	Number with recommen-dations	Percentage non-custodial
Low	134	85.1	49	85.7
Medium	73	78.5	53	86.8*
High	87	66.6	52	73.1

*χ^2=0.70, 1 df, p<0.40.

The conclusion that has inevitably to be drawn is that the differences in the sentences imposed cannot be attributed to the recommendations made by the probation officers. The judges who dealt with cases at the Dudley courts between them only imposed the sentence recommended for blacks in 19 per cent of the cases, whereas they accepted the recommendation in 36 per

Table 30: Recommendations in social inquiry reports at the Dudley courts and Birmingham for whites and blacks* (males)

Recommendation	Dudley courts		Birmingham	
	Whites	Blacks	Whites	Blacks
Custody/susp. sentences/No rec.	21.8	18.2	25.8	31.4
CSO	33.7	44.2	29.7	30.8
Prob. order	34.4	29.2	31.0	25.5
Fine or other	10.2	8.4	13.4	12.3

*Comparing CSO with other recommendations the White/Black difference was χ^2=4.3, 1 df, p<0.38.

cent of the white cases. In comparison, the judges at Birmingham accepted the recommendations for blacks in 38 per cent of instances. Yet again, therefore, evidence was found that there was a distinctive practice shared by a number, but of course by no means all, of the judges at the Dudley courts which, when aggregated over a sufficient number of cases, was unfavourable to black defendants.

11

SENTENCING WOMEN

As mentioned at the outset of this report, much concern has been expressed about the large over-representation of Afro-Caribbean women in the prison population. It has also been suggested that while women, in general, may less often be sentenced to custody than men, those who are not integrated into conventional female roles are, in fact, more prone to be sentenced to a penal institution. In this context it has been feared that black women have been 'doubly' discriminated against: first because they are black and secondly because of the kind of women black offenders are said to be.[1] This chapter examines the evidence in relation to both of these concerns.

1. Comparing the Sentences Imposed on Women of Different Ethnic Backgrounds

Because of the relatively small number—76—of black females who were sentenced at these courts during 1989, and the even smaller number—14—of Asian women, the analyses could not be as detailed as those which have been reported for male offenders. Too few were dealt with at several of the court centres and too few were sentenced by any individual judge for meaningful comparisons to be made.

Like their male counterparts, black female defendants were over-represented at least six-fold in relation to their number in

---

[1] See, for example, the discussion in Allison Morris, *Women, Crime and Criminal Justice*, (1987), at pp 88 and 101.

the population of the West Midlands as a whole. Asian women, on the other hand, were very rarely before the Crown Courts.

Custodial sentences, as Figure 29 shows, were used much less often for women than for men, whatever their ethnic background.[2]

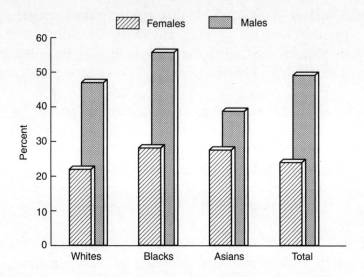

Figure 29 Percentage of females and males of each ethnic group sentenced to custody

Although, as already explained, the number of cases was too small to place much reliance on comparisons,[3] it is nevertheless interesting to note that the pattern of variations between cases

---

[2] The difference is remarkably similar to that found by David Moxon, 28% of the females and 52% of the males in his sample of offenders sentenced at 18 Crown Court centres were sentenced to custody, op. cit., p. 18.

[3] For these reasons Asian women are not included in the analyses which follow.

dealt with at different court centres was very similar to that found for males (see Table 31). Again, judges at Coventry between them sent the highest proportion to custody, those at Birmingham and the Dudley courts sentenced at a similar rate overall, but the judges at the Dudley courts, on aggregate, committed a much higher proportion of black women to a penal institution.

Table 31: Percentage of females sentenced to custody by court*

	Whites		Blacks		Total	
Court:	Number sentenced	Per cent to custody	Number sentenced	Per cent to custody	Number sentenced	Per cent to custody
Birmingham	173	22.0	49	24.5	227	23.3
Dudley courts	99	19.2	25	36.0	133	22.6
Coventry	41	39.0	1	–	42	38.1
Total	342	22.5	76	28.9	433	24.0

*The number dealt with at Stafford and Warwick was too small to make this comparison

Could these variations, and the 6 percentage points overall difference (equivalent to 28 per cent) between the proportionate use of custody for blacks and whites, be explained by the characteristics of black defendants? They were, in several respects, different. They were much more likely to have appeared charged with an indictable-only offence, to have been found guilty of three or more charges, to have not been the sole offender, to have used violence and caused injury, to have been convicted of robbery or a section 20 wounding with grievous bodily harm, to have had a prior conviction for violence, and to have been first convicted at a young age. Furthermore, considerably fewer of them were married and more were said to be socially unsettled and in a socially or economically disadvantageous position. Table 32 sets out these findings.

There were far fewer variables in respect of which there were

Table 32: Percentage of white and black female offenders with various characteristics†

Attributes	Whites	Blacks
Committed for trial on indictment		
(i.e. not an either-way offence)	30	45*
Either-way offence—elected trial	12	5*
Found guilty 3 or more offences of different		
types	39	54
Convicted of robbery	4	18
Victim Black	1	8*
Under 16	7	12 n.s.
Convicted of violent offence as main/and or a		
subsidiary charge	6	16
Theft motive of violence	3	18
Knife used	10	20
Injuries caused	23	33*
Convicted S20 GBH	6	11 n.s.
Convicted of drugs offence involving cannabis	2	8*
Convicted of household burglary	6	3 n.s.
Convicted of fraud	30	22 n.s.
Sole Offender	46	34*
Expressed remorse	58	43*
1+ prior convictions for violence	10	22
2+ previous custodial sentences for offence of		
similar type to current conviction	1	7
Previously on CSO: breached	2	7*
Married	35	9
Unsettled/disrupted home life	17	38
Socially/economically disadvantaged	25	40*

All comparisons are significant $p<0.01$, unless indicated; *$p<0.05$; n.s. not significant.

substantial and significant differences between the proportions
of white and black women who received a custodial sentence
(see Appendix 7), but the largest related to the following three
variables:

- A much higher proportion of black women who were aged
  under 21 were sentenced to detention in a young persons'
  institution (42% blacks v 18% whites).
- More than twice as many blacks with a co-defendant who
  was also black were committed to custody than whites with
  white co-defendants (39% v 16%).
- More black women with no previous convictions got a custodial sentence (28% v 10% of whites).

Following the procedures outlined in Chapter 5, a Probability
of Custody Score was devised specifically for females cases.
Taking the women as a whole, the variables which were most
highly correlated with the use of custody, when all other variables had been taken into account, were similar to those found
for men: type of offence, whether remanded in custody,
whether in breach of a court order, the number of offences of
which found guilty, the amount of money involved, whether
injury was caused, number of previous proved offences. But
when all of these had been considered, there was also a social
variable which was significant, namely, if the person was of no
fixed abode or living in a rented room or flat: a variable highly
correlated with evidence of living an unsettled or unstable
lifestyle.[4] It should be noted, however, that black women were

---

[4] The model is presented in Table 7 of Appendix 8. It will be seen, by comparing
this with Table 1 of the same Appendix, that many fewer attributes were significant for
women than for men. However, with the exception noted above, the significant attributes affecting the use of custody for women were also significant for men. This is a different finding from that reported for a Magistrates Court by David Farrington and
Allison Morris, 'Sex, Sentencing and Reconviction', *Brit J Criminol*, (1983), Vol. 23,
pp 229–248 at pp 244–5. This may be due to the different range of offences considered
in that study from those in this enquiry. It is also at variance with the American study
by Ilene Nagel which found that the severity of the offence and the number of previous

not more disadvantaged in this respect, nor more likely, if they were, to get a custodial sentence. It should also be noted that two variables which were significantly associated with a higher custody rate for black women when considered in isolation— being under 21 and having a co-defendant of the same race—

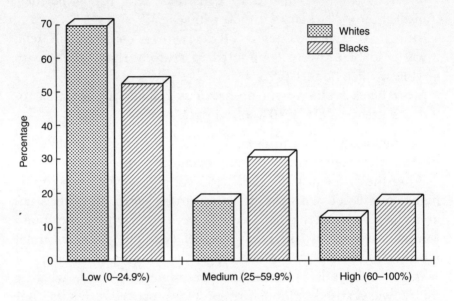

Figure 30 Percentage of white and black women in low, medium and high risk custody groups (FPCS)

were no longer significant when the other variables were taken into account.

For purposes of analysis the Risk of Custody Score was divided into three categories: low (0–24.9%), medium (25–59.9%) and high (60–100%) risk of custody. It will be apparent from Figure 30 that significantly fewer of the black cases fell into the low risk category.

convictions did not significantly affect the severity of sentences for women, whereas marital status did. Reported in Morris, op. cit., pp 87–88.

When probability of custody was taken into account, the observed proportions of custodial sentences imposed on both white and black women were almost identical with what would be expected. In other words, the difference in the white and black custody rates was fully explained by the characteristics of the cases.[5]

However, while no differences between the observed and expected rates for white and black women were found among the cases dealt with at Birmingham, differences once again were revealed at the Dudley courts. Although only 25 black women had been dealt with by judges at that court, 36% of them got a custodial sentence rather than the 26% expected from the profile of their cases.

Only a small proportion (12%) of women had pleaded not guilty. Like the men who had done so they received longer sentences on average than those women who pleaded guilty. But, unlike the findings for men, there were no significant differences between the length of sentences imposed on blacks and whites, whether they pleaded guilty or not guilty or were adults or young adults.[6] In general, the women sentenced to prison got much shorter sentences than did the men: 43% 6 months or less compared with 21% of men, and 8% over 3 years compared with 13% of men.[7]

The differences in the pattern of non-custodial penalties (see Table 33) imposed on black and white women, particularly in

---

[5] 22 black women were sentenced to custody compared with 23 expected. This small difference was not statistically significant. The number of white women given a custodial sentence (77) was exactly the same as the number expected. This is confirmed by the significance of the coefficient for race in the logistic model. See Table 7 Appendix 8, $p < .83$ (Wald Statistic).

[6] In fact, the number involved was too small for any reliable comparisons to be made: only 3 black women pleaded not guilty out of a total of 13 adult black women sentenced to custody.

[7] Moxon found that 'almost twice as many females (16%) received a sentence of three months or less, whilst men were more than twice as likely to receive a custodial sentence in excess of 2 years', op. cit., p 32.

Table 33: Number and percentage of women who were sentenced to various non-custodial penalties

Non-Custodial Penalty	Adults				Women under 21			
	Whites		Blacks		Whites		Blacks	
	Number	Per cent of total sentenced	Number	Per cent of total sentenced	Number	Per cent of total sentenced	Number	Percent of total sentenced
Susp. Sent.	81	41	19	46	—	—	—	—
CSO	17	9	4	10	9	13	3	23
Probation	50	25	14	34	36	53	6	46
Fine/ Comp.	13	7	—	—	7	10	2	15
Discharge	36	18	4	10	16	24	2	15

the use of suspended sentences of imprisonment, was found to be explained by the fact that more of the black women had characteristics which placed them in a relatively high risk group of receiving custody. There were no statistically significant race of defendant effects in the pattern of penalties imposed when risk of custody was taken into account.[8]

The proportion of women who were sentenced without a Social Inquiry Report being available to the court was very small: 6% of whites, 5% of blacks. And there was no evidence

---

[8] Of the women put on probation 9.3% were subject to a condition of receiving psychiatric treatment. The figure for men was 6.5%. The numbers were too small to place any reliability on this difference. It does however qualify Hilary Allen's statement 'that if convicted a woman is more likely than a man to be ordered to receive psychiatric treatment instead of a normal penalty', *Justice Unbalanced: Gender, Psychiatry and Judicial Decisions*, (1987), p xi. Her qualitative study was, however, based largely on homicide cases and on cases which had been referred for psychiatric assessment.

that black women were more likely to have had a recommendation which explicitly or implicitly implied that a custodial sentence would be appropriate. Nor, overall, did more black women get a sentence greater than that recommended by a probation officer. But, again, there were differences between the courts. A higher proportion of black women than whites at the Dudley courts got a greater sentence (57% v 44%) and so did the white women at Coventry (60%). As with the male sample, this reflected the observed differences in the proportionate use of custody by these courts.

2. Comparing the Sentences Imposed on Females and Males

Although it was not the prime focus of this study, the data collected, can shed some light on the controversial question of how women offenders are dealt with in the courts as compared with men. As already mentioned, it has sometimes been suggested that some women, and black women in particular, fare worse than men before the courts. One way of studying this was to apply to the female cases the Probability of Custody Score which had been calculated for the males. In other words, to test whether, when the weights give to the variables which best explained the use of custody for males were applied to the same characteristics in female cases, women were as likely to get a custodial sentence as men. Figure 31 shows, for both white and black women, that the observed proportion given a custodial sentence was considerably lower than that which would have been predicted if their characteristics had been responded to by the courts in the same way as for males. There was no evidence here that black women were treated, in respect of this comparison, differently from white women: in fact, the observed rate for blacks was even lower in relation to what could be expected than it was for whites.

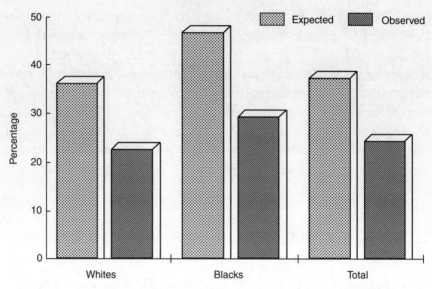

Figure 31 Percentage of women observed sentenced to custody compared with percentage expected when the male probability of custody score (TPCS) was applied to white and black female offenders

As a check on these findings, the male and female samples were joined and a combined probability of custody score computed (MFPCS, see Table 8 Appendix 8). When the observed and expected proportions of females sentenced to custody were compared the results were remarkably similar to those shown in Figure 31. White women were given a custodial sentence 34 per cent less often than would be expected given the characteristics of their cases and black women 37 per cent less often.[9] The odds of a women being sentenced to custody were very significantly less than the odds for a man.[10] But there was no

---

[9] For white females the observed custody rate was 22.5% and the expected 34% (Obs-Exp −11.5, Obs-Exp/Exp −33.8). 28.9% of black females got a custodial sentence compared with the expected rate of 45.7% (Obs-Exp −16.8, obs-Exp/Exp −36.8).

[10] p < .0000 (Wald statistic). See Table 8, Appendix 8.

significant differences in the odds of a black or a white woman receiving a custodial sentence.

These findings are more favourable to the so-called 'chivalry' or 'paternalistic' hypothesis than those of other researchers in England, such as Eaton and Farrington and Morris, who found that at magistrates courts 'men and women received similar treatment when they appeared in similar circumstances'.[11] They are more in line with American studies, which have typically dealt with felony cases as well as misdemeanours. The best of these studies have revealed that, in general, females do fare better than males.[12]

The 'paternalistic' hypothesis has, however, recently been refined by a number of feminist scholars. They suggest that the reason why women, in general, are more leniently dealt with is not because of the chivalry of male judges but because the courts are concerned to shield families and children from the unpleasant and destructive consequences of the incarceration of a major 'carer'. This 'family-based justice' as Kathleen Daly calls it, means that family ties are hypothesised to have a mitigating effect on sentences for both men and women, but particularly for the latter. Furthermore, her analysis of American data led her to the view that 'gendered family interactions spawning a more lenient response . . . will be greatest for black defendants'.[13] The West Midlands data gave no support to either hypothesis.

---

[11] Mary Eaton, *Justice for Women? Family, Court and Social Control*, (1986), p 12. Also Farrington and Morris, op. cit., p 239. On the 'chivalry hypothesis', see, for example, Frances Heidensohn, 'Women and Crime in Europe' in F. Heidensohn and M Farrell (eds.), *Crime in Europe*, (1991), pp 55–71 at pp 67–68, and Mary Eaton, op.cit., at pp 22–25.

[12] See, for example, Ilene H. Nagel 'Sex Differences in the Processing of Criminal Defendants' in A. Morris(ed), *Women and Crime*, (1981), pp 104–124 and Ilene H. Nagel and John Hagan, 'Gender and Crime: Offense Patterns and Criminal Court Sanctions' in M. Tonry and N. Morris(eds), *Crime and Justice: An Annual Review of Research*, Vol. 4 (1983), pp 91–144 at pp 127–134.

[13] Kathleen Daly 'Neither Conflict Nor Labeling Nor Paternalism Will Suffice: Intersections of Race, Ethnicity, Gender and Family in Criminal Court Decisions' *Crime*

The women were classified in respect of family ties by two criteria: first whether they had children and, secondly, whether they were married or cohabiting with their partner and/or had children. In neither case was it found that these variables affected the probability of receiving a custodial sentence.[14] Nor were there any differences between black and white women.[15] Nor were there any statistically significant differences between the proportion of women with and without such family ties receiving a custodial sentence (either black or white) when the probability of custody—whether low, medium or high—was controlled for.

But, of course, general support for the 'paternalistic' hypothesis does not prove that all women are more leniently treated than men. For example, some commentators have suggested that women are more likely than men to receive a custodial sentence earlier in their criminal careers. Nancy Seear and Elaine Player, for example, stated that 'in 1984 proportionately more adult women than adult men were sentenced to prison for their first offence. Almost one in four women sentenced to immediate imprisonment in 1984 had no previous convictions in comparison with only one in seventeen of the men'.[16] And a recent NACRO report argued that 'the tendency for women [in prison] to have fewer previous convictions than men suggests that many are imprisoned after having experienced only

and Delinquency, vol. 35, (1989) pp 136–168 at p 160. See also for a useful review of this debate, Lola Odubekun, 'A Structural Approach to Differential Gender Sentencing', *Criminal Justice Abstracts*, (June 1992, pp 343–360. I am grateful to Allison Morris for bringing these to may attention.

[14] Of the women who were married or cohabiting and/or had children 24.1% received a custodial sentence. Of those who were neither living with a partner nor had children 23.8% were incarcerated.

[15] White women: married/cohabiting/children 22.1% to custody; neither 23.6% to custody. Black women: married/cohabiting/children 28.9% to custody; neither 29.0% to custody.

[16] N. Seear and E Player, *Women in the Penal System*, (1986), Howard League for Penal Reform, p 4.

one or two community based options rather than the full range'.[17]

No such tendency was evident in the data collected for this study. As Table 34 shows, at all levels of previous convictions, women—black as well as white—were sentenced to custody less, not more, frequently than were men dealt with by the same courts.[18] Furthermore, while black males with two or

Table 34: Percentage of males and females sentenced to custody in relation to number of previous convictions

	Males				Females			
	Whites		Blacks		Whites		Blacks	
Number of previous convictions	Number of cases	Per cent to custody	Number of cases	Per cent to custody	Number of cases	Per cent to custody	Number of cases	Per cent to custody
None	832	31.9	164	30.5	167	10.2	29	27.6
1	454	41.3	120	45.0	67	20.9	13	15.4
2–4	958	49.2	148	58.5	65	41.5	21	28.6
5–7	621	57.9	196	67.9	25	40.0	6	50.0
8–10	447	58.4	96	75.0	18	50.0	7	42.9
11+	432	61.9	60	76.9				

[17] NACRO, *A Fresh Start for Women Prisoners: The Implications of the Woolf Report for Women*, (1986), p 2.

[18] The only exception appears to be (See Table 34) black women with no previous convictions. Comparing black and white women with no previous convictions, the proportion of black women sentenced to custody is significantly higher. $\chi^2 = 5.25$, 1 df, p $< .002$. However, the fact that black women as a whole were not sentenced to custody at a higher rate than expected, when all the other significant variables were controlled for, suggests that those with no previous convictions had committed more serious offences. In fact, 24% of the black women were convicted of robbery and 0.6% (1) white. If these robbery cases are discounted, the proportion of black and white women with no previous convictions who were sentenced to custody was very similar.

more previous convictions were significantly more likely than white males to receive a custodial sentence, there were no such differences between the proportion of white and black females sentenced to custody, whatever their number of prior convictions.

But, of course, females were proportionately much more often convicted of the property offences without violence— theft, fraud and handling—than were males, a higher proportion of whom were convicted of offences involving violence. It was possible, therefore, that when this was taken into account the incarceration rate for women was, indeed, higher than would have been expected if the men had had a similar profile of offences recorded against them. Pat Carlen, for example, has written of 'a grave cause for concern about women's imprisonment because the recent statistical analysis of female incarceration rates reveal . . . that women tend to be sentenced to prison for less serious offences than men'.[19] A comparison was therefore made (See Table 35) solely of the proportion of males and females who had been convicted of one of these less serious property offences who were sentenced to custody for the first time, taking into account their number of prior convictions.

There was no evidence here of unfavourable treatment for women as compared with men.[20] At all levels of previous convictions fewer females were sentenced to custody than males. Nevertheless, although only 13 per cent of the women first offenders were sentenced to custody compared with 31 per cent of the men, they accounted for the same **proportion** (35 per

[19] Pat Carlen, *Women, Crime and Poverty*, (1988), p 4. Carlen was here drawing on two documents published by NACRO: *Women in Prison* (1987) and *Women, Cautions and Sentencing* (1987).

[20] It is interesting to compare this with Moxon's finding that, among those convicted of theft and fraud 'women were significantly more likely to receive a non-custodial sentence after allowing for offence and criminal record. For example, males with no previous convictions were almost twice as likely as females to receive un-suspended custody (37% compared with 19%). The differences were less marked for those with previous convictions, but they remained substantial'. Op. cit., p 54.

Table 35: Offenders with no prior custodial sentence.
Percentage of males and females amongst those convicted of theft, fraud and handling sentenced to custody in relation to number of previous convictions

Number of previous convictions	Males (N=1122)			Females (N=376)		
	Percentage of cases	Percent sentenced to custody	Percent of all those in custody	Percentage of cases	Percent sentenced to custody	Percent of all those in custody
0	43.7	31.2	35.2	55.1	13.0	35.1
1	21.1	41.1	22.4	20.5	20.8	20.8
2–4	27.3	44.7	31.5	18.9	38.0	35.1
5–7	6.5	54.7	9.1	4.3	37.5	7.8
8–10	1.2	51.3	1.6	1.1	25.0	1.3
11+	0.2	40.0	0.2	—	—	—
			100.0			100.0

cent) of all those sentenced as did the men with no prior record. This is a good illustration of why it is wrong to make inferences about sentencing from the proportion of persons with no previous convictions who are in custody (see p. 177 below).

But was it possible that there was a distinctive group of socially deprived women who were particularly at risk of a custodial sentence in comparison with men who had similar social circumstances? Pat Carlen, amongst others, has pointed out that 'a number of criminological studies have indicated that, once women break the law, they are judged not only in terms of the seriousness of their crimes but also—and often predominantly- in terms of their conformity to idealised notions of proper femininity and women's proper place in the idealised nuclear family'.[21]

It was not, of course, possible to investigate this hypothesis as thoroughly as one would wish from the data gathered in this study, not least because to do so would require research on the perceptions of judges. Nevertheless, it was possible to identify those women who had been first convicted before their 17th birthday, who had already been convicted on five or more occasions, and whose backgrounds in the reports were described as unsettled, irresponsible or unstable, and to compare the proportion of them sentenced to custody with men who had the same combination of characteristics. Bearing in mind the small number, Table 36 reveals strong evidence to support the hypothesis: the proportion of such women who got a custodial sentence was high compared with the general probability of women being incarcerated. Yet there was no evidence to suggest that black women with these attributes were treated worse than whites, and no evidence that such women were worse treated than men who had similar characteristics.

Why, therefore, has it often been said that women, and particularly black women, are more severely dealt than men? The main reason is that there have been very few English studies which have examined sentencing practices relating to women and none, so far, which have compared black and white females.[22] This has resulted in the practice of drawing inferences about sentencing from the distribution of the characteristics of women in the prison population despite the fact that both Allison Morris and Nigel Walker, more than a decade

[21] Pat Carlen, *Women, Crime and Poverty*, (1988), p 143. See also, Allison Morris, op. cit., at p 101.

[22] The only study in the Crown Courts is David Moxon's, which included a sample of 223 females, but no information was given about their ethnic origin, op. cit, pp 52–55. The research by David Farrington and Allison Morris was based on only one Magistrates' Court at which only a tiny minority of the women received a custodial sentence, 'Sex, Sentencing and Reconviction', *Brit J Criminol*, pp 229–248.

Table 36: Comparison of the percentage of females and males with various disadvantageous indices who were sentenced to custody

	Males		Females	
	Number	Percentage to Custody	Number	Percentage to Custody
Whites	159/259	61.4	11/21	52.4
Blacks	93/132	70.5	3/6	50.0

ago, pointed out that such inferences led to patently false conclusions.[23] For example, when Carlen wrote recently that 'disproportionate numbers of women from ethnic minorities are **imprisoned**'(our emphasis), she was, presumably, referring to the existing evidence that more are '**in prison**'.[24] Similarly, Seear and Player's conclusion (cited above on page 172) that proportionately more women than men were sentenced **to prison** for a first offence was based on the fact that a higher proportion of women than men **in prison** had no prior convictions. Obviously, these are erroneous inferences to draw: a much higher proportion of women than men convicted in the courts are convicted of theft or have no previous convictions. Therefore, even though a smaller proportion of women than men are sentenced to custody for theft or with no prior convictions, they are still over-represented in the prison population in comparison with men.

Similarly, the over-representation of black women in prison has been greatly affected by the relatively small number who

[23] See, Allison Morris with the assistance of Loraine Gelsthorpe(eds.) *Women and Crime*, (1981), Cropwood Conference Series No. 13, Cambridge, at p 138, and Nigel Walker, 'Feminists' Extravaganzas', *Criminal Law Review*, (1981), pp 379–386, at pp 379–80.
[24] Pat Carlen, 'Criminal Women and Criminal Justice: The Limits to, and the Potential of, Feminist and Left Realist Perspectives', in Roger Matthews and Jock Young (eds.), *Issues in Realist Criminology* (1992), pp 51–69, at p 65.

receive long prison sentences for acting as 'mules' in importing drugs into this country. Thus, almost half (48.5%) of the West Indian, Guyanese and African women in prison service establishment on 30 June 1990 were serving sentences for drugs offences compared with 14 per cent of the white women. If foreign women convicted of drugs offences were discounted, the proportion of black women in the prison population would be about 13 per cent not 24 per cent.[25]

Yet in the West Midlands sample there were only four cases involving women who had imported drugs, two of them white and two black. And of the few women (6% of whites and 7% of blacks) who were convicted of other drugs offences (mostly supplying cannabis), exactly the same proportion of black women were sent to custody as whites: and it was a much smaller proportion—only a fifth—than the proportion of men given a custodial sentence for the same type of offence. There was strong evidence, therefore, that when offences of importing drugs are laid to one side, black women were not more prone to being given a custodial sentence than were white women—at least in the Crown Courts of the West Midlands—and that there was no evidence to support the claim either that women are more severely treated than men or that black women are 'doubly discriminated against'.

---

[25] See A Maden, M Swinton and J Gunn, 'The Ethnic Origin of Women Serving a Prison Sentence', *Brit J Criminol*, Vol. 32 (1992), pp 218–221.

12

DISCRIMINATION IN THE COURTS?

This study has confirmed what has for long been suspected, namely that, to a very substantial degree, the over-representation of Afro-Caribbean males and females in the prison system is a product of their over-representation among those convicted of crime and sentenced in the Crown Courts. The best estimate that it is possible to make from this study is that 80 per cent of the over-representation of black male offenders in the prison population was due to their over-representation among those convicted at the Crown Court and to the type and circumstances of the offences of which black men were convicted. The remaining 20 per cent, in the case of males but not of females, appeared to due to differential treatment and other factors which influence the nature and length of the sentences imposed: two thirds of it resulting from the higher proportion of black defendants who pleaded not guilty and who were, as a consequence, more liable on conviction to receive longer custodial sentences.

From Crown Court records it was not possible to shed much light on the circumstances and factors which might produce a higher rate of convictions amongst the black population, but there were some clues which are worthy of further investigation. A higher proportion of black people were charged with offences which could only be dealt with on indictment at the Crown Court: considerably more being charged with robbery, often of the kind normally referred to as 'mugging'. One should not minimise the distress caused by such behaviour, especially when women are the victims, nor the general sense of unease which it breeds, but as a form of violent or property crime it is often not more serious in its consequences than grievous bodily harm or housebreaking, both of which can be dealt with summarily if the court and defendant consent. This would not, of course, have meant that all of these black defendants would have accepted summary trial. The reason is that considerably more of them had, early on in the procedure, signified their intention to plead not guilty: 46 per cent of blacks and Asians compared with 34 per cent of whites charged with robbery. Nevertheless, the unavailability of discretion to deal with these offences either-way inevitably brings more black defendants into the arena of the Crown Court and its greater propensity to inflict a custodial penalty.[1]

Black offenders were also disproportionately involved in the supply of drugs, usually cannabis, and these convictions regularly arose from police activity rather than from a complaint by citizens. This is not the place to open the debate about the seriousness of illegal dealings at street level in cannabis. It is only to say that if these offences were excluded the proportion of black males dealt with at the West Midlands courts would have been 13.7 rather than 17.2 per cent, equivalent to 20 per cent lower. By contrast, excluding such cases amongst whites and Asians would have reduced their number by only 0.6 and 0.9 per cent respectively. Of course, it is impossible to say whether these persons would have committed other offences but it is incontrovertible that the continued legal proscription of cannabis and the insistence that trading in it, even on a small or moderate scale, is an offence which should always be com-

---

[1] See, Carol Hedderman and David Moxon, *Magistrates' Court or Crown Court? Mode of Trial Decisions and Sentencing*, (1992), Home Office Research Study No. 125. This study showed, after cases had been matched on nine variables, that 'custody was used almost three times as often and sentences were, on average, about two and a half times longer in elected cases than in comparable cases at Magistrates' Courts. In other words, the Crown Courts impose more than seven times as much custody as do Magistrates' Courts for cases having similar characteristics', at p 37.

mitted to the Crown Court for trial,[2] is a substantial factor influencing the number of black persons in the prison population.

Furthermore, black defendants were at a disadvantage both because of decisions they made and decisions made about them during the processing of cases before they appeared for sentence. They were more likely to be remanded in custody by magistrates who committed them for trial, even taking into account the seriousness of the charges against them and other factors which might legitimately have had an effect on the decision whether to give bail. They were much less likely to have had a social inquiry report prepared on their background, mainly because a considerably higher proportion of them signified their intention to plead not guilty, but also because fewer who pleaded guilty were reported on, although, the reasons for this are not known.

Being already in custody, pleading not guilty, and not having a report were all associated with a higher probability of receiving a custodial sentence or with a lengthier sentence. And all of them, of course, limit the possibilities for effective pleas in mitigation. Those who have been in custody have less opportunity to show that they have been of exemplary behaviour or have sought to make amends by, say, entering regular employment since they were charged with the offence. Those who deny the offence cannot suddenly, on being found guilty, convincingly express remorse. For those without social inquiry reports there is often insufficient information on hand to put the offence in its social context and no opportunity to take advantage of a specific proposal from a probation officer for an alternative sentence to custody. It would appear, therefore, that ethnic

---

[2] In his Practice Note: (Mode of Trial Guidelines), the Lord Chief Justice Lord Lane laid down that supply or possession with intent to supply a class B drug should be committed for trial 'unless there was only small scale supply for no payment' *The [1990] 1* WLR, 1439 at 1442.

minority defendants were inadvertently subjected to a form of indirect discrimination at the point of sentence due to the fact that they chose more often to contest the case against them. Because of the way that the system works to encourage guilty pleas through a 'discount' on sentence, which has been shown to produce a substantial reduction,[3] and because it is the policy of the Probation Service not generally to make social inquiry reports on those who intend to contest the case against them, black defendants obviously put themselves at greater risk of custody and longer sentences.

No criticism should be levelled against the judges on this issue: they were, of course applying the policy as laid down by the Court of Appeal. And there would, of course, be resistance to changing the policy of giving a substantial credit for guilty pleas given the pressure on the workload and costs of the courts and the judicial desire to be able to respond to expressions of genuine remorse. Nevertheless it is time to consider all the implications of a policy which favours so strongly those who plead guilty, when ethnic minorities are less willing to forgo their right to challenge a prosecution. For, as Andrew Ashworth has argued, 'there are grave dangers of injustice in its practical operation'.[4]

---

[3] See D. Moxon, *op. cit.*, p 32. D. A. Thomas's, *Current Sentencing Practice*, (1983 continuing), Section A 8.2., states that the Court of Appeal has approved reductions of between one quarter and one third. As mentioned above, at fn 5 p 125, the average discount for male adults in the West Midlands appeared to be about a third. Recently (June 1992), a Working Party of the General Council of the Bar (Chairman Robert Seabrook QC) has suggested that the amount of discount should be linked to the stage at which the defendant decided to plead guilty. Those who notified their intention to do so at the committal stage would get a minimum of 30 per cent discount; those who did so before the first listing of the case in the Crown Court would get a minimum of 20 per cent; and those who only decided to plead guilty between the first Crown Court listing and arraignment in court would only be eligible for a minimum of 10 per cent. This is intended to decrease the number who change their plea at a late stage, causing 'cracked trials' and administrative inconvenience. *The Efficient Disposal of Business in the Crown Court* (1992), p 38. It would be important to monitor any ethnic differences before putting such a proposal into effect.

[4] Andrew Ashworth, *Sentencing and Penal Policy*, (1983), at p 314. For a more

Some headway may be made in dealing with this problem after Section 3(1) of the Criminal Justice Act 1991 comes into effect on 1st October 1992. This will make it mandatory for the court to obtain and consider a pre-sentence report (the designation for a new style of social inquiry report) when the court is considering the imposition of a custodial sentence on either of the grounds laid down by the Act: namely, the seriousness of the offence and one other offence associated with it, or, where the offence is a violent or sexual offence, the protection of the public from serious harm from the offender. However, the Act does make an exception to this requirement where 'the offence or any other offence associated with it is triable only on indictment' and the court considers that a pre-sentence report would be 'unnecessary'.[5] This provision was inserted so that reports would not have to be prepared in cases which were inevitably bound for custody. But the evidence of this study suggests that if this exception is used for a wider range of indictable-only offences, it will bear far more on black and Asian defendants than on whites in the Crown Court. There is a danger that it will not address sufficiently the issue of indirect discrimination in the amount and type of information available to judges in deciding whether or not a custodial sentence should be imposed.

This research has also revealed a rather complex pattern of racial disparities in the sentences imposed. It should be recognized that there was no evidence of a 'blanket' race or colour discrimination against all ethnic minority defendants, male or female. In most respects, Asian offenders did not fare worse than whites nor did all Afro-Caribbeans. Whether they did or did not depended on a number of factors: the seriousness of the

recent discussion see the new edition of Professor Ashworth's book *Sentencing and Criminal Justice* (which was published as this report was in Press): (1992) pp 130–133.

[5] For a very useful discussion of this Sub-Section see Martin Wasik and Richard D. Taylor, *Blackstone's Guide to the Criminal Justice Act 1991*, (1991), pp 22–23.

case, age, employment status, whether they had pleaded not guilty, and, above all, the court centre to which they had been committed for trial the judge before whom they appeared for sentence, some of whom appeared to sentence a considerably lower proportion of black defendants to custody than would have been expected. At Coventry, for example, white defendants were much more likely to receive a custodial sentence than whites dealt with elsewhere in the West Midlands, particularly at nearby Birmingham. On the other hand, although blacks at Coventry more often got a custodial sentence than blacks at Birmingham, they were more leniently treated that either whites or Asians at Coventry.

Taking the total number of male cases dealt with over the whole of the West Midlands, and controlling for the nature of the offences and several other legally relevant variables, the apparent differences in the proportionate use of custody between white, black and Asian males dealt with by these courts was considerably reduced from 8 percentage points to about 2.5 points. Thus, a relatively small difference remained. Depending on the basis of the comparison, a black offender had a probability of receiving a custodial sentence about 5 to 8 per cent higher than a white offender. Asians, on the other hand, had about a 4 per cent lower probability. Given the number of cases which appeared before these courts in the course of a year, these differences were sufficiently large to be to the disadvantage of a considerable number of black defendants especially when combined with the longer sentences imposed on the higher proportion of them who had pleaded not guilty.

But does this amount to evidence of discrimination? Or, to put it another way: is the evidence consistent with a pattern of discrimination rather than a residue of unexplained variation?

It is true, of course, that no statistical study can control for all the variables which might affect differences between cases. But it has to be recognised that the analysis carried out for this inquiry was based on a substantial number of cases, used multi-variate techniques to control for the influence of some 15 legally relevant variables, and used a variety of bases for making comparisons: a risk of custody score based on all cases, disaggregated to show court and race variations; a score based on the white cases only so as to compare the weight given to variables for whites with their weight when applied to blacks; a score based solely on the Birmingham cases, so as to compare the weights given to variables by that court to the weights attached to same variables at other courts. All these scores produced the same pattern of results and very similarly sized differences. And, as a further check, a probability of custody score was devised using an entirely different statistical method, a method widely in use by the probation service in devising risk of custody indices. This, too, produced similar results. It is difficult to imagine what other legally relevant variables not already taken into account could explain the fact that for every 100 black males sentenced to custody at Birmingham about 130 black males were given a custodial sentence at the Dudley courts, and even more at Warwick or Stafford.

It is, of course, always hazardous to move from correlation to explanation. But the marked differences in the apparent treatment of black and whites offenders amongst those who had been sentenced at one of the Dudley courts needs some interpretation, particularly because there was a much lower proportion of blacks sentenced to custody in the neighbouring Birmingham Crown Court. Nevertheless the fact that a similar high custody rate for blacks was observed at Warwick and Stafford suggests that there may be nothing unique about the Dudley courts.

The judges who were relatively severe on black offenders compared with whites dealt with a higher proportion of the cases at the Dudley courts than at Birmingham, but on aggregate the other judges at the Dudley courts—taken together—

were also comparatively more likely to sentence black offenders to custody than colleagues at Birmingham. There were other indices of a different sentencing pattern. Black defendants at the Dudley courts got a sentence greater than that recommended by a probation officer much more often than did blacks at Birmingham. Moreover, blacks at the Dudley courts received sentences generally further up the scale of penalties; and if they were recommended for probation or community service they were more likely to get a more severe penalty than was a white defendant.

In attempting to understand what may have produced this divergent pattern, it was at once noticeable that the differences were greatest not in the mid to upper band of cases where difficult decisions were being made about whether to use custody or not, but in the range of cases at the lower end of the scale of severity. There was strong evidence to suggest that factors which would have been regarded as mitigating the seriousness of the case if the defendant was white were not given the same weight if the defendant was black in the cases dealt with at Dudley courts. Yet, they were given a similar weight for black offenders dealt with at Birmingham. For instance, blacks at the Dudley courts were sentenced to custody in a significantly higher proportion of cases whether they were employed or unemployed, whether they were under 21 or over 21, whether they had only one prior conviction or 2 or more, whether they pleaded guilty or not guilty.

A much higher proportion of the black offenders at the Dudley courts (amongst those in the lower band of seriousness) who had been convicted with at least one other black defendant were sentenced to custody at the Dudley courts. Here the difference between the observed and expected rate, given the nature of the cases, was so big that it explained half of the difference between the observed an expected rate of custody for all black cases at the Dudley courts. An examination of these cases failed to find any distinctive differences between them and cases where whites had been convicted with other whites. Nor were the black cases at Birmingham, where custody was, in contrast, rarely used, substantially different in character. It appears reasonable to assume that the judges at the Dudley courts viewed these cases in a different light to those involving groups of whites. While it is true that there were slightly more black offenders who were committed with other black offenders at the Dudley courts than at Birmingham, there were substantially more whites at the Dudley courts who had been convicted alongside other whites. Furthermore, blacks were sentenced more often to custody than either whites at the Dudley courts or blacks at Birmingham when they were the sole offender. On the whole, there was nothing to suggest that the judges who dealt with the Dudley courts' cases were confronted with a worse impression of black criminality than were the far more lenient judges at Birmingham. On the contrary, black defendants were a lower proportion of the caseload of the Dudley courts, and the seriousness of the cases dealt with, as measured by their risk of custody score, was no different from the cases at Birmingham.

Could it be that black offenders sentenced at the Dudley courts had been less well served by the pleas of mitigation made on their behalf? There was no way of measuring the performance of barristers and probation officers, but this hypothesis seems implausible for a number of reasons. First, a higher proportion of blacks at the Dudley courts than at Birmingham pleaded guilty (83% v 75%) and had social inquiry reports available about them (63% v 56%): both factors which are an aid to mitigation. Secondly, as already mentioned, it was in the less serious range of cases, where mitigation would normally be more readily accepted, that the largest differences between the use of custody for blacks and whites existed. Thirdly, the fact that the sentences imposed on blacks at the Dudley courts were of greater severity than those recommended by probation officers where the defendant was black rather than white, or was a black dealt with at Birmingham, also suggested that it was not the quality of the mitigation, but the different practice of the Dudley courts when faced with a black defendant, that accounted for the racial differences observed.

It is therefore apparent that the failure to find a large overall difference in the use of custody for blacks, whites and Asians in the West Midlands as a whole was a product of the fact that by far the largest proportion of cases in the sample had been dealt with at Birmingham Crown Court, a court with no over-all racial bias in its sentencing patterns as far as use of custody was concerned. Leaving Birmingham aside, there were substantial racial differences in the sentencing patterns of the other courts and it seems inconceivable that similar variations would not be found in other regions of the country. It would not need very many courts to behave as the Dudley courts and Warwick and Stafford appear to do, for it to have a considerable impact on the proportion of black offenders in the prison system: especially when one bears in mind that not only are they more readily sentenced to custody but, because they are more likely to contest the case, they have longer sentences to serve. Furthermore, it seems that if they are not given a custodial sentence they are more likely, and much more likely in some courts, to receive a suspended sentence of imprisonment or a community service order which puts them more at risk of being sentenced to custody if they should re-offend.

When one contrasts the overall treatment meted out to black Afro-Caribbean males one is left wondering whether it is not a result of different racial stereotypes operating on the perceptions of some judges. The greater involvement of black offenders in street crime and in the trade in cannabis, their higher rate of unemployment, their greater resistance to pressures to plead guilty, and possibly a perception of a different, less deferential, demeanour in court may all appear somewhat more threatening.[6] And, if not threatening, less worthy of mitigation of punishment. It was significant that being unemployed increased the risk of a black male getting a custodial sentence, but not, in general, for a white or an Asian offender. In contrast, the better financial and employment status of the Asians and their more socially integrated households, when judged by white standards, as well as the fact that they were much more likely to be first-time offenders, may have meant that they were probably able to present themselves as less threatening, and more worthy of mitigation than either whites or blacks. Only in respect of the length of sentences received by those who were sentenced to prison did Asian adult males fare worse. But without research which would allow the investigation of judicial attitudes towards, and perceptions of, racially related differences in crime patterns and in cultural responses to the criminal justice system, all this for the moment must remain speculation. It cannot be doubted that such a programme of research is now needed.

The findings regarding women will surprise many, especially given the very large over-representation of black women in penal institutions. The evidence in general supports the so-called 'chivalry' or 'paternalistic' hypothesis that judges give much more weight to mitigating features of the case in sentencing women offenders, whether white or black. No differences were found between the use of custody, of alternatives, or in sentence length between white and black women when variables relating to the seriousness of the offences were controlled for. Black women were just as likely as the whites to have had a social inquiry report prepared about them prior to sentence

---

[6] This was not something that could be investigated without interviews with judges, but the Oxford pilot study of Crown Courts suggested 'that the defendant's demeanour and 'attitude' in court were regarded as legitimate and indeed significant matters to be taken into count', Andrew Ashworth, *et al.*, *Sentencing in the Crown Court*, (1984), *op cit.*, pp 22–23.

and were no more likely than the whites to have been given a sentence greater than that recommended by the probation officer. Furthermore, compared with black men, black women were dealt with relatively leniently just as white women were dealt with leniently compared with white men. Nevertheless, when a particularly disadvantaged group were singled out—those who had various attributes which could be associated with failure to conform to female stereotypes—a relatively high proportion of them were sentenced to custody: yet, no more blacks than whites and no more females than males. One thing is certain. If considerations relating to their gender did not mitigate the punishment of women, and they were treated as men are, there would be many more in custody than at present.[7]

What conclusions of a practical kind can be drawn from this study? First, that the research has revealed a complex picture of the way in which race appears to have affected the pattern of sentencing. In doing so, it has led to some uncomfortable conclusions for those whose duty it is to sentence offenders. It will not be possible any more to make the claim that all the differences in the treatment of black offenders occur elsewhere in the criminal justice system. At least some of it occurs in the courts, and more often in some localities than others. Much will be achieved if judges recognise this. One aim of studying sentencing by empirical methods is to help stimulate reassessment of attitudes and judicial responses. Previous research has shown how unaware judges may be of their own practices, let alone those of their colleagues.[8] It may be that some are not yet sufficiently sensitive to the way in which racial views and

---

[7] In the United States, where Sentencing Commissions have sought to establish equality in the treatment of men and women, there is evidence from Minnesota that sentencing severity for women increased to the level for males within three years of the establishment of the Guidelines (I am grateful to Professor Michael Tonry for this information). Overall, the State and Federal Incarceration rates for women have been growing at a much faster rate than for men. See 'Female Prison Population Growing Faster than Males' *Overcrowded Times* May 1991, p 3.

[8] See Andrew Ashworth, et. al., *Sentencing in the Crown Court*, op. cit., pp 50–56.

beliefs may influence their judgement. If this research can stimulate such self-awareness and re-evaluation it will have made a modest contribution towards the positive self conscious appreciation of the need to take the question of race seriously which the Judicial Studies Board has now recognized by the setting up of its Ethnic Minorities Advisory Committee.

Secondly, this study draws attention to the way in which the criminal process may contribute to indirect discrimination against black people. There is clearly a need to consider the implications of the policy which favours so strongly those who plead guilty, when ethnic minorities are less willing to let a prosecution go unchallenged. This has implications, in particular, for the range and value of the information available to the courts in deciding whether or not to impose a custodial sentence as well as the type of non-custodial sentence. And, for the reason already mentioned, it will be necessary to monitor carefully the way in which the courts exercise their discretion, under the Criminal Justice Act 1991, to pass sentence without a pre-sentence report when the case is one triable only on indictment.

Thirdly, there are obvious implications relating to the duty placed on the Secretary of State by Section 95 (1)(b) to 'publish such information as he considers expedient for the purpose of . . . facilitating the performance . . . [by persons engaged in the administration of criminal justice] . . . of their duty to avoid discriminating against any persons on the grounds of race or sex or any other improper ground.' To do this it will be essential for the Crown Courts to monitor the ethnic origin of all persons appearing before them. If the self-reflection on sentencing performance mentioned above is to be achieved, information on sentencing dispositions, analysed by ethnic origin, should be communicated to each judge and to the court as a whole annually. Only then will it be possible to detect whether sentencing patterns which might prove to be unfavourable to any ethnic minority are becoming established. Judges may regard this as an unnecessary imposition, or even as a slight on their integrity and impartiality. But in all walks of public life, servants of the Crown are being expected to monitor their performance, both with regard to its quality and to its evenhandedness with respect to ethnicity and gender. There can be no good reason for judges to be excepted from this demand. Indeed it is essential if the principle promulgated by the Judicial Studies Board in its Report for 1987–1991 is to be made a reality:

> *It is axiomatic that no court should treat a defendant differently from any other simply because of his race or ethnic origin. Any court that exhibited prejudice against a defendant from an ethnic minority would be failing in its basic duty to treat all defendants before it equally*

When this research was originally envisaged, it was hoped to sample a large number of cases at each of the various stages of the criminal process. For the reasons already explained this proved to be an impossible task with the resources available. It is therefore recommended that a study should be set in train, officially supported by all the agencies in the criminal justice system, which would follow a large number of cases in all the major areas where there are sufficient concentrations of ethnic minorities, as they progress from arrest to final disposition in the courts. Only when this flow of cases is properly monitored will it be possible to identify the points at which any discrimination may occur and to quantify their cumulative effect on the number and proportions of ethnic minorities who eventually enter the prison system.

A SUMMARY OF THE MAIN FINDINGS

1. This study, which was funded by the Commission for Racial Equality, is the first large scale statistical attempt to try to assess whether defendants of different ethnic origin are treated equally when sentenced in the Crown Courts. Aims and Method

2. It arose from the concern engendered by the very substantial over-representation of males and females of Afro-Caribbean origin in the prisons and young offenders institutions of England and Wales. They now comprise over 10 per cent of the male sentenced population, between eight and nine times their proportion in the population at large. And they account for almost a quarter of female prisoners, although a substantial number of black female prisoners are foreigners imprisoned for importing drugs.

3. The study was carried out in the Crown Court Centres which service the region covered by the West Midlands Police: at Birmingham, Dudley (now Wolverhampton), Coventry, Warwick and Stafford Crown Courts. It is based on an analysis of all the information that could be gleaned from the Crown Court files about every identified ethnic minority male convicted and sentenced at these courts in 1989 and from an equivalent sized random sample of male white offenders. Altogether 1,441 persons were described in police records and other sources in such a way that they could confidently be identified as 'black', usually meaning of Afro-Caribbean origin, or Asian, meaning from the Indian subcontinent or of 'other' racial origin. There were 886 black offenders, 536 Asian and 16 from other backgrounds.

A sample of 1,443 white males was drawn, making a total of 2,884 cases. This is the largest sample of Crown Court cases studied in this country. In addition, information was gathered from the files of all 433 women sentenced by these courts, 76 of them being black, 14 Asian and one 'other'. The male and female samples were analysed separately and the outcomes compared.

Race
Differences
to be
Explained

4. Ethnic minority defendants accounted for 28 per cent of the males sentenced at the West Midlands Crown Courts in 1989. This was two and a half times greater than their proportion in the population at large, which was about 11 per cent. This was because Afro-Caribbeans were generally over-represented, making up 21 per cent of the those found guilty at Birmingham and 15 per cent at the Dudley Courts (which sat in court rooms at Dudley, Wolverhampton and Birmingham) although they accounted for less than 4 per cent of the general male population in the age range of 16 to 64. Asian males, on the other hand, were convicted in the Crown Court only slightly more often than would be expected from their number in the population at large.

5. Any differences in the sentences imposed on ethnic minorities as compared with whites have to be set in the general context of a considerable amount of variation, irrespective of race, in the percentage of males sentenced to custody (including imprisonment, a partially suspended sentence, and detention in a young offenders' institution). This varied from 61% of these dealt with at Coventry to 46% of the men sentenced at Birmingham.

6. Differences in the proportions of each ethnic category—white, black or Asian—given a custodial sentence were marked. Taking the sample as a whole, the proportion of blacks sentenced to custody was just over 8 percentage

points higher than for whites (56.6% v 48.4%). Asians, on the other hand, were sentenced to custody less often than either whites or blacks (39.6%).

7. Variations between the proportions of ethnic minorities sentenced to custody at the different Crown Court Centres were even larger. The black: white 'custody ratio' was particularly high for those sentenced by the Dudley courts, amounting to a difference of 17 percentage points (65% v 48%). There was a similar high black: white ratio at Warwick and Stafford, although the numbers dealt with there were much smaller. Only at Coventry were more whites and Asians sentenced to custody than blacks.

8. It was possible to examine the pattern of sentences of 18 judges, (17 Circuit Judges and one Recorder) each of whom had dealt with at least 45 cases in the sample, and who, between them, had sentenced over half of all the cases. They varied a great deal in their overall use of custody (i.e. for all cases irrespective of race) ranging from one judge who had sentenced 29 per cent of the cases he dealt with to custody to another who sentenced 69 per cent. As regards race, three judges had sentenced considerably fewer blacks to custody than whites, eight appeared to be relatively even-handed, and five sentenced a much higher proportion of blacks than whites to custody: the difference ranging from 11 to 42 percentage points, equivalent to a greater proportion of black offenders getting a custodial sentence of between 41 and 111 per cent. When judges were ranked in order of their severity (measured by proportion to custody) for each ethnic group, there was a very low level of concordance between them. In other words, they appeared to vary a great deal in their relative severity on defendants of different ethnic backgrounds.

9. To what extent could these disparities be accounted for by variability in the nature of the cases dealt with by these

Differences in Patterns of Offending

judges at the various courts covered by the study? A comparison was first made of the nature and circumstances of the offences and the legally relevant characteristics of the defendants in each ethnic group. This showed that, although more black offenders had appeared at the Crown Court charged with offences which could only be tried on indictment at such a court, there were no significant differences in the proportions of blacks and whites convicted of the most serious crimes of personal violence. More blacks were, however, charged with and convicted of robbery and of supplying drugs (mostly cannabis), although there were proportionately fewer sentenced for housebreaking, theft or fraud. Their *modus operandi* for illegally obtaining money was clearly often different. As far as social characteristics were concerned, more blacks were unemployed and in receipt of welfare benefits, but it appeared that fewer had an unsettled or disrupted social life or were impaired by alcohol at the time of the offence. Although fewer blacks had no prior convictions a higher proportion of whites had eight or more. The pattern of these convictions differed somewhat, the black offenders being more likely to have a record for robbery or a drugs offence. Nevertheless, a smaller proportion of them had been convicted in the past of the same broad type of offence as that of which they had currently been convicted. It was particularly noticeable that more of the blacks pleaded not guilty and contested the case against them before a jury. As a consequence of this a considerably smaller proportion had a Social Inquiry Report (SIR) prepared about them by the probation service.

10. When the cases involving Asians were examined there was much to suggest that the lower proportion of them sentenced to custody was largely due to the fact that they were less involved in criminal acts than either whites or blacks.

Although more had been charged with indictable only offences, fewer had more than one indictment laid against them and fewer had multiple charges or other offences taken into consideration. A much lower proportion had been previously convicted or had already served a custodial sentence. Furthermore, considerably fewer were unemployed or came from obviously unsettled backgrounds. They, too, had more often pleaded not guilty than had whites, and they too less often had an SIR.

11. In order to test whether the observed differences could be explained by the combination of factors in each case and the weighting given to them, a statistical method was used to 'match' cases as closely as possible in terms of those variables which were shown to have had the most significant impact on whether an offender was committed to custody or not. This was done by using standard multivariate statistical techniques to calculate a 'probability of custody' score for each case, a score which summarised the probability of an offender with that particular combination of attributes getting a custodial sentence. In deriving this score more than 80 variables were analysed and 15 chosen which described 50 legally relevant attributes of the offence and the offender's criminal record. These variables correctly predicted whether an offender would receive custody or not in 75% of cases. To what extent did the observed race differences in the proportion of blacks, whites and Asians sentenced to custody disappear when their probability of custody, as determined by these other factors, was taken into account? *Variations in the Use of Custody*

12. A higher proportion of blacks than whites did fall into the category with the highest risk of custody, and fewer in the category with the lowest probability of receiving such a sentence. Asian offenders, on the other hand, were much

less likely to be in the highest risk of custody group and were much more frequently in the lowest.

13. When this was taken into account the black-white difference in the sample as a whole of 8.2 percentage points in the proportion sentenced to custody was reduced to a difference of about 2.5 percentage points. Given the fact that the white custody rate was just under 50 per cent this amounts to a 5 per cent greater probability of a male black defendant being sentenced to custody than a white male. When a comparison was made on the basis of a probability of custody score derived only from the black defendants the difference was rather lager: whites being 7.6 per cent less likely to get a custodial sentence. Five per cent is not as large a 'residual race difference' as many commentators have suggested, but in a sample of this size it can be estimated that the number of blacks who received a custodial sentence would, if race had had no effect at all, have been 479 rather than 503 in the year 1989. It is important to bear in mind that this does not refer to any *particular cases*, only to the *aggregate difference* between the observed and expected *probability* of receiving a custodial sentence.

14. The substantially lower proportion of Asian males sentenced to custody was largely explained by the less serious nature of the cases. Even so, it was still a little lower than expected.

15. The black:white difference in the proportion sent to custody was at its greatest in the band of cases which could be described as of medium seriousness (with a probability of custody ranging from 45 to 80 per cent). Here the 68% custody rate for blacks was significantly higher than the 60% rate for whites: a difference which amounts to a 13 per

cent greater probability of a black offender receiving a custodial sentence than a white in this range of cases.

16. After taking into account the seriousness of cases, two other variables were related to racial differences in the use of custody. These were age and employment. There were no differences between the use of custody for blacks and whites aged under 21: all of the difference occurring amongst the adult offenders. The same pattern was found in relation to employment: the comparatively higher custody rate for blacks being found not amongst those who were employed but only amongst the unemployed. Indeed, if the defendant was black, being unemployed was a factor significantly associated with receiving a custodial sentence, when all the other variables were controlled for, but not if he was white or Asian.

17. When the seriousness of the cases dealt with at the different court centres was controlled for, it was found that the observed differences between the proportions sentenced to custody by judges at these centres remained substantial and significant. In other words, the overall average relatively small 'race of defendant effect' concealed considerable variations between cases dealt with by judges sitting at different court centres. Variations Between Courts and Judges

18. At Birmingham Crown Court the proportion sentenced to custody was below what would have been expected, with no significant differences between the observed and expected rates for any of the ethnic groups. In other words, no overall 'race of defendant effect' existed amongst cases dealt with at that court. As half of the cases in the sample had been dealt with at Birmingham, this obviously had an impact on the overall findings.

19. The proportion of blacks committed to custody amongst those dealt with at the Dudley courts remained, however,

considerably higher than expected from the characteristics of the cases: more than 12 percentage points higher than for whites, which is equivalent to an increased probability of receiving a custodial sentence of 23 per cent. Although the numbers were much smaller, and therefore the conclusions less reliable, the black defendants were similarly more likely to get a custodial sentence at Warwick and Stafford. Comparing blacks dealt with at the Dudley courts with those dealt with at Birmingham, the probability of receiving a custodial sentence was 29 per cent higher amongst cases at the former venue. Several other analyses and comparisons confirmed these findings.

20. The different pattern of disposal of cases sentenced at the Dudley courts and Birmingham appears to result from a different approach to dealing with cases of the less serious type. The large difference between the treatment of blacks and whites at the Dudley courts occurred mainly (although not entirely) amongst those cases with a predicted probability of custody of less than 45 per cent. In this category the proportion of blacks getting a custodial sentence at the Dudley courts was 44% compared with 24% of the whites and with 17% of the blacks and 21% of the whites dealt with at Birmingham. This difference remained even in respect of offenders who had attributes which would normally be considered as mitigating factors in sentencing. Where black defendants had been convicted with black co-defendants the proportions sentenced to custody was much higher. This could not be explained by the known characteristics of these cases. It may be that there were different perceptions of, and reactions to, black offenders among at least some of the judges who sat in the Dudley courts during 1989 than amongst most of their colleagues who sat at Birmingham. It was not, however,

possible to investigate this as permission was not granted to interview judges.

21. The analysis of the sentencing patterns of the judges showed that Assistant Recorders were relatively lenient compared with more senior and experienced Circuit Judges and Recorders. They were also comparatively less severe on black defendants, of whom only 37% per cent got a custodial sentence when the expected rate for the type of cases they had dealt with was 46%.

22. With only a few exceptions, the variations between individual judges was largely unaffected by taking into account the characteristics of the cases they each dealt with. There were very high correlations between the relative severity of their 'observed' use of custody and their relative severity when the seriousness of the cases they had dealt with had been controlled for.

23. When the practice of judges who had dealt with cases at the Dudley courts were compared with those who had sentenced them at Birmingham Crown Court, it was found that there were some relatively severe judges at both courts, judges whose use of custody for black defendants was 10 or more percentage points higher than for whites. These judges sentenced more black defendants than expected to custody whichever court they sat in. However, amongst those judges who dealt with relatively few cases each (and whose sentencing patterns could therefore not be analysed separately) those who heard cases in the Dudley courts sent considerably more blacks to custody than expected, while those at Birmingham sent less to custody. Although it must be stressed that not every judge sitting in the Dudley Courts was comparatively more severe on blacks than whites, the aggregate effect was to raise the probability of a

black defendant receiving a custodial sentence so that it
was considerably higher than if the case had been dealt
with in the Birmingham Crown Court. How or why such a
pattern should have emerged amongst independent judges
sitting at three different court sites (Dudley, Wolverhampton and in courts provided in Birmingham) is another
question this study was unable to investigate.

**Variations
in
Sentence
Lengths**

24. A significantly higher proportion of black and Asian adults
received a sentence of over 3 years (17.4% and 15.1%)
compared with whites (10.6%) and their average length of
sentence was also longer.

25. The average sentence lengths were not, however,
significantly different for those who pleaded guilty, only for
those who pleaded not guilty, especially amongst those convicted of the most serious offences.

26. When all relevant variables which affected the length of
sentence were controlled for, and extreme cases removed
from the analysis, the average length of the prison sentences imposed on Asians who pleaded not guilty was 9
months longer, and for blacks 3.4 months longer, than for
whites who pleaded not guilty.

27. There were, however, no significant differences in the average lengths of sentences given to offenders under the age of
21 from different ethnic backgrounds once the seriousness
of the cases had been taken into account.

**Estimating
the Size of
the 'Race
Effect'**

28. A calculation was made to estimate the cumulative effect of
race differences—in the proportion of cases sentenced to
custody, in the proportion pleading not guilty, and in the
average length of sentence imposed in such cases—on the
substantial over-representation of black males in the prison
population. Bearing in mind the difficulties of such an exer-

cise and the degree of error therefore involved, it appears that, in this West Midlands sample, about 80 per cent of the difference between the proportion of black males in the general population and their proportion among those serving prison sentences, can be accounted for by the greater number of black offenders who appeared for sentence in the Crown Court and by the nature and circumstances of the crimes they were convicted of. The remaining 20 per cent could be attributed to their subsequent different treatment by the courts: one third of this (7%) to more being sentenced to custody than expected and two-thirds (13%) to more pleading not guilty and to the consequent longer sentences imposed.

29. There were significant race differences in the way that sentences were distributed along the scale from imprisonment to discharge and in the alternatives to custody which were considered appropriate. Controlling for those variables which best explained severity of sentence, blacks were placed higher up the scale than were whites, especially amongst those sentenced at the Dudley courts. Variations in the Use of Alternatives to Custody

30. Black offenders were more often given a fully suspended sentence of imprisonment and less often a probation order or a community service order than were whites. These differences were found to be concentrated amongst those blacks who had a medium risk of receiving a custodial sentence.

31. Asians were also less likely to be placed on probation but more likely to have been fined or conditionally discharged. They generally suffered less intrusive penalties than either blacks or whites.

32. Amongst young people, black offenders with a medium risk of receiving custody were more likely than whites to get a

Community Service Order or to be sent to an Attendance Centre, and less likely to be placed on probation. Again, Asians tended to be more often fined and discharges and so were comparatively favourably dealt with.

33. Probation officers less frequently recommended a probation order for blacks or Asians. But even when blacks were recommended they were less likely to receive it than whites and more likely, if they did not go to prison, to get instead a more severe alternative sentence: either a suspended term of imprisonment or a CSO. The same was true for those recommended for a CSO: substantially more blacks got, instead, a suspended sentence of imprisonment. This evidence supports the contention that blacks are, indeed, placed higher up the 'tariff' and therefore put more at risk of receiving a custodial sentence should they re-appear on fresh charges.

The Influence of Pre-Sentence Factors

34. An examination was made of how the incident which gave rise to the conviction came to light in order to see whether more of the black offenders had entered the criminal process as a result of a stop and search or some other action initiated by the police. Of course, nearly all the drug offences were the result of police action and they accounted for 15 per cent of all the convictions of the black offenders but only 3 and 2 per cent respectively of those of the Asians and whites. But, in addition, a much larger proportion (27%) of the offences of black males who were convicted of non-domestic burglary and theft were 'discovered' by the police compared to only 15 and 6 per cent of those for which whites and Asians were convicted. Furthermore, a higher proportion of blacks were apparently known to the police when they were arrested on suspicion (6% compared with 3 per cent of whites and even fewer Asians). This suggests that differential police activity may play a

somewhat greater role in the prosecutions brought against blacks at the Crown Court than it does for whites or Asians.

35. Over 80 per cent of those who had been remanded in custody prior to trial and sentence, in all ethnic groups, were subsequently sentenced to custody. But a higher proportion of blacks (26%) than whites (20%) and Asians (18%) had been remanded without bail. An analysis was undertaken to see if this was the result of an equal application of the criteria which appeared to determine whether an offender would be remanded in custody or given bail. After taking these factors into account it was estimated that blacks had been remanded in custody at a rate of between 3.5 and 4 percentage points higher than whites, which on the basis of an expected rate for blacks of 22% amounted to a greater probability of about16 per cent.

36. A significantly higher proportion of blacks and Asians were sentenced without a Social Inquiry Report from the probation service being available to the court when deciding on the sentence. This was partly due to the fact that a higher proportion of blacks and Asians had indicated that they intended to contest the charges against them. But even among those pleading guilty a significantly lower proportion of blacks and Asians had a report prepared about them.

Variations in Social Inquiry Reports and Recommendations

37. Black offenders with no Social Inquiry Report, whether they were pleading not guilty or guilty, were significantly more likely to have received a custodial sentence. In part this was due to the fact that a much higher proportion of blacks with no SIR had been convicted of serious offences and, in any case, therefore, had a high probability of going into custody. Even so the observed proportion sent to

custody was, after taking into account the characteristics of the cases, still 4 percentage points higher than for whites. Again, differences between cases dealt with at the various Crown Court centres were evident: the proportion of blacks sentenced to custody at the Dudley courts among those without an SIR was over 13 percentage points higher than expected by the type of cases: equivalent to a 26 per cent greater use of custody.

38. Among those for whom an SIR had been available, there were again differences in the proportion who received a custodial sentence at one of the Dudley courts compared with Birmingham. This was related to the fact that, at the former courts, a much higher proportion of black offenders got a sentence greater than that recommended by the probation officer in her or his report. Indeed blacks dealt with by the Dudley courts got a greater sentence than recommended 20 per cent more often (79% v 59%) than did blacks at Birmingham. The conclusion is that the differences between the sentences imposed on black offenders at these two court centres was largely due to different judicial perceptions and practices, not to recommendations made by the probation service.

Sentencing
Women

39. The analysis of cases where women had been convicted at one of these five Crown Courts revealed that black females were over-represented at least six-fold in relation to their number in the population of the West Midlands as a whole. Asian women, on the other hand, were very rarely before the Crown Courts.

40. A higher proportion of black than white women (29% v 23%) received a custodial sentence, but, when the types of crime they had been convicted of and other relevant characteristics were taken into account, the observed propor-

tions of both white and black women sentenced to custody were almost identical to what would be expected. In other words, the difference between the white and black custody rate was explained by the characteristics of the cases in which a black women was the defendant.

41. Although the small group of women who pleaded not guilty received longer sentences than those who pleaded guilty, there were no significant differences due to race. Nor, once the characteristics of cases had been controlled for, were there any differences in the range and severity of non-custodial sentences imposed; nor in the proportion of black and white women sentenced without a Social Inquiry Report; nor were black women more likely to get a sentence greater than that recommended by a probation officer.

42. Although the numbers dealt with at each court were rather small, there was again evidence that black women were more likely to get a custodial sentence at one of the Dudley courts than at Birmingham.

43. Females, whether black or white, were less often sentenced to custody than males. This was true even when women with characteristics most associated with high use of custody were compared with males with similar characteristics. There was no evidence that black women were 'doubly discriminated against', first as women and then because they were black. The conclusion was that, at least in the West Midlands, the substantial over-representation of black women amongst those sentenced to custody was due entirely to the number and the legally relevant characteristics of those appearing for sentence in the Crown Court and not to any overall discrimination in the way in which they were treated by the courts.

APPENDICES

APPENDIX 1

CODING FRAME USED FOR

ABSTRACTING INFORMATION FROM COURT RECORDS

PRIVATE AND CONFIDENTIAL

University of Oxford

Centre for Criminological Research

———————————

Race and Criminal Justice

<u>Summary of Records Available: TICK BOX</u>

Form 5089

Indictment

Depositions

Police Antecedents & List

of Prior Convictions

Social Inquiry Report

Medical Report

Other Reports

Specify...

SECTION I: FORM 5089

1.   CODE NUMBER

2.   CROWN COURT OF TRIAL
   1. Birmingham
   2. Coventry
   3. Dudley/Wolverhampton
   4. Warwick
   5. Stafford

3.   DATE OF BIRTH

4.   AGE AT TIME SENTENCED   yrs

5. SEX
    1. Male
    2. Female

6. RACIAL/ETHNIC ORIGIN [To be obtained from Police files]
    1. White/European
    2. Afro-Carib/West Indian
    3. Indo-Asian
    4. Sino-Asian
    5. Arab
    6. Other

    Specify...

7. MIXED RACE
    1. Yes
    2. No

8. NAME OF DEFENCE COUNSEL (at Sentence)
. . . .

9. NAME OF SOLICITORS (at Sentence)

. . . .

10. DEFENDANT LEGALLY AIDED
    1. Yes
    2. No
    3. No Info.

11. NAME OF PROSECUTING COUNSEL

. . . .

12. PROSECUTING SOLICITORS
    1. C.P.S.
    2. Other

    Specify...

13. STATUS OF JUDGE DELIVERING SENTENCE

    1. High Court Judge
    2. Circuit Judge
    3. Recorder
    4. Assistant Recorder

    ....

14. NAME OF MAGISTRATES COURT COMMITTED FROM

    ....

15. NATURE OF COMMITTAL

    1. For trial
    2. For sentence

16. MODE OF COMMITTAL

    1. On bail
    2. In custody

17. APPEARED AT CROWN COURT

    1. For trial
    2. For plea
    3. For sentence

18. APPEARANCE FOR SENTENCE

   1. On bail
   2. In custody

19. LENGTH OF TIME BETWEEN COMMITTAL AND TRIAL

   weeks

20. LENGTH OF TIME BETWEEN COMMITTAL AND SENTENCE

   weeks

21. TOTAL LENGTH OF TIME BETWEEN COMMITTAL AND
    SENTENCE IN CUSTODY
   weeks

22. REMANDED BETWEEN TRIAL AND SENTENCE FOR REPORTS

   1. Yes
   2. No

   IF NO - GO TO Q. 23

22a. IF REMANDED FOR REPORTS: LENGTH OF TIME BETWEEN
     CONVICTION AND SENTENCE
     Enter time
   weeks

22b. IF REMANDED
     1. In custody
     2. On bail

23. NUMBER OF SEPARATE INDICTMENTS

Enter number

24. TOTAL NUMBER OF OFFENCES (COUNTS) CHARGED ON ALL INDICTMENTS

Enter number

25. MULTIPLE COUNTS
(i.e. If more than one offence charged)

1. Most serious charge proceeded with.
2. Most serious charge not proceeded with by prosecution (including – to lie on file).

26. IF MOST SERIOUS CHARGE <u>NOT</u> PROCEEDED WITH: DEFENDANT CHANGED PLEA FROM NOT GUILTY ON LESSER ALTERNATIVE CHARGE TO GUILTY AT COURT

1. Yes
2. No
3. Already pleading guilty
4. D.N.A. (most serious charge proceeded with).

27. IF MOST SERIOUS/SOLE CHARGE PROCEEDED WITH: DEFENDANT PLEADED NOT GUILTY TO MOST SERIOUS/SOLE CHARGE BUT CHANGED PLEA TO GUILTY AT COURT

1. Yes
2. No

28. PLEA AND CONVICTION

1. Plead guilty to most serious or sole charge (regardless of second/further charges).

2. Plead not guilty to most serious or sole charge and convicted of most serious or sole charge (regardless of second/further charges).

3. Plead not guilty to sole/all charges, acquitted of major charge but convicted of lesser charge.

4. Plead not guilty to sole/all charges, acquitted of sole/most serious charge on judges order but convicted of lesser charge.

5. Plead not guilty to sole/all charges, acquitted of most serious charge at judges direction but convicted of lesser charge.

6. Plead not guilty to most serious charge but guilty to lesser charge – acquitted of most serious charge but sentenced on the lesser charge.

7. Plead not guilty to most serious charge but guilty to lesser charge – acquitted of most serious charge on judges order but sentenced on the lesser charge.

8. Plead not guilty to most serious charge but guilty to lesser charge – acquitted of most serious charge at judges direction but sentenced on the lesser charge.

9. Plead not guilty to most serious charge but guilty to lesser charge - most serious charge left to lie on file but sentenced on the lesser charge.

10. Other combination (specify).

....

29. MOST SERIOUS/SOLE OFFENCE CHARGED
(Copy description on Indictment)

....

....

30. IN BREACH OF COURT ORDER

1. Yes
2. No

30a. IF YES, BREACH OF:

1. Suspended Sentence
2. Probation Order
3. Conditional Discharge
4. Other, specify.......................................

31. IN BREACH OF BAIL

1. Yes
2. No

32. OFFENCES TAKEN INTO CONSIDERATION (TICS)

Enter Number or 0

33. TOTAL NUMBER OF CHARGES CONVICTED (F.G.) OF:
(i.e. the number sentenced for. Do not count here breaches of orders)

Enter Number

34. MOST SERIOUS/SOLE OFFENCE CONVICTED OF:

Specify..

35. OTHER OFFENCES CONVICTED OF:

Specify

1..

2..

3..

4..

5..

6. Summarise any further charges.....................

....

7. D.N.A.

36. TOTAL NUMBER OF CHARGES FOUND GUILTY FOR SAME BROAD TYPE OF OFFENCE AS MOST SERIOUS CONVICTED OF (one or more)

Enter Number

37. IF CONVICTED OF MORE THAN ONE OFFENCE

1. All of same broad type of offence
2. Mixture of offences
3. D.N.A.

37a. NUMBER OF SEPARATE INCIDENTS INVOLVED

Enter Number

38. SENTENCE FOR MOST SERIOUS/SOLE OFFENCE/FOUND GUILTY.

    1. Imprisonment immediate
    2. Imprisonment partially suspended
    3. Imprisonment fully suspended
    4. Youth detention (YOI)
    5. Hospital order with restriction
    6. Hospital order without restriction
    7. Community service order
    8. Probation order
    9. Fine
    10. Conditional discharge
    11. Absolute discharge
    12. Supervision order
    13. Care order
    14. Attendance centre order
    15. Bound over
    16. Other
    17. Compensation order (sole sentence)

39. IF IMMEDIATE IMPRISONMENT OR YOUTH DETENTION

39a. Length of sentence for Most Serious Offence F.G.

..........Months

39b. Total length of sentence for <u>All</u> offences F.G.

..........Months

39c. If F.G. of more than one offence were sentences

    1. All concurrent
    2. Consecutive (some or all)

40. IF FULLY SUSPENDED SENTENCE

40a. Length of sentence for Most Serious Offence F.G.

..........Months

40b. Total length of sentence for <u>All</u> offences F.G.

..........Months

40c. Supervision Order attached

    1. Yes
    2. No

40d. Length of time sentence suspended for

..........Months

40e. If F.G. of more than one offence were sentences

    1. All concurrent
    2. Consecutive (some or all)

41. IF PARTIALLY SUSPENDED SENTENCE

41a. Total length of sentence for most serious offence F.G.

..........Months

41b. Total length of sentence for <u>all</u> offences F.G.

..........Months

41c. Length of sentence to be served in custody for most serious offence F.G.

..........Months

41d. Total length of sentence to be served in custody for <u>all</u> offences F.G.

..........Months

41e. If F.G. of more than one offence were sentences

1. All concurrent
2. Consecutive (some or all)

42. IF PROBATION/SUPERVISION ORDER

42a. Enter Length ....Months

42b. Conditions attached

1. Yes
2. No

42c. If Conditions attached

1. Psychiatric Treatment
2. Supervised Activity Centre
3. Place of Residence
4. Other

Specify.....................................

42d. If Conditions: Period of Attendance

Enter Time   ....Weeks

43. IF COMMUNITY SERVICE ORDER

43a. Length for most serious/sole offence F.G..........Hours

43b. Length for <u>all</u> offences F.G.   ....Hours

43c. If F.G. of more than one offence were sentences

    1. All concurrent
    2. Consecutive (some or all)

44. IF HOSPITAL ORDER WITH RESTRICTION

    Enter Length ....Months

45. IF FINE

45a. Amount for most serious/sole offence F.G. £..........

45b. Total amount for <u>all</u> offences F.G.   £..........

46. COMPENSATION/RESTITUTION ORDERED IN ADDITION TO ANOTHER PENALTY

    1. Yes
    2. No

47. IF COMPENSATION AWARDED

47a. Amount for most serious offence F.G.   £..........

47b. Total amount for <u>all</u> offences F.G.   £..........

48. COMBINED PENALTIES IMPOSED

    1. Yes
    2. No

48a. IF YES:

1. Imprisonment and non-custodial penalty
2. Probation and C.S.O.
3. Probation and fine
4. Probation and other non-custodial penalty
5. Other combination *

* Specify...

49. PENALTIES PLUS COMPENSATION (Code most serious main penalty)

1. Yes
2. No

49a. IF YES:

1. Custody and compensation
2. Fully suspended sentence and compensation
3. Probation and compensation
4. Fine and compensation
5. C.S.O. and compensation
6. Hospital Order and compensation

7. Other (specify)..................... + compensation.

50. TOTAL FINANCIAL PENALTY

1. Yes
2. No

50a. IF YES:

Total amount of fine and compensation: £..........

51. COSTS: (Costs awarded against defendant)

    1. Yes
    2. No

51a. IF YES: Amount of total financial penalty = fine + costs + compensation.

    £...

52. WAS PROPERTY FORFEITED/CONFISCATED/DESTROYED

    1. Yes *
    2. No
    3. D.N.A.

      * Specify...

53. WERE DRUGS CONFISCATED?

    1. Yes
    2. No
    3. D.N.A.

54. CO-DEFENDANTS CHARGED:

Number (If NONE enter 0)

If None go to Q. 57

54a. IF YES: Co-defendant(s) found guilty

Number (If NONE enter 0)

54b.   IF YES: Did any Co-defendant receive:

1. Lesser total sentence than defendant
2. More severe total sentence than defendant
3. All received same sentence

55. RACE OF CO-DEFENDANTS CHARGED

1. All same as defendant
2. Some or all different from defendant

   Specify...

Write in names and D.O.B. of Co-defendants

....

....

....

....

56. SEX OF CO-DEFENDANTS CHARGED

1. All same as defendant
2. Some or all different from defendant

   Specify...

SECTION II: DEPOSITIONS

CIRCUMSTANCES OF CRIME REPORT AND ARREST:

57. PERSON REPORTING INCIDENT:

    1. Aggrieved person
    2. Relative/friend of aggrieved person
    3. Manager/proprietor/employee of premises where incident occurred.
    4. Hospital
    5. Offender
    6. Other person
    7. Discovered by police
    8. Police victim on duty
    9. No information

    Specify who (e.g. father of A.P. passerby, etc.):

    ....

58. HOW DEFENDANT ARRESTED:

    1. Arrested at scene of offence
    2. Defendant arrested after identification by victim(s)
    3. Defendant arrested after identification by witness(s)
    4. Defendant arrested after information given to police
    5. Defendant known to police and arrested on suspicion
    6. Defendant not previously known to police and arrested on suspicion.
    7. Defendant traced from other clues
    8. Defendant surrendered to police
    9. No information

    Specify details...

    ....

59. WHERE DEFENDANT ARRESTED:

1. On the street
2. At home
3. At pub/club etc.
4. At work
5. At police station
6. Elsewhere
7. No information

Specify...

60. DEFENDANT'S STATEMENTS

1. Defendant agreed to make statement without a lawyer present.
2. Defendant only made statements with lawyer present.
3. Some with some without lawyer present

Specify...

....

61. PROSECUTION INITIATED BY

1. Police
2. Customs and Excise
3. Inland Revenue
4. DHSS
5. Local Authority
6. British Rail Police
7. Other

Specify...

CIRCUMSTANCES OF THE MAIN/SOLE OFFENCE(S)
FOUND GUILTY

WRITE SHORT SYNOPSIS OF MAIN CIRCUMSTANCES OF THE CASE: I.E. OF THOSE OFFENCES OF WHICH THE DEFENDANT WAS FOUND GUILTY.

. . . .

. . . .

. . . .

. . . .

. . . .

. . . .

. . . .

. . . .

. . . .

. . . .

. . . .

. . . .

62. WAS DEFENDANT THE SOLE PERSON INVOLVED IN THE CRIME?

    1. Yes
    2. No
    3. No Info.

62a. IF ACCOMPLICES: Defendant described as:

1. Playing leading role ('prime mover')
2. Playing equal role with accomplices
3. Playing lesser/minor role
4. D.N.A.

In each case specify....................................

....

63. WAS VIOLENCE USED OR THREATENED?

(The Most Serious Offence for this purpose is the one which received the most severe penalty. If several charges received the same most severe penalty code the most serious offence charged)

1. Only in most serious offence F.G.
2. In most serious and lesser offence F.G.
3. Only in a lesser offence F.G.
4. No evidence of violence

IF NO EVIDENCE OF VIOLENCE: go to Question 64

63a. IF VIOLENCE USED OR THREATENED: OBJECT OR MOTIVE OF VIOLENCE?

1. In pursuit of theft
2. In pursuit of sexual gratification
3. In resisting arrest
4. In a dispute
5. No clear motive: unprovoked attack

63b. IF VIOLENCE USED OR THREATENED, WEAPON USED:

1. A firearm
2. A knife/axe or other sharp implement

3. A blunt implement
4. Fist, head, feet or other part of body
5. Other

Specify..

63c. IF VIOLENCE USED OR THREATENED, was the weapon:

1. Used to injure
2. Used to threaten only
3. Unclear

63d. IF VIOLENCE USED OR THREATENED, was the victim physically harmed?

1. Yes
2. No
3. No info.

63e. IF YES: describe nature and degree of injury:

1. Bruises/grazes/cuts no requiring stitches
2. Wounds requiring stitches but no internal injuries
3. Broken bones/fractured limbs/skull etc.
4. Severe internal injuries

63f. IF YES: was the victim medically treated?

1. Yes
2. No
3. No info.

63g. IF YES: was the victim hospitalised?

1. Yes

2. No
3. No info.

63h. IF YES:

Enter number of days
(count 'overnight' as one day)

63i. WAS ANY EVIDENCE GIVEN OF CONTINUING IMPAIRMENT?

1. Yes
2. No

Specify..

64. DID THE OFFENCE INVOLVE THEFT OF PROPERTY?
(Including handling/receiving stolen property)

1. Only in most serious offence F.G.
2. In most serious and a lesser offence F.G.
3. Only in a lesser offence F.G.
4. Not a property offence

65. IF PROPERTY STOLEN WAS ANY RECOVERED?
1. Yes
2. No
3. No info.

65a. IF YES: WAS ALL RECOVERED?
1. Yes, all
2. Partly

Specify..

65b. NATURE AND VALUE OF PROPERTY STOLEN
(Write down main items and total value if recorded)

. . . .

. . . .

66. WAS IT DESCRIBED AS A BREACH OF TRUST?

   1. Yes
   2. No
   3. No info.

67. WAS IT A DRUGS OFFENCE?

   1. Only most serious offence F.G.
   2. Most serious and a less serious offence F.G.
   3. Only a less serious offence F.G.
   4. Not a drugs offence

   IF NOT A DRUGS OFFENCE: go to Question 68

67a. IF DRUGS OFFENCE: WERE DRUGS SEIZED/RECOVERED?
   1. Yes
   2. No
   3. No info.

67b. MOST SERIOUS TYPE OF DRUG INVOLVED?

1. Heroin	5.	Extasy
2. Cocaine	6.	Amphetamines
3. Cocaine crack	7.	Cannabis
4. L.S.D.	8.	Other

   ....

67c. WAS A STREET VALUE SPECIFIED?

   1. Yes
   2. No

67d. IF YES: Enter value £

67e. WAS AN AMOUNT SPECIFIED?

   1. Yes
   2. No

67f. IF YES: Enter amount   gms

67g. PURPOSE OF POSSESSION

   1. Personal use only
   2. Supply: small scale implied
   3. Supply: moderate scale implied
   4. Supply: large scale drug dealing implied
   5. No clear indication

   Specify...

   ....

68. WAS EVIDENCE GIVEN OR IMPLIED THAT THE OFFENCE WAS
PLANNED/PREMEDITATED?
   1. Evidence of planning
   2. Arose on spur of moment
   3. Not sufficient evidence
   4. Other

69. WERE OTHER AGGRAVATING FEATURES MENTIONED?
(e.g. victim abducted, sexually abused, undue brutality)

Specify (If NONE, enter NONE)............................

....

70. DEFENDANT SURRENDERED TO POLICE
    1. Yes
    2. No
    3. No info.

71. DEFENDANT MADE OR OFFERED COMPENSATION
    1. Yes
    2. No
    3. No info.

71a. IF YES: specify...

THE VICTIM

72. WAS THE VICTIM (CRIME DIRECTED AT):
    1. An individual victim
    2. A household
    3. A business
    4. A public utility
    5. Other (specify)
    6. No known victim

72a. IF AN INDIVIDUAL VICTIM: Enter number

72b. SEX OF VICTIM(S)
    1. Male

2. Female
3. Male and female victims

72c. WAS ANY VICTIM A CHILD AGED 12 OR LESS?
1. Yes
2. No

72d. WAS ANY VICTIM A JUVENILE AGED 13-16?
1. Yes
2. No

72e. WAS ANY VICTIM AN AGED ADULT (OVER 65)?
1. Yes
2. No

72f. WAS ANY VICTIM IN SAME AGE GROUP AS DEFENDANT(S)?
1. Yes
2. No

72g. MAJOR INJURED PARTY
1. Husband/wife (incl. common law).
2. Ex – husband/wife (incl. common law).
3. Parent.
4. Child.
5. Sibling.
6. In-law.
7. Other family member.
8. Paramour/present or past/opposite sex.
9. Paramour/present or past/same sex.
10. Friend/or ex-friend.
11. Neighbour.
12. Other (casual) acquaintance - defendant known to victim.
13. Other (casual) acquaintance - victim know to defendant.
14. Other (casual) acquaintance - defendant/victim known to each other.
15. Relationship established just prior to offence - (i.e. drinking together).

16. Employer/or ex-employer.
17. Employee/or ex-employee.
18. Other business associate.
19. Current or prior confederate in crime.
20. Rival criminal group.
21. Stranger.
22. Police officer.
23. Prison officer
24. No information.

72h. WAS THERE ANY INDICATION OF THE VICTIM'S RACE?
1. White/European
2. Afro-Carib./West Indian
3. Indo-Asian
4. Sino-Asian
5. Arab
6. Mixed race
7. Other
8. No info

Specify...

73. IF <u>MORE</u> THAN ONE VICTIM:

1. Victims <u>all</u> of same race/ethnic origin as offender.
2. Victims <u>all</u> of different race/ethnic origin than offender.
3. Victims of various ethnic origins.
4. D.N.A.

73a. IF MULTIPLE VICTIMS/DEFENDANTS: SPECIFY RACIAL CHARACTERISTICS

Specify...

....

....

74. ANY FACTORS RELATING TO VICTIM AGGRAVATING
    OFFENCES?
    (e.g. Victim mentally impaired, especially frail)

    Specify..

    ....

SECTION III: POLICE ANTECEDENTS, PROBATION S.I.R.
AND MEDICAL REPORTS

75. SOCIAL INQUIRY REPORT PREPARED

    1. Inquiry and no recommendation on sentence
    2. Inquiry and definite recommendation on sentence
    3. Inquiry and implied recommendation on sentence
    4. No inquiry made

75a. IF 2.: Specify........................../D.N.A.

75b. IF 3.: Specify........................../D.N.A.

75c. Was sentence imposed?:

    1. Greater)
    2. Same   ) than sentence recommended
    3. Lesser   )
    4. D.N.A.

    Specify...

76. MEDICAL   REPORT   SUBMITTED

76a 1. Medical report and no recommendation on sentence
   2. Medical report and definite recommendation on sentence
   3. Medical report and implied recommendation on sentence
   4. No medical report

76b IF 2.: Specify.................................../D.N.A.

76c IF 3.: Specify.................................../D.N.A.

76d IF 2. or 3.: Was sentence imposed?:

   1. Greater)
   2. Same   ) than sentence recommended
   3. Lesser)
   4. D.N.A.

77. PLACE OF BIRTH

1. England and Wales	8. Far East
2. Ireland	9. Australia/NZ/Canada
3. Scotland	10. Africa
4. European Country	11. West Indies
5. Middle East	12. U.S.A.
6. India	13. Elsewhere
7. Pakistan	

   Specify...

78. NATIONALITY
   1. British
   2. Foreign

79. RELIGION

1. No information	3. Non-Conformist
2. C. of E.	4. Catholic

5. Hindu   8. Jewish
6. Muslim   9. Other
7. Sikh

80. SOCIO-ECONOMIC CLASS
     1. No information   8. Police
     2. Professional Group 1   9. Armed Forces
     3. Professional Group 2   10. Student
     4. Clerical non-manual   11. Housewife
     5. Skilled manual   12. Never had occupation
     6. Semi-Skilled
     7. Unskilled

     Specify occupation.....................................

81. CURRENT WORK STATUS
     (i.e. at time of commital)

     1. Employed
     2. Unemployed
     3. Self-employed
     4. Student
     5. Retired
     6. Housewife

82. WELFARE STATUS
     If unemployed:
     Receiving State Benefit:

     1. Yes
     2. No
     3. D.N.A.

83. REGULARITY OF EMPLOYMENT
     1. Regularly in employment
     2. Frequent periods of unemployment (at least once a year)
     3. Regularly umemployed
     4. Not sufficient information

Specify...

....

84. EDUCATIONAL HISTORY
    1. No information
    2. No education beyond 16
    3. No education beyond 18
    4. Part-time higher education
    5. Full-time higher education

85. EDUCATIONAL ACHIEVEMENT

    1. No information
    2. Left school with no formal qualification
    3. Left school with CSE/GCSE/GCE 'O' Levels
    4. Left school with GCE 'A' Levels - no further education
    5. Further qualifications - Diplomas, Certificates etc
    6. Degree level qualification.

    Specify...

86. MILITARY EXPERIENCE
    1. Yes
    2. No
    3. No info.

86a. IF YES: Enter length   yrs

87. LIVING ARRANGEMENTS PRIOR TO APPREHENSION
    1. No information
    2. Living alone no children
    3. Living alone plus children
    4. Living with spouse (with common law wife) no children
    5. Living with spouse (with common law wife) plus children

6. Living with parents or close family member
7. Living with girlfriend/boyfriend, no children
8. Living with girlfriend/boyfriend, plus children
9. Living with friends
10. Living 'rough' (N.F.A.)
11. Resident of a hostel or institution
12. Other

Specify..

88. ADDRESS

Street Name...

Area........................Postcode....................

89. TYPE OF RESIDENCE
1. Owner/occupier house/flat
2. Private rented house/flat
3. Corporation house/flat
4. Private rented room/lodgings
5. Hostel
6. No fixed abode (NFA)
7. No information

90. MARITAL STATUS
1. No information
2. Married and living with spouse
3. Married and separated from spouse
4. Divorced
5. Widowed
6. Cohabiting
7. Single

91. CHILDREN
1. No information
2. From current association only

3. From previous association only
4. From current and previous association
5. No children

92. WAS EVIDENCE GIVEN SUGGESTING THAT THE DEFENDANT
HAD AN UNSETTLED/IRRESPONSIBLE/UNSTABLE LIFESTYLE?
1. Yes
2. No

92a. IF YES: Specify ....

....

93. EVIDENCE OF COMMITTING CRIME SINCE CHARGED WITH
FIRST OF THE OFFENCES
1. Yes
2. No

94. WAS EVIDENCE GIVEN OF EFFORTS TO REFORM?
1. Yes
2. No

94a. IF YES: Specify...

....

95. DEFENDANT PROVIDED EVIDENCE AGAINST CO-ACCUSED OR
OTHER OFFENDERS (See also the Depositions)
1. Yes
2. No
3. No info.
4. D.N.A.

96. DEFENDANT EXPRESSED REMORSE/REGRET
    1. Yes
    2. No
    3. No info.

97. EVIDENCE OF DEFENDANT USING DRUGS IMMEDIATELY
    PRIOR TO CRIME
    1. Yes
    2. No

97a. IF YES: Degree of impairment
    1. Defendant greatly impaired
    2. Defendant moderately impaired
    3. Defendant slightly/not impaired
    4. Not impaired at all
    5. No information

    Specify...

98. EVIDENCE GIVEN OF DEFENDANT USING ALCOHOL
    IMMEDIATELY PRIOR TO CRIME
    1. Yes
    2. No

98a IF YES: Degree of impairment
    1. Defendant greatly impaired
    2. Defendant moderately impaired
    3. Defendant slightly/not impaired
    4. Not impaired at all
    5. No information

    Specify...

99. EVIDENCE OF DEFENDANT ADDICTED (TO DRUGS, ALCOHOL,
    OR GAMBLING)

1. Yes
2. No
3. No info.

99a. IF YES: Specify ....

100. EVIDENCE THAT DEFENDANT ACTED UNDER INFLUENCE OF OTHERS
    1. Yes
    2. No
    3. No info.

100a IF YES: Specify...

101. WAS EVIDENCE GIVEN THAT DEFENDANT WAS PROVOKED?
    1. Yes
    2. No

101a IF YES: Specify..

    ....

102. WAS EVIDENCE GIVEN THAT DEFENDANT ACTED UNDER MENTAL/EMOTIONAL STRESS/DISTURBANCE?
    1. Yes
    2. No
    3. No info.

103. DID DEFENDANT HAVE A HISTORY OF MENTAL/EMOTIONAL ILLNESS?
    1. Yes
    2. No
    3. No info.

103a IF YES: Specify...

....

104. DEFENDANT OFFERS TO/OR IS/ UNDERGO(ING) TREATMENT
FOR ADDICTION (DRUGS, ALCOHOL, GAMBLING)
1. Yes
2. No
3. No info.

104a IF YES: Specify...

....

105. EVIDENCE THAT DEFENDANT IS IN SOME OTHER
WAY IN DISADVANTAGEOUS POSITION e.g. EXTREME
POVERTY/PHYSICAL HANDICAP/SOCIAL ISOLATION
1. Yes
2. No

105a IF YES: Specify...

....

106. EVIDENCE GIVEN OF UNSETTLED/DISRUPTED DOMESTIC LIFE
1. Yes
2. No

106a IF YES: Specify...

....

SECTION IV: RECORD OF PREVIOUS CONVICTIONS

NOTE: Count all previous <u>court appearances</u> which resulted in at least one <u>conviction</u> for an offence. Do NOT count <u>current</u> court appearance. Do NOT count appearances for summary (minor) motoring offences.

107. TOTAL NUMBER AS AN ADULT (I.E. NOT THOSE DEALT WITH IN A JUVENILE COURT)
      (If none, enter 0)

108. TOTAL NUMBER (INCLUDING JUVENILE)
      (If none, enter 0)

      IF NONE: move to Q. 122

108a NUMBER INVOLVING OFFENCES OF VIOLENCE AGAINST THE PERSON (S.18, S.20, S.47)

108b NUMBER INVOLVING ROBBERY/ATTEMPTED ROBBERY/AGGRAVATED BURGLARY

108c NUMBER INVOLVING RAPE/ATTEMPTED RAPE/ INDECENT ASSAULT/BUGGERY/INCEST

108d NUMBER INVOLVING RIOT/VIOLENT DISORDER /AFFRAY

108e   NUMBER INVOLVING CARRYING/POSSESSION OF
OFFENSIVE WEAPON/FIREARMS

108f   NUMBER INVOLVING DRUNKENNESS/CRIMINAL
DAMAGE/THREATENING BEHAVIOUR/ARSON/
COMMON ASSAULT/ASSAULT P.C./BREACH OF
PEACE

108g   NUMBER INVOLVING BURGLARY

108h   NUMBER INVOLVING OTHER OFFENCES OF
DISHONESTY

108i   NUMBER INVOLVING DRUG OFFENCES

108j   SUMMARY: NUMBER INVOLVING SAME BROAD TYPE AS
PRINCIPAL OFFENCE FOR WHICH
CURRENTLY CHARGED

TOTAL NUMBER OF PREVIOUSLY PROVED OFFENCES

NOTE: Count every offence (except minor motoring offences) which has
resulted in a conviction (i.e. If charged with five offences at one appearance
enter 5).

109. TOTAL NUMBER
(If none, enter 0)

110. IF PREVIOUSLY CONVICTED: AGE AT FIRST CONVICTION

IF NOT PREVIOUSLY CONVICTED: move to Question 122

Age (years)

D.N.A.

111. LENGTH OF TIME SINCE LAST CONVICTION

NOTE: Calculate on the basis of the dates of court <u>appearances</u>. <u>If</u> sentenced
to imprisonment assume that the defendant served H of the sentence unless
earlier parole date given. (i.e. a six year sentence = 3 years in custody).

Enter time   mths

112. TOTAL NUMBER OF PREVIOUS <u>COURT APPEARANCES</u>
RESULTING IN IMMEDIATE <u>CUSTODIAL</u> SENTENCES

NOTE: Include <u>partial</u> but <u>not</u> wholly suspended sentences and detention centre and borstal training (but not approved school, or care order)

Total number
(If NONE, enter 0)

113. PREVIOUSLY SERVED A DETENTION CENTRE SENTENCE?
1. Yes
2   No

114. PREVIOUSLY SERVED A BORSTAL SENTENCE?
      1. Yes
      2. No

115. PREVIOUSLY SERVED YOUTH CUSTODY?
      1. Yes
      2. No

116. PREVIOUSLY SERVED A PRISON SENTENCE?
      1. Yes
      2. No

116a IF YES: TOTAL NUMBER OF MONTHS PREVIOUSLY
      SENTENCED TO IMPRISONMENT
      (NOTE: Take all custodial sentences. Take care to distinguish
      concurrent from consecutive sentences).

      Enter number

117. TOTAL NUMBER OF PREVIOUS CUSTODIAL SENTENCES FOR
      OFFENCES OF THE TYPE CURRENTLY FOUND GUILTY
      (NOTE: Include partial but not wholly suspended sentences and include
      detention centre and borstal training (but not approved school, or care
      order).

      Total number
      (If NONE, enter 0)

117a TOTAL NUMBER OF MONTHS PREVIOUSLY SENTENCED TO
      IMPRISONMENT FOR OFFENCES OF THE TYPE CURRENTLY
      FOUND GUILTY

      Enter number

118. MOST SERIOUS PREVIOUS SENTENCE
    1. No previous convictions
    2. Detention centre
    3. Borstal
    4. Youth custody
    5. Imprisonment
    6. Partially suspended sentence
    7. Suspended sentence
    8. Probation
    9. C.S.O.
    10. Fine
    11. Other/specify

    ....

119. PREVIOUSLY ON PROBATION
    (or if a juvenile previously on a supervision Order)
    1. Yes
    2. No

119a IF PREVIOUSLY ON PROBATION – RESPONSE (See S.I.R.)
    1. Good response to supervision
    2. Erratic or poor response to supervision
    3. Not recorded

    Specify..

119b PREVIOUS PROBATION BREACHED?
    1. Yes
    2. No

120. PREVIOUSLY ON C.S.O.
    1. Yes
    2. No

120a IF PREVIOUSLY ON C.S.O. WHETHER BREACHED
    1. Yes
    2. No

121. PREVIOUS RELEASE ON PAROLE
    1. Previously paroled
    2. No previous parole
    3. No information
    4. D.N.A. (no prior custody or no parole eligible sentences i.e. 18 months or more).

121a IF PREVIOUSLY ON PAROLE (See S.I.R.)
    1. Good response to supervision
    2. Erratic or poor response to supervision
    3. Not recorded

    Specify..

SECTION V: COMMITTAL

122. CASE TRIABLE EITHER-WAY
    1. Yes
    2. No

122a IF YES:
    1. Defendant elected trial
    2. Magistrates committed for trial
    3. No information

APPENDIX 2

A NOTE ON THE STATISTICAL ANALYSES

1. The Approach

The main goal of the statistical analysis developed throughout this study has been to determine whether or not the ethnic origin of the offender is a variable which significantly effects the probability of receiving a custodial sentence when all other variables which have an effect on that decision have been controlled for.

Statistical models were computed to quantify the relative seriousness of crimes and other legally relevant variables which, at statistically significant levels, best explained the use of custody. Controlling by this relative measure of case seriousness it was possible to compare the proportions of each ethnic group—white, Afro-Caribbean (black) and Asian—sentenced to custody, the size of these differences and whether or not they were significant.

The most appropriate statistical technique to model variables, such as the decision whether or not to sentence to custody, is logistic regression which applies to dichotomous dependent variables and independent variables which are highly skewed in their distribution and non linear in their effects. Through logistic regression models it is possible to obtain an index that expresses, for each case, its probability of receiving custody. Controlling for this predictor of custody one can obtain, for each ethnic minority, the odds of receiving a custodial sentence when compared with 'similar' white cases. In Appendix 8 the final logistic regression models for custody are presented: two models based on the total male sample (TPCS: Table 1 and TPCS(RC) Table 2); a model for each ethnic group taken separately (white WPCS, black BPCS and Asian APCS: Tables 3, 4 and 5); a model based on the cases sentenced at Birmingham Crown Court which dealt with half of the male sample (BirmPCS: Table 6); a separate model calculated for the female sample (FPCS: Table 7); and, finally, a model based on the combined male and female samples (MFPCS: Table 8).

Other models were developed for different dependent variables. A logistic regression model was used to study the remand status of the offender—whether he appeared for trial already in custody or on remand, in order to investigate any possible discrimination at this earlier stage of the sentencing process (PRCS Appendix 9). For the study of the 'Severity Scale', and for the Length of Custody (Imprisonment or Detention in a Young Offender Institution) OLS (Ordinary Least Squares) models were developed, separately for adults and young offenders (Appendix 10).

2. The Data base

The data base for this study comprised of 2,884 cases of male defendants and 433 females. The total number of cases when weighted according to the size of the sampling fraction at each court was 5,185. About 130 basic variables were collected for each case. They relate to all the information that was relevant and possible to collect from Crown Court case files (see Appendix 1).

In the first stage of the analysis all these variables were submitted to an extensive screening in order to detect missing data or mistaken coding by testing their limits and compatibility. Through these checks it was possible to ensure that for all variables included in the analysis there were no cases with missing data.

The second stage examined the distribution of these variables, several of which were transformed in order to emphasize the most significant attributes expressed by each of them. Several composed variables and indices were also computed.

3. Bivariate Analysis

The correlation coefficients between all the basic variables and all the dependent variables (custody, remand status, 'severity scale' and length of imprisonment) were computed separately for the total male and female samples and by each ethnic group and also for the two courts which had the largest number of cases in this study (Birmingham and the Dudley courts), again by each ethnic group.

Independent variables which revealed high correlations with the dependent variable were then selected and the correlations between a large number of independent variables were also analyzed. Independent variables which revealed high correlations were combined in composed variables or grouped in sub-sets of variables to consider in the multivariate analysis. Their inclusion in the subsequent models was carefully scrutinized in order to avoid multicollinearity.

4. Multivariate analysis: Modelling the Custody Decision

i) Selection of Variables

All the variables which the previous stage of statistical analysis had showed to have significant correlations with the dependent variable were considered for inclusion in each model. The variables were also submitted to an *a priori* selection in order to consider all information which might be relevant in gauging the seriousness of the case and to exclude inappropriate variables. The male custody model began with at least 70 variables involving about 100 attributes.

Multivariate techniques made it possible to reduce the number of variables, while still retaining the essential information reflected by the omitted variables. The variables selected were those which, by themselves, had the greatest impact on the custody decision and at the most significant levels, or those which, by themselves, could better summarize the impact of others which were excluded.

Discriminant analysis and OLS were used as the first method of selecting the main variables or sub-set of variables to include in the logistic regression models. Although all variables included in this selection process were plausibly related to the sentencing outcome, there were a few variables for which multiple regression analysis produced a regression coefficient whose sign was contrary to that which was expected *a priori* . For example, a mitigating variable might produce a positive regression coefficient signifying that it had an aggravating effect. Such a coeficient might reflect perverse effects or the existence of multicollinearity. This indicated that the inclusion of such variables in the model was inappropriate.

For each model shown in Appendices 7 and 8 the Tables show the explanatory variables, the logistic coefficients, their standard errors, significance for the Wald statistic, the partial correlation with the dependent variable (R Statistic) and the odds multiplier.

All the included variables have a high level of significance. However, in certain cases of categorical variables (nominal variables with several attributes) there were some attributes for which the coefficients were close to zero with low significance. This revealed that the cases with these attributes had close to the average custody rate when all the other explanatory variables are controlled for[1].

[1] The logistic regression coefficients should be carefully interpreted. If they relate to

The following variables which had significant coefficients were excluded from the model for the TPCS: i) if there were statements in the file indicating that the defendant had made efforts to reform since charged; ii) if the defendant was unemployed; and iii) if there was evidence to suggest that the crime had been planned. The reasons for these exclusions were that information about the first and third variables was difficult to assess, and was regarded, therefore, as too unreliable. Unemployment was excluded because it is not a legally relevant variable and ethnically biased in its distribution. All these variables were added in subsequent models. Their inclusion did not change any of the results regarding either race or court differences in the use of custody with the exception of the variable unemployment, which had a significant influence on the use of custody at Coventry (See below p. 262).

In order to test for the presence of multicollinearity in the models the correlation coefficients between independent variables were computed and found to be generally low (below .35). Moreover, there was no instability in the coefficients for variables when other variables were added or dropped from the models, nor when a random sub-sample was selected. This indicates that there were no signicant effects of multicollinearity in the model. The discriminant power of the TPCS model is 76% for custody and 74% for non custody which corresponds to a reduction of error in prediction of 50%. [2]

ii) Logistic Regression

In logistic regression models the logarithm of the odds of custody is an exponential function of the regression coefficients. Consequently, the regression coefficients for the characteristics of a given case measure the difference in the logarithm of the odds of custody for cases with and without these characteristics, when all the other variables present in the model have been controlled for. The probability of a defendant receiving custody is given by the formula

nominal variables with only two categories e.g. 'appearing for sentence on remand in custody/on bail' the coefficient of 1.26 obtained for offenders appearing in custody (which corresponds to an odds of 3.52) expresses the average impact of that characteristic compared with cases appearing for sentence on bail. If they relate to nominal variables with several categories (such as the 12 categories of offence included in the model), they can be treated as 'categorical' or blocks of dummy variables, so that their coefficients measure the impact of each category of that variable (e.g. household burglary) as compared with the average custody rate for all categories included in the variable (in this case all offences). Thus, the regression coefficient shows how much more or less each category is associated with receiving custody compared with the average effect over all categories.

[2] If the three variables referred to above had been included in the model its discriminant power would only have been increased by 1%.

$$P(\text{custody}) = e^{b0 + b1 \times 1...bi \times i} / 1 + e^{b0 + b1 \times 1...bi \times i}$$

which can be transformed into

$$P(\text{custody}) = 1/ 1 + e^{-z}$$

Where z is the linear combination of the coefficients (bo,b1...bi), x (x1,x2...xi) the explanatory variables for the custody model, and e is the base of the natural logarithms, approximately 2.718.

For each case the offender's characteristics were weighted by their coefficients and a combined odds ratio was computed expressing the odds of that case receiving custody.

The formula o=p/1–p converts odds into probabilities and conversely the formula P=o/1+o converts probabilities into odds. Where o = odds and p = probability of custody.

The odds multiplier for each variable shows the average impact of that characteristic if present in any individual case. Negative logistic coefficients produce an odds multiplier of less than one which indicates that the variable expressed by it, when present, reduces on average the odds of receiving a custodial sentence. Conversely, positive coefficients relate to features which increase the probability of custody. The larger the size of the coefficient the greater the impact that variable has, on average, on the use of custody and, therefore, on the Probability of Custody Score.

Due to the aggregate nature of the logistic probability scores computed for each case, the impact of an aggravating factor such as 'previously served a custodial sentence for the same type of offence' which, on average, multiplied the odds of a custodial sentence by 1.8:1, may be partly cancelled by the presence of mitigating factors such as 'no harm to victim' which multiplied the odds by .54:1. Thus, it is possible for cases with similar probabilities of custody to have very different combinations of characteristics.

The significance level for the Wald statistic is obtained by squaring the ratio of the coefficient and its standard error. The R statistic measures the aggregate influence of each characteristic over all the cases. It shows the contribution of each variable to the model. For example, in the TPCS model, the most influential variable is the type of crime followed by the remand status. Yet a variable may have a high odds multiplier but may nevertheless not contribute much to the model. The variable 'Breach of Suspended Sentence, C.S.O. or a combination of penalties' had a substantial impact in those cases in which it occurred (increasing their odds by 2.04) but its impact on the model as whole, as measured by R(.039), is comparatively small since this characteristic was relatively rare.

In each Table a second model is presented which includes the variable race. The coefficients for black and Asian cases express the magnitude of the difference between the predicted custody rate for whites and for these two ethnic minorities after adjustment for all the legitimate variables in the model. The odds multiplier for black cases in the TPCS model is 1.19 which indicates that, on average, the defendant's odds of receiving custody are 1.19 times higher if he is black than if he is white. It is estimated that a coefficient of this size will be produced by a sampling error in less than 8 times out of 100.[3] For the sample as a whole this coefficient is not very high but it indicates that, on average, black defendants were sentenced to custody 5% more often than would be predicted given the legitimate variables considered in the TPCS model.[4] The coefficient for the Asian cases indicates that their odds of being sentenced to custody were less than 'similar' white cases but the difference is not statistically significant.

The results relating to race and Court (see Tables 1B and 1C of Appendix 8) were consistent whichever of the several probability scores which were obtained for the male sample – the total sample, for whites, blacks, Asians and for Birmingham cases – was used. The coefficients by court, race and court, type of Judge and even by individual judges were analysed and the significant coefficients identified. In order to investigate whether these coefficients could be explained by variables other than those included in the score, variables originally considered, as well as others that could have influenced the decision, were added to the score. Several interactions between explanatory variables and race were also considered. The main results of this analysis were:

Analysis by Court:
Two courts had sentencing patterns different from the average: Birmingham, with an odds of 0.7 (sig.=0.0001, R=-.06) indicating a sentencing pattern generally more lenient; Coventry with odds of 1.6 (sig.=0.0002, R=.04) indicating

---

[3] See the discussion on this level of significance in Chapter 5, pp 80–81 above.

[4] The impact of the odds multiplier when converted into percentage points is not the same over the whole range of cases. For example, the impact of the odds of 1.19 for black offenders compared with whites will differentially change their probability score for cases at different points on the scale, being at its greatest in the medium range of cases where there is more room for discretion. Therefore, if the probability of custody produced by all the legitimate variables was 10% for whites it would be, on average 11.7% for black offenders. If it were 50% for whites it would be 54.3% for blacks, and if 70% it would be on average 73.5% for blacks. Thus, the overall difference in percentage points in the use of custody for different ethnic groups will be substantially affected by the way that cases are distributed across the scale of seriousness.

a sentencing pattern generally more severe. When these two courts were considered as variables in the TPCS model, the coefficient for the black cases became more significant (sig=0.02) and the odds increased to 1.26.

Interactions between race and court:

No significant racial differences in Birmingham or Coventry.

Significant differences for blacks compared to white cases at the Dudley Courts. Their odds of a custodial sentence were 2.0 (sig=0.0001, R=.10).

At Warwick and Stafford Crown Courts (combined), the odds for blacks cases was 2.3 (sig=0.037, R=.02). Although this is a significant coefficient, it should be noted that it relates to a small sample of cases.

No significant differences were found at any courts between the odds of custody for Asian and white offenders.

A detailed analysis was carried out of the cases dealt with at Coventry Crown Court which showed that, when the following two variables—being unemployed and having breached previously a C.S.O. sentence—were included in the model, the difference between the use of custody at this court and the average custody rate disappeared. The odds for the first variable in Coventry were: 2.0 (sig=0.003, R=0.12) and for the second one 3.8 (sig=0.005, R=0.11).

The cases dealt with at the Dudley courts were exhaustively analysed. Again, any other variables which could possibly have explained the size of the difference between white and black custody rates were added to the model (TPCS). No legal or social-related variables which could explain the difference were detected.

The variable that emerged with the greatest explanatory power, after controlling for the TPCS score, was 'being black' and 'having been charged with co-defendants of the same race'. This latter variable was not significant either for whites or for Asian cases. After controlling by the TPCS score, the odds of receiving custody for black offenders with black co-defendants was 6.7 (sig=0.000, R=0.06). Black cases with no codefendants or with co-defendants of mixed ethnic origin had higher custody rates than whites but the difference was much smaller (odds=1.3, sig=0.14, R=0.005).

The cases of black offenders who had been charged only with other black offenders were analysed in detail in order to detect any mis-specification or hidden effects. Several legal or social-related variables which could have affected the custody decision at the Dudley courts were added to the model, namely: if the offence had been planned; if there was evidence that the defendant had made efforts to reform; recommendation in the Social Inquiry Report; if the defendant was unemployed; under the age of 21; type of crime, including a differentiation between 'organised and planned' robberies of premises, security vans etc. and street 'muggings'. None of these variables changed the size and significance of the coefficient for black cases as a whole, or for blacks convicted with black codefendants. It was also found that the impact of race was greatest for cases in the first half of the probability of custody score.

All the results were consistent in the magnitude and significance of the coefficients whichever of the four basic models for custody was employed: the TPCS, the WPCS, the BPCS or the BirmPCS.

5. The Accuracy of the Logistic Models for the Custody Decision

Some critics might be concerned about the discriminant capacity of the custody models. For the total male sample (TPCS) it is 75% (76% for custody and 74% for non custody). This corresponds to a 50% reduction of error when compared with a random sample.

It is not possible to predict decisions in the social sciences with the same degree of accuracy as in the natural sciences. This is mainly due to the fact that several explanatory variables are nominal; that it is virtually impossible to collect all the information available about factual circumstances which might affect the decision; and that there is always some variation due to the way individuals use criteria in the decisions they make—in this case judges (as can be seen in Chapters 3 and 7). Thus, the discriminant power of a model should be understood as a relative measure of its accuracy in comparison with alternative models.

It is true that a significant amount of variation remained unexplained, but there is no reason to believe that this unexplained fraction significantly affected any differences in the use of custody for each ethnic group in a way that could invalidate the results obtained. On the contrary, for cases dealt with at the Dudley courts (and also at Warwick and Stafford together), the discriminant power of the model was not increased when other variables relating to the seriousness of the cases were added to the model. Yet when race (being black) was added, its predictive power was improved.

It was possible to compare the discriminant power obtained by the (TPCS) model with others developed in research studies of sentencing and race where there have been a reasonable number of cases and variables collected. Among these studies one that stands out, both because of the similarity of the problem and the impressive number of cases involved, is the Rand Corporation research by Stephen Klein, Joan Petersilia, and Susan Turner, 'Race and Imprisonment Decisions in California', *Science*, vol. 247 (1990) pp 812-816.

This study was based on data collected by the California Board of Prisons Terms for all the offenders sentenced to prison in California in 1980 and for a sample of those sentenced to probation in the same year by the Superior Court, making a total of 11,553 offenders convicted of Assault, Robbery, Burglary, Theft, Forgery and Drugs offences. This data base contained information on the offender's criminal, personal, and socio-economic characteristics as well as aspects of the way the case was processed. The goal was to detect any discrimination due to race on sentencing to probation or custody and on the length of sentences.

All the variables available in the Californian study were also considered in the West Midlands Crown Court sample. On the other hand, several variables were included in this study which were not considered in the Californian study. The statistical analysis developed is similar to that carried out in this study, with the important difference that the much larger size of their sample allowed them to develop independent models for each broad category of crime whereas the TPCS model included the whole range of offences.[5] Despite this significant advantage, the discriminant power of the Californian and English models is not substantially different. The discriminatory power for the six offence types in the Californian study varied between 83% for drugs offences and 76% for forgery. Applying TPCS to the much smaller number of cases in each offence category in the West Midlands the discriminant power varied between 73% and 79%.

None of the other studies consulted which involved a substantial number of cases relating to all types of crime have had a discriminant power higher than 80%. It can thus be concluded that the TPCS model produced an adequate discriminatory power for the purpose of this study.

To test the stability of the TPCS model the sample was, first, randomly divided in half and the model applied to each sub-sample. Secondly, a score, based on the same variables as those included in the TPCS, was obtained for a random sample of 50 percent of the cases and then applied to the other 50 percent. The discriminant power was remarkably close to 75% in all the samples, indicating that the model obtained did not vary substantially when

[5] This study, however, did not use logistic regression but instead estimated the dichotomous variable custody/probation by the Fisher linear discriminant function.

applied to different samples of the same cases. The discriminant capacity of the model was also tested by subdividing the sample by court and type of crime. This revealed that: for Birmingham cases the discriminant power of the main model is 77%; 74% for Coventry cases; 73% for Dudley cases; and 75% for Warwick and Stafford cases combined. For the Coventry cases, when the variables 'unemployment status' and 'previous C.S.O. breached' were added to the model, the discriminant power increased by 2% to 76%. When 'being black' and 'being black and acting with black co-defendants' was added to the model applied to the cases dealt with at the Dudley courts, its predictive power also increased by 2%, to 75%. Thus, the TPCS was quite consistent in its discriminant power across all courts.

6. An Alternative Method for Calculating Risk of Custody

As explained in Chapter 1 (page 20), it would have been possible to use another method to compute a probability of custody score: a method which has been quite extensively used by the probation service. This method assigns a weight to an attribute which is the difference between the percentage of cases receiving a custodial sentence among cases with that attribute and the average percentage for all cases. Thus, if the overall average proportion sentenced to custody is 50% and the average for cases with no previous convictions is 30 %, all cases with no previous convictions would be given a score of –20 points. The probability of custody for each case is simply calculated by summing the points (plus or minus) for every attribute possessed by a case. Therefore, attributes which are highly inter-correlated are given the same weight as are those attributes each of which is independently related to the use of custody and this obviously introduces a great deal of multi-collinearity into the model. Furthermore, it is particularly hazardous to use this "summed percentage difference" method for a total sample which may include quite heterogeneous sub-samples, as in this case where the sample was composed of white, black and Asian defendants. This is because attributes may be very differently distributed in these ethnic sub-samples and also related to other attributes in different ways. For, example, Asian offenders were much less likely than either white or black offenders to have previous convictions, but a higher proportion of Asians were convicted or the more serious offences (see Chapter 3 p 60). It is well known that the weight given to mitigation for having no prior record is less when offences are especially serious, and yet, under this scoring system each case would be given the same weight for this variable. The net effect, of course, is that the Asian cases would have too much weight given to having no previous convictions and the many variables (such as no prior custody) which are correlated with it. This means that the score would make the Asian cases appear less serious and less likely to receive a custodial sentence than they really were.

For purposes of comparison with the model based on logistic regression a scoring system based on this "summed percentage" method was calculated. The Observed and Expected rates of custody were as follows:

	White	Black	Asian
Obs—Exp.	−1.4	+4.3	+2.5
Obs—Exp/Exp	−2.8	+8.2	+6.7

This score produced a larger difference between the observed and expected custody rates for black and white offenders: 5.7 percentage points which is equivalent to an increased probability of custody for black offenders compared with whites of 11%. But, as predicted above, it also produced an observed custody rate for Asians which was considerably higher than expected, whereas the logistic regression model showed their observed rate to be lower than expected. It was also found that the "summed percentage" score did not discriminate as well between the various levels of the use of custody and that its overall discriminatory power was considerably less than that of the logistic regression model: 69% correctly predicted outcomes v 75%. It was particularly less successful in predicting the custodial (as opposed to non-custodial) decision: 60% as compared with 76% for the logistic regression model. For all these reasons it was decided that the "summed percentage" method was inferior to the logistic regression method employed for the purposes of this study.

APPENDIX 3

SIGNIFICANT DIFFERENCES IN PROPORTIONS OF MALE CASES

COMMITTED TO CUSTODY WITH VARIOUS ATTRIBUTES

TABLE 1
COMPARISON OF WHITE AND BLACK OFFENDERS

	Whites	Blacks	Chi Square p<
Aged 21–44	49.5	60.1	.0000
Circuit Judge	50.4	57.4	.004
Recorder	44.2	58.1	.0003
Committed for trial on Bail	41.5	47.7	.003
Committed for trial in Custody	81.1	8.6	.02
Appeared for sentence on Bail	40.0	46.4	.003
1 Indictment	41.9	57.4	.0000
1–2 Offences Charged	38.8	49.2	.0000
Most serious charge proceeded with	9.1	69.1	.0000
Not in Breach of Court Order	44.8	53.4	.0000
Not in Breach of Bail	47.1	56.5	.0000
No TICs	46.3	54.5	.0000
2+ TICs	60.3	80.4	.0006
No Evidence of Violence	42.4	54.7	.0000
Most Serious Off. involved theft	39.5	53.3	.0000
Most & less serious off. involves theft	58.1	72.6	.003
Property Recovered	50.5	58.1	.03
Not Recovered	49.6	66.4	.002
Household/Personal/Cash stolen	53.2	65.7	.0001
Valued £0–499	45.6	54.4	.0000
No Breach of Trust	48.7	56.8	.0000
Most & Less Serious Off. involved drugs	43.0	68.9	.008

	Whites	Blacks	Chi Square
Offence Planned/Premeditated	52.4	65.2	.0000
Did **not** surrender to Police	48.2	57.1	.0000
No offer of compensation	49.2	57.2	.0000
Crime directed at Household	53.8	66.7	.04
at Business	40.8	53.7	.006
No Victim	36.6	53.1	.0006
Less than 3 Victims	47.0	56.7	.0000
Major Injured Party – Rival Group	84.9	30.8	.0007
Sentence Imposed was same as			
Recommended	6.4	16.0	.0001
Occupation	47.3	55.0	.0003
Unemployed	54.6	63.5	.0002
On Welfare	51.7	62.4	.0000
No Regular Employment	52.5	60.5	.0002
Married	45.0	56.0	.01
Not Married	49.8	56.1	.001
No Children	48.5	55.9	.007
No Unsettled/Irresponsible/Unstable			
lifestyle	42.8	53.1	.0000
Evidence of committing crime since			
charge	65.9	73.8	.04
No Evidence given against others	44.9	61.0	.0003
No evidence of Remorse/Regret	50.8	60.7	.0000
No evidence of drug use prior to			
offence	48.0	56.5	.0000
No evidence of addiction	45.7	55.8	.0000
Not acting under influence of others	48.6	57.0	.0000
Defendant **not** provoked	49.1	58.3	.0000
Acting under mental/emotional			
stress	42.3	55.2	.0000
Not Acting under mental/emotional			
stress	49.1	56.6	.0002
No history of mental stress	47.8	56.3	.0000
Not in a disadvantageous position	47.6	56.9	.0000
Evidence of Unsettled/disrupted			
Family	56.8	64.6	.05
No Evidence of Unsettled/disrupted			
Family	44.5	54.5	.0000
2–4 Previous Convictions	49.2	58.5	.01

	Whites	Blacks	Chi Square
5–7	57.9	67.9	.02
8–10	58.4	75.0	.004
11 +	61.9	76.7	.04
No Prev. cons. for violence	44.9	50.7	.01
One	54.0	66.5	.003
No Prev. cons. for robbery	47.0	52.4	.01
No Prev. cons. for rape/indecent ass.	47.9	56.1	.0000
No Prev. cons. for Public Order	52.4	62.5	.0000
No Prev. cons. for Offensive Weapon	51.6	60.7	.0001
One	54.6	66.4	.04
No Prev. cons. for Drug Offences	41.7	51.5	.0000
One	53.1	65.7	.002
No Prev. cons. for same as Current			
Main Off.	42.0	48.3	.01
2 +	56.5	72.6	.0000
4–5	41.1	63.0	.001
11 +	61.0	74.4	.0001
Aged 14–16 at first conviction	54.4	64.6	.0007
17–24	45.8	59.7	.0000
No Previous Custodial Sentence	41.6	52.0	.001
2 or more	62.1	73.3	.0006
Previous Detention Centre	60.4	69.9	.01
No Previous Detention Centre	48.7	59.0	.0000
Previous Borstal	55.3	72.2	.003
No Previous Borstal	51.8	60.7	.0001
No Previous Youth Custody	48.9	59.9	.0000
Previous Prison Sentence	58.6	70.0	.002
No Previous Prison Sentence	49.8	58.7	.0004
No Previous time in any Custody	41.6	52.5	.0008
25–61 mnths Previous Custody	62.3	75.0	.002
No Prev. cust. for same as Current			
Main Off.	42.7	51.7	.0000
1 +	63.3	73.1	.01
1–6 months	53.7	73.4	.004
25 months +	65.3	79.0	.005
Most Ser. Previous Sentence –			
Imprisonment	58.8	70.7	.002
Most Ser. Previous Sentence – CSO	48.4	71.7	.01
Most Ser. Previous Sentence – Fine	34.9	45.9	.04

	Whites	Blacks	Chi Square
Previously Paroled	61.6	82.2	.01
No Previous Parole	50.0	58.7	.0002
Poor Response to Parole/Supervision	54.1	100	.02
Triable Either-Way offence	42.1	48.1	.01
Magistrates committed for trial	43.6	50.8	.005
Offences arose from one Incident only	40.2	51.2	.0000
Pleaded Guilty to main charge	49.4	59.2	.0002
Found Guilty of one charge	37.5	46.0	.0007
Found Guilty of 2 charges – same type	42.0	62.8	.0001
Found Guilty of 3 charges – same type	51.6	72.5	.03
No Co-Defendants	48.9	55.9	.004
Co-Defendant same race	46.0	59.5	.0003
Sole Offender	50.4	55.9	.04
Played Leading Role	52.0	65.6	.02
Played Equal Role	47.9	60.2	.0007
Inquiry Recommended CSO	45.6	54.6	.03
No Inquiry	41.5	56.4	.0000
No use of Alcohol prior to Offence	46.5	56.8	.0000
No Probation/Probation not breached	49.1	60.9	.0000
No Previous CSO	44.7	50.8	.005
Previous CSO – Not Breached	54.4	71.1	.0007
– Breached	65.1	77.8	.03
First Conviction Over 17	40.1	48.7	.001
First Conviction Under 17	56.8	64.9	.003
Not Vulnerable Victim (ie not aged/under 16)	46.0	54.9	.0000
Convicted of Blackmail/Rob/Kidnap	86.3	76.7	.03
Convicted of Household Burglary	54.8	73.1	.007
Convicted of Supplying Drugs	52.2	70.4	.06

Appendix 3

TABLE 2
COMPARISON OF WHITE AND ASIAN OFFENDERS

	Whites	Asians	Chi Square p<
Appeared at Crown Court for Trial	46.9	39.7	.04
Appeared at Crown Court for Plea	49.4	39.8	.004
Aged 14–20	48.5	41.0	.04
Aged 17–20	48.6	40.2	.03
Aged 21 or more	48.4	38.7	.002
Aged 21–44	49.5	38.6	.0007
Defendant Legally Aided	48.2	39.3	.0002
Circuit Judge	50.4	38.5	.0000
Committed for trial on Bail	41.5	32.0	.0001
Appeared for sentence on Bail	40.0	29.2	.0000
1 Indictment	41.8	34.5	.004
1–2 Offences Charged	38.8	30.1	.003
Most serious charge not proceeded with	42.2	28.2	.003
Pleaded Guilty to Lesser Charge	45.5	26.8	.02
Already Pleading Guilty	38.5	21.8	.004
Not in Breach of Court Order	44.8	38.3	.008
Not in Breach of Bail	47.1	38.6	.0004
No TICs	46.3	38.1	.0008
Violence used in Most Serious Offence	50.3	32.1	.0000
Motive for Violence – theft	79.3	55.3	.0009
Dispute	40.4	27.6	.005
No clear motive	56.1	32.7	.003
Weapon – Blunt Instrument	53.9	34.0	.0008
Fist/Part of Body	52.4	38.2	.007
Used to Injure	55.7	40.9	.0001
Threaten	58.9	32.8	.0003
Victim was medically treated	55.0	41.9	.003
Not treated	63.0	34.6	.01
No Information	59.5	23.5	.02
Evidence of continuing impairment	72.3	39.1	.002
No impairment	53.4	39.4	.0007
Offence did Not involve theft of property	46.8	35.7	.0007
Property Stolen – Valued £0–499	45.6	38.1	.006
Breach of Trust	46.3	31.9	.03
No Breach	48.7	41.0	.003

	Whites	Asians	Chi Square p<
Offence did not involve drugs	48.3	38.8	.0001
Offence Planned/Premeditated	52.4	45.1	.02
Did **not** surrender to Police	48.2	39.7	.0005
No offer of compensation	49.2	39.1	.0001
Crime directed at Individual	52.6	38.3	.0000
at Business	40.8	29.4	.01
No Victim	36.6	57.1	.02
3 or more victims	68.1	34.1	.0001
Victim was male	48.5	31.5	.0000
Same age as defendant	54.7	41.4	.002
Not same age	52.4	38.3	.004
Major Injured Party – Group	84.9	15.4	.0000
Stranger	55.0	41.0	.004
Victim was White	55.1	38.9	.002
Asian	52.2	31.5	.003
Not Asian	48.3	42.9	.05
Sentence Imposed greater than			
Recommended	78.3	69.3	.01
Unemployed	54.6	46.5	.02
No Regular Employment	52.5	39.9	.0000
Not Married	49.8	39.0	.0002
No Children	48.5	36.5	.0002
Residence – N.F.A.	88.9	54.5	.01
No Unsettled/Irresponsible/Unstable			
lifestyle	42.8	35.2	.003
No Evidence of committing crime since			
charge	42.9	35.7	.005
No evidence of Remorse/Regret	50.8	40.1	.0007
No evidence of drug use prior to offence	48.0	39.7	.0004
No evidence of addiction	45.7	38.7	.004
Not acting under influence of others	48.6	40.3	.0009
Defendant **not** provoked	49.1	41.8	.004
Acting under mental/emotional stress	42.3	62.5	.01
Not Acting under mental/emotional stress	49.1	37.7	.0000
No history of mental stress	47.8	39.6	.0006
Not in a disadvantageous position	47.6	38.1	.0001
No Evidence of Unsettled/disrupted			
Family	44.5	37.0	.004

	Whites	Asians	Chi Square p<
No Prev. cons. for violence	44.9	38.3	.01
No Prev. cons. for robbery	47.0	38.7	.0005
No Prev. cons. for rape/indecent ass.	47.9	39.6	.0004
3+ Prev. cons. for criminal damage	64.8	33.3	.01
Aged 30–34 at first conviction	31.8	69.2	.04
Prev. Prison Sentence – 1–6 mnths	55.0	34.4	.04
Prev. custodial Sentence for same – 7–12mnths	63.6	27.3	.04
Most Ser. Previous Sentence – Det. Centre	62.2	25.0	.007
Triable Either-Way offence	42.1	34.4	.02
Triable only on Indictment	65.3	45.4	.0000
Magistrates committed for trial	43.6	36.1	.03
Offences arose from one Incident only	40.2	34.0	.02
Pros. withdrew Main Charge – pg to lesser	40.6	26.7	.003
Pleaded Guilty to main charge	49.4	39.8	.004
Plead Changed to Guilty at Trial	50.5	69.4	.05
Found Guilty of one charge	37.5	28.0	.001
Co-Defendant different race	59.5	32.4	.0001
Played Equal Role	47.9	32.8	.0003
Victim was **not** harmed	55.1	38.7	.01
Required stitches	61.8	33.8	.0000
No Inquiry	41.5	33.5	.03
No use of Alcohol prior to offence	46.5	39.8	.009
Evidence of Alcohol	54.5	39.2	.02
No Previous CSO	44.7	38.1	.008
Not Vulnerable Victim (ie not aged/under 16)	46.0	36.6	.0002
Charged with Blackmail/Rob/Kidnap	79.7	52.6	.0000
Charged with Household Burglary	52.4	79.3	.008
Charged with Public Order	43.3	20.0	.0006
Charged with Minor Violence	30.3	14.3	.02
Convicted of Blackmail/Rob/Kidnap	86.3	65.6	.0004
Convicted of Household Burglary	54.8	80.0	.01
Convicted of Burglary/Theft	41.9	27.8	.02
Convicted of Public Order	45.8	17.6	.0000
Convicted of Minor Violence	33.2	9.5	.0003

TABLE 3

COMPARISON OF BLACK AND WHITE OFFENDERS SENTENCED
AT BIRMINGHAM CROWN COURT

	Whites	Blacks	Chi Square p<
Sentenced by a Circuit Judge	45.4	54.9	.05
One indictment only	38.8	46.0	.02
Charged 1–2 Offences	34.6	41.9	.04
Charged 4 plus Offences	63.8	74.5	.04
Most Serious Chg Proceeded with	55.4	66.3	.01
Pleaded Guilty to main charge	44.5	54.3	.01
Not in Breach of Court Order	41.5	49.0	.01
Not in Breach of Bail	43.0	51.0	.01
No other offences TIC	43.8	49.8	.04
2 plus offences TIC	36.5	77.4	.03
F.G. 2 charges of same type	36.5	56.6	.01
Equal Role with Co–Defendant	41.7	54.4	.02
Most Serious offences involved property stolen	32.7	48.9	.0008
No property Recovered	43.8	64.7	.01
Cash, household or personal property	49.9	63.3	.004
No Breach of Trust involved	45.8	51.8	.04
Did **not** surrender to police	44.6	52.1	.01
No SIR prepared	38.3	53.4	.0009
21 years and older	45.2	54.3	.01
Unemployed	50.9	59.8	.01
In receipt of Welfare Benefits	47.5	57.0	.01
No Regular Employment	48.3	56.4	.01
Made Verbal Threats/No Weapon	38.7	47.2	.03
Value of Property stolen £0–499	42.6	50.4	.01
No Unsettled/Irresponsible/Unstable lifestyle	37.4	44.8	.03
No evidence crime since charged	39.4	46.7	.02
No expression remorse/regret	46.3	56.4	.004
No evidence defendant provoked	45.7	53.2	.01
No evidence of Mental Stress	45.6	51.5	.05
No history of Mental Stress	44.7	51.1	.02
Not socially disadvantaged	43.4	51.0	.01

	Whites	Blacks	Chi Square p<
14–16 at first conviction	51.5	60.4	.05
17–24 at first conviction	42.9	57.6	.004
Previously sentenced to D.C.	54.0	65.6	.05
Not previously sentenced to D.C.	46.8	55.2	.02
Not previously sentenced to Borstal	47.6	55.8	.01
Not previously sentenced to Y.O.I.	45.4	55.6	.003
Previously sentenced to imprisonment-	53.3	64.7	.04
Not previously sentenced to imprisonment	47.1	54.8	.04
Prev. cust. same type as current Main Charge	58.0	70.2	.03
2 plus previous ct apps resulting in custody	57.8	69.5	.02
7–10 previous proved offences	43.0	63.9	.005
11 plus previous proved offences	58.6	68.4	.05
5–7 previous convictions (ct.app.)	47.6	61.9	.03
1 prev con for burglary	49.3	63.4	.03
2 prev conv for same type current conv.	51.3	66.7	.01
Previously on Probation – **not** breached	46.0	56.5	.003
Prev cons but **No** prev cust. sentence	39.8	49.2	.05
Prev cons and 1 plus prev cust. sentences	55.7	64.1	.04

TABLE 4

COMPARISON OF BLACK AND WHITE MALE OFFENDERS
SENTENCED AT THE DUDLEY COURTS

(* indicates that this attribute was also statistically significant at Birmingham.)

[+] Figures in square brackets refer to variables where the numbers were too small for the Chi Square value to be meaningful. The value of the Phi coefficient is given instead.

	Whites	Blacks	Chi Square[+] p<
Aged 17–20	45.7	62.1	.04
* Aged 21 and over	48.4	66.5	.0003
* Sentenced by a Circuit Judge	48.5	64.1	.001
Sentenced by a Recorder	45.7	75.0	.002
Committed on bail	40.0	60.0	.0000
* One Indictment only	40.0	62.9	.0000
* Charged 1–2 Offences	41.3	60.9	.0000
* Most Serious Chg Proceeded with	53.7	73.7	.0006
Convicted of Serious violence	58.1	78.1	[phi.21]
Convicted of Public Order offence	56.3	73.3	[phi.16]
* Convicted of House Breaking	54.4	72.0	[phi.17]
Convicted of Theft	36.1	80.0	.002
Convicted of Handling	22.7	47.8	[phi.26]
Convicted of fraud	35.3	83.3	[phi.42]
Convicted of a Drugs offence	20.0	62.5	[phi.29]
* **Not** in Breach of Court Order	42.7	61.7	.0000
* **Not** in Breach of Bail	46.8	66.5	.048
* **No** other offences TIC	44.7	163.9	.0000
F.G. 1 charge of same type	37.6	57.3	.0007
* F.G. 2 charges of same type	41.8	73.5	.005
F.G. 2 charges of mixed type	48.1	72.7	[phi.25]
F.G. 3 charges of same type	42.3	66.7	[phi.24]
Race Co–defendant Same	46.7	80.7	.0000
Sole Offender	50.0	62.7	.035
Played Leading Role	39.7	76.2	.008
* Equal Role with Co–Defendant	52.3	74.1	.01

	Whites	Blacks	Chi Square[+] p<
Violence in a dispute	33.3	60.0	.009
Use of a knife	56.7	76.9	[phi.21]
* F.G. of offences involving property	49.6	69.0	.0004
Property Recovered	47.2	65.9	.0078
* No property recovered	54.4	75.0	[phi.19]
* Cash, household or personal property	51.9	71.6	.007
Property value under £100	36.7	68.0	.04
* Property value £100–499	30.4	60.9	.03
Property value £1000–4999	49.2	78.9	.043
* No Breach of Trust involved	47.9	66.2	.0000
* Drugs offence	33.3	66.7	[phi.24]
Offence Planned/Premeditated	50.5	73.0	.0000
* Did Not Surrender to police	47.2	65.8	.0000
* Victim a business	47.0	71.1	.019
Victim a female	50.0	72.9	.044
Victim from family	47.6	75.0	[phi.28]
Victim a stranger	51.3	71.4	.039
* No SIR prepared	42.7	64.1	.004
SIR recommended SS or CSO	45.7	64.6	.013
* Unemployed	51.7	70.0	.0003
* In receipt of welfare benefits	50.5	69.8	.0003
Regularly employed	35.9	56.4	.036
* No Regular employment	52.9	67.1	.002
Married	44.9	70.0	.005
* Made verbal threats/no weapon	44.1	66.4	.0001
Victim needed stitches	50.0	72.0	[phi.22]
Has children	50.6	66.7	.014
* No Unsettled/Irresponsible/Unstable lifestyle	43.8	64.6	.0000
* No evidence crime since charged	41.9	60.6	.0001
No evidence given against others	40.9	76.2	.002
Expressed remorse/regret	42.3	62.3	.0077
* No expression remorse/regret	51.3	66.7	.0024
* No evidence defendant provoked	48.4	67.7	.0000
Evidence of mental stress	40.0	72.7	[phi.32]
* No evidence of Mental Stress	47.9	65.0	.0001
* No history of mental stress	46.4	65.5	.0000
* Not socially disadvantaged	47.3	66.4	.0000
No evidence unsettled domestic life	40.0	72.7	[phi.32]

	Whites	Blacks	Chi Square[+] p<
2–4 previous convictions	44.7	66.2	.009
8–10 previous convictions	60.0	87.5	.02
No prev con. for violence	42.8	61.9	.009
1 prev con. for violence	52.9	71.0	.042
No prev con. for robbery	45.9	62.1	.0003
* 17–20 at first conviction	41.8	68.6	.004
* Not previously sentenced to D.C.	48.3	68.3	.0002
* Not previously sentenced to borstal	51.6	69.7	.0001
* Not previously sentenced to Y.O.I.	49.6	70.8	.0001
* Not prev. sentenced to imprisonment	48.2	65.5	.0011
* Not prev. served custodial sentence	41.3	62.7	.004
Prev. custody totalling 7–12 months	48.0	78.3	[phi.31]
Prev. custody totalling 25–36 months	59.1	80.8	[phi.24]
Most serious prev sentence – imprisonment	64.4	80.6	.04
Most serious prev sentence – CSO	33.3	90.0	.01
Most serious prev sentence – fine	36.1	60.0	[phi.21]
* Previously on probation – not breached	48.5	69.8	.0000
No previous CSO	43.2	58.9	.002
Previous CSO – not breached	52.8	81.0	.008
Magistrates committed either–way for trial	42.5	62.8	.0001
No prev cons for burglary	35.0	56.8	.0003
* 1 prev con for burglary	49.3	70.4	.031
3 prev cons for burglary	59.3	81.3	[phi.23]
1 prev con for dishonesty	45.6	66.0	.05
2 prev cons for dishonesty	50.0	76.3	.02
4–5 prev cons for dishonesty	56.4	75.0	[phi.19]
No prev cons for drugs	47.6	63.7	.0004
No prev cons same type as current Main Off.	38.9	55.7	.006
* 2–4 prev cons same type	62.5	79.3	[phi.18]
5–7 prev cons same type	50.0	77.8	[phi.27]
4–5 prev proved offences	39.4	71.4	.04
11 plus prev proved offences	64.2	79.8	.02
* Prev cons but No prev custodial sent.	41.3	62.7	.004

GROUPING OF CRIMES

NUMBER OF MALES AND FEMALES CONVICTED AND PERCENTAGE SENTENCED TO CUSTODY

Offence Type	Males		Females	
	N	% Custody	N	% Custody
1. Sex Offences:–				
Attempted Buggery	4	25.0		
Attempt to Procure	1	100.0		
Buggery	7	57.1		
Conspiracy Live on Prostitution			1	0.0
Conspiracy Prostitution			6	66.7
Expose	1	0.0		
Incest	2	50.0		
Indec. Ass. Child	10	40.0		
Indec. Ass. Female	46	65.2		
Indec. Ass. Male	8	62.5	1	100.0
Live on Prostitution	10	80.0		
Permit Sex with Under 13	1	0.0		
Sex with Under 16	5	60.0		
2. Blackmail/Robbery/Kidnap:–				
Abduct	3	100.0		
Abduct Child	1	100.0	1	0.0
Admin. O P Substance	2	100.0		
Assist Offender	3	66.7	1	0.0
Assist Illegal Entry	1	100.0		

Offence Type	Males		Females	
	N	% Custody	N	% Custody
Assault with intent to Rob	13	61.5	1	100.0
Attempted Kidnap	1	100.0		
Attempt to Perv. Justice	1	100.0		
Attempted Robbery	17	70.6	1	100.0
Blackmail	9	77.8	3	0.0
Conspiracy to Rob	13	76.9		
Escape	2	100.0	1	0.0
False Imprisonment	2	100.0		
Kidnap	22	68.2	2	0.0
Robbery Aid and Abet	1	100.0		
Robbery	199	76.4	20	70.0

3. Violent & Serious Crimes

Aggravated Burglary	6	83.3		
Arson 2A	11	63.6	5	60.0
Arson 2B	4	75.0	2	50.0
Assault to Resist Arrest	8	62.5	1	100.0
Attempted Arson 2	1	100.0		
Attempted Rape	12	91.7		
Bomb Hoax	1	100.0		
Conspiracy to Import Drugs	1	0.0		
Conspiracy to Supply Drugs	3	100.0		
Criminal Damage with intent	2	100.0		
Import Drugs	13	100.0	3	100.0
Infantic	1	0.0		
Manslaughter	14	85.7	2	100.0
Make Explosion	1	100.0		
Possess Arms with intent	4	100.0		
Possess Explosives	3	100.0		
Rape	24	100.0		
Section 18 GBH	72	95.8	11	54.5
Section 18 Aid and Abet	1	0.0		
Threat to Kill	7	71.4	1	0.0

Appendix 4

Offence Type	Males		Females	
	N	% Custody	N	% Custody
4. Burglary Household:–				
Burglary in a Dwelling House	299	59.9	22	18.2
5. Supplying Drugs:–				
Possess Drugs with intent	73	64.4	6	33.3
Supplying Drugs	48	68.8	6	33.3
6. Reckless Driving:–				
Driving Disqualified	16	50.0	1	0.0
Death by Reckless Driving	8	50.0		
Reckless Driving	45	53.3	1	0.0
7. Others:–				
Allow to be Carried	3	0.0		
Attempt to Possess Drugs	1	0.0		
Bigamy	1	0.0		
Gross Indecency	5	0.0		
Obscene Art	3	0.0		
Open Private Post	2	0.0		
Permit Use of Drugs	2	0.0	1	0.0
Possess Drugs	37	8.1	11	9.1
Possess Racial Material	1	0.0		
Wilful Delay of Post	1	0.0		
8. Burglary/Theft:–				
Attempted Burglary	18	38.9		
Attempted Theft	10	0.0		
Burglary	192	46.9	9	22.2

Offence Type	Males		Females	
	N	% Custody	N	% Custody
Conspiracy to Burgle	1	100.0		
Conspiracy to Steal	25	40.0	3	33.3
Equipped to Steal	14	57.1		
Taking and Driving Away	16	43.8		
Theft	285	36.8	84	17.9

9. Public Order:–

Affray	86	26.7	6	0.0
Ammunition with no Certificate	1	0.0		
Arms with no Certificate	6	50.0		
Arson 1	24	54.2	5	0.0
Att. Arson 1	3	66.7		
Cons. Arson	2	0.0		
Cons. Perv. Justice	2	50.0	1	0.0
Criminal Damage	18	33.3	3	0.0
Obstructing Police	2	50.0		
Pervert Justice	21	42.9	6	0.0
Possess Arms	1	0.0		
Threatening Behaviour	53	15.1	2	0.0
Transport Ammunition	1	0.0		
Transport Arms	1	0.0		
Violent Disorder	140	47.9	4	0.0

10. Fraud/Receiving:–

Abstract Electricity	3	0.0	4	0.0
Attempted Deception	9	11.1	5	20.0
Attempted Fraud	1	0.0		
Attempted Handling	3	0.0		
Attempted Non Payment	1	0.0		
Conspiracy Cheat Inland Revenue	1	100.0		
Conspiracy to Deception	26	61.5	11	9.1
Conspiracy to Fraud	2	50.0	1	0.0
Conspiracy to Handling	2	50.0		
Cheat Inland Revenue	1	100.0		

Offence Type	Males		Females	
	N	% Custody	N	% Custody
Corrupt	2	0.0		
Counterfeit	1	0.0		
Deception	82	35.4	41	22.0
False Accounting	8	37.5	2	0.0
False Instrument	7	42.9	8	50.0
False Statement	1	0.0		
Forgery	15	33.3	12	33.3
Fraudulent Evasion	1	0.0		
Fraudulent Trade	3	33.3	1	0.0
Fraudulent Use	1	0.0		
Fraud regarding VAT	3	66.7		
Gambling Machines	2	0.0		
Handling	144	30.6	37	24.3
Non Payment	1	0.0		

11. Minor Violence:–

	N	% Custody	N	% Custody
Attempted Section 47	1	100.0		
Conspiracy to Assault	18	0.0		
Conspiracy to commit Section 47	4	25.0	2	0.0
Conspiracy to Violent Disorder	6	50.0		
Common Assault	17	11.8	3	0.0
Cruel to Child	1	0.0	8	25.0
Offensive Weapon	19	15.8		
Section 47	222	27.5	27	11.1

12. Section 20 GBH:–

	N	% Custody	N	% Custody
Conspiracy to commit Section 20	1	0.0		
Section 20	243	49.4	32	25.0

TABLE 1

PERCENTAGE TO CUSTODY COMPARISON OF OBSERVED AND EXPECTED (TPCS) BY COURT AND RACE (MALES)

	Whites	Blacks	Asians	w:b	w:a
Birmingham					
Observed	45.1	51.7	37.1	+6.6	−8.0
Expected	48.7	54.7	41.5	+6.0	−7.2
Obs–Exp	−3.6	−3.0	−4.4	+0.6	+0.8
Obs–Exp Exp	−7.4	−5.5	−10.6	−	−
Obs–Exp White Exp	−	−	−	+1.2	+1.6
Dudley Courts					
Observed	47.5	65.4	39.5	+17.9	−8.0
Expected	46.5	53.1	39.4	+6.6	−7.1
Obs–Exp	+1.0	+12.3	+0.1	+11.3	−0.9
Obs–Exp Exp	+2.2	+23.2	−0.3	−	−
Obs–Exp White Exp	−	−	−	+24.3	−1.9
Coventry					
Observed	62.3	54.3	58.3	−8.0	−4.0
Expected	51.1	46.9	44.2	−4.2	−6.9
Obs–Exp	+11.2	+7.4	+14.1	−3.8	+2.9
Obs–Exp Exp	+21.9	+15.8	+31.9	−	−
Obs–Exp White Exp	−	−	−	−7.4	+5.7

Appendix 5

	Whites	Blacks	Asians	w:b	w:a
Warwick & Stafford					
Observed	52.3	74.4	50.0	+22.1	−2.3
Expected	53.3	60.3	48.1	+7.0	−5.2
Obs–Exp	−1.0	+14.1	+1.9	+15.1	+2.9
Obs–Exp Exp	−1.9	+23.4	+4.0	−	−
Obs–Exp White Exp	−	−	−	+28.3	+5.4

TABLE 2
COMPARISON OF THE PROPORTIONATE USE OF CUSTODY
FOR WHITE OFFENDERS COMPARED WITH THE EXPECTED RATE
BY JUDGES SITTING AT BIRMINGHAM AND THE DUDLEY COURTS

White Offenders Sentenced at Birmingham Crown Court

	Percent of Cases Dealt	Percent to Custody	Number to Custody	Number Expected	Number Obs–Exp
Judges(4) Higher Bl/Wh	17.8	44.2	69	79	−10
Judges(6) Equal (2) or Lower (4) Bl/Wh	33.1	46.2	134	145	−11
Judges(88) Less 35 cases each	49.0	44.8	192	202	−11
Total		45.1	395	426	−32

White Offenders Sentenced at the Dudley Courts

	Percent of Cases Dealt with	Percent to Custody	Number to Custody	Number Expected	Number Obs–Exp
Judges(4) Higher Bl/Wh	37.6	44.1	67	73	−6
Judges(3) Equal (2) or Lower (1) Bl/Wh	24.0	57.7	56	45	+11
Judges (31) Less 31 cases each	38.4	44.5	69	70	−1
Total		47.5	192	188	+4

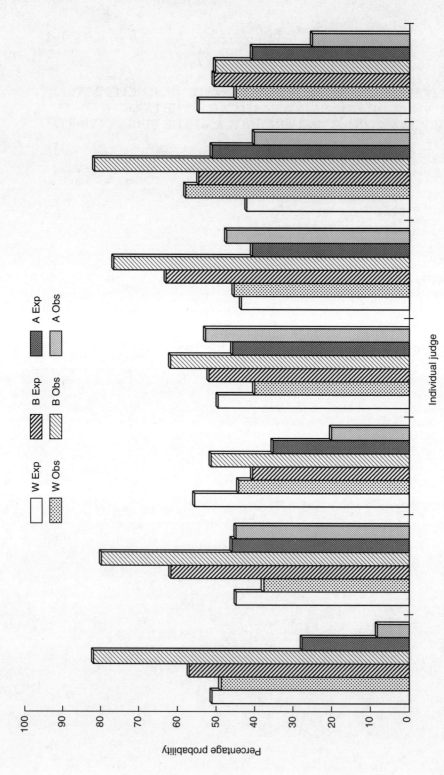

Figure 1 Observed and expected percentages sentenced to custody by race and relative severity (males)
I. Judges relatively severe on black offenders : 7 judges

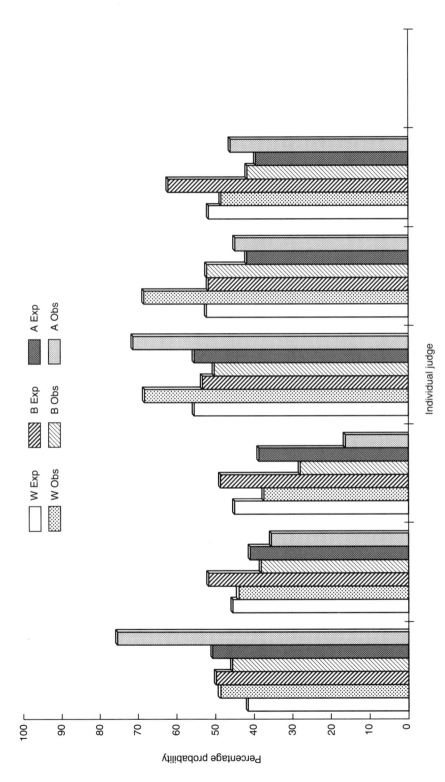

II. Judges relatively lenient with black offenders : 6 judges

Percentage probability

Individual judge

W Exp
W Obs

B Exp
B Obs

A Exp
A Obs

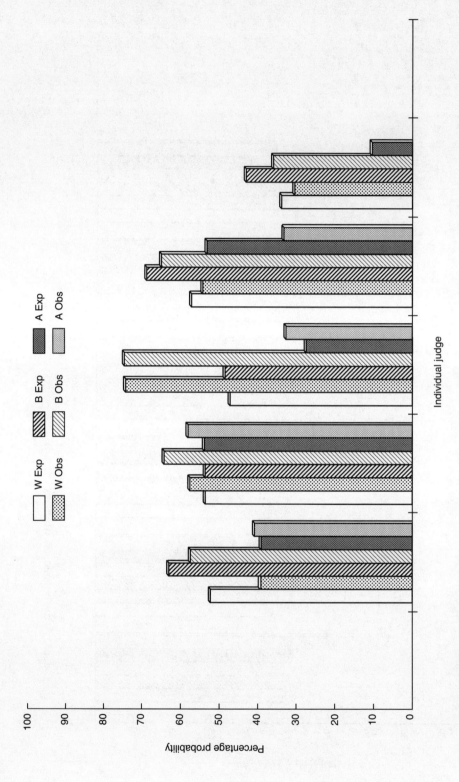

III. Judges relatively even-handed with black and white offenders : 5 judges

APPENDIX 6

PERCENTAGE OF MALE OFFENDERS WITH NO SOCIAL INQUIRY REPORTS ACCORDING TO TYPE OF PLEA

	Entered Guilty Plea	Pleaded Guilty at Trial to Lesser Charge	Changed Plea to Guilty at Trial	Pleaded Not Guilty
Whites	19	37	33	59
Blacks	29	45	49	63
Asians	25	56	50	73

Entered Guilty Plea:

w/b χ^2 = 21.53, 1 df, p< .0000
w/A X^2 = 5.7, 1 df, p< .017

Pleaded Guilty to Lesser Charge:

w/b χ^2 = 3.59, 1 df, p< .06
w/A χ^2 = 15.76, 1 df, p< .0001

Changed Plea to Guilty at Trial:

w/b χ^2 = 6.06, 1 df, p< .014
w/A χ^2 = 3.2, 1 df, p< .07

Pleaded Not Guilty:

w/b χ^2 = 0.66, 1 df, p< .42
w/A χ^2 = 5.56, 1 df, p< .02

APPENDIX 7

SIGNIFICANT DIFFERENCES IN PROPORTIONS OF FEMALES COMMITTED TO CUSTODY RELATED TO VARIOUS ATTRIBUTES COMPARISON OF WHITE AND BLACK OFFENDERS

	Whites	Blacks	Chi Square p<
Aged 17 – 20	17.9	42.1	.0513
Gave evidence against others	17.8	36.7	.0391
Co–defendant of same race	15.9	39.3	.0104
Low level of Violence*	7.7	55.6	.009
Victim was male	16.1	57.1	.0109
No Previous Offences	10.2	27.6	.0219
No Previous Convictions	10.2	27.6	.0219
No Previous Probation	10.6	30.0	.011
No Previous Parole	10.2	27.6	.0235

* This was the lowest score on the degree of violence scale.
See p 106 fn. 11, above.

APPENDIX 8

LOGISTIC MULTIPLE REGRESSION MODELS

ESTIMATED FOR THE CUSTODY/NON CUSTODY DECISION

TABLE 1A

TOTAL PROBABILITY OF CUSTODY SCORE FOR MALE SAMPLE (TPCS)

Outcome Variable: Custody

5185	Weighted Observations
2650	non custody = 0
2535	custody = 1

Discriminant power 75% (74% non custody, 76% custody)

VARIABLE	ORIGINAL				ADDING RACE			
	Coeff. (Standard Error)	Wald. Sig	R Statistic	Odds Multiplier	Coeff. (Standard Error)	Wald Sig	R Statistic	Odds Multiplier
Constant	.90 (.1712)	.0000			.88 (.1720)	.0000		
Appeared for sentence in Custody	1.26 (.1017)	.0000	.145	3.52	1.25 (.1019)	.0000	.144	3.50
No Breach of Court Order	-.54 (.1325)	.0000	-.045	.58	-.54 (.1326)	.0000	-.045	.58
Breach of SS/CSO/Other Combination	.71 (.2010)	.0004	.039	2.04	.70 (.2011)	.0005	.038	2.02
No. & Type of Offences Found Guilty		.0000	.143			.0000	.144	
One Charge	-.63 (.0596)	.0000	-.123	.54	-.63 (.0598)	.0000	-.124	.53
2 Same Type	-.38	.0000	-.052	.69	-.38	.0000	-.052	.69

	(.0817)				(.0818)			
2 Mixed type/3 Same Type	-.07 (.0844)	.4205	.000	.93	-.07 (.0844)	.4118	.000	.93
3 Mixed Type/4 Same Type	.37 (.1014)	.0003	.040	1.45	.37 (.1014)	.0003	.039	1.44
4 Mixed Type +	.70 (.0936)	.0000	.087	2.01	.71 (.0938)	.0000	.103	2.03
Total No. of Previous Proved Offences		.0000	.078			.0000	.073	
None	-.48 (.0730)	.0000	-.076	.62	-.46 (.0739)	.0000	-.072	.63
1-3	-.03 (.0701)	.6692	.000	.97	-.03 (.0702)	.6863	.000	.97
4-5	-.00 (.0992)	.9993	.000	1.00	-.00 (.0994)	.9905	.000	1.00
6-10	.30 (.0733)	.0001	.045	1.34	.29 (.0736)	.0001	.043	1.33
11 +	.22 (.0780)	.0058	.028	1.24	.20 (.0786)	.0098	.030	1.23
Previously Served a Custodial Sentence for the same type of Offence	.60 (.1013)	.0000	.067	1.81	.60 (.1015)	.0000	.068	1.82
Previously Served & Breached C.S.O.	.30 (.1201)	.0123	.024	1.35	.30 (.1202)	.0122	.024	1.35
Convicted Offence Type (12 Groups)		.0000	.204			.0000	.201	
Convicted of Sex Offence	.47 (.1802)	.0095	.026	1.60	.48 (.1807)	.0077	.027	1.62
Convicted of Blackmail/Robbery/Kidnap	1.38 (.1678)	.0000	.095	3.96	1.37 (.1685)	.0000	.094	3.93
Convicted of Violent/Serious Crime	2.03	.0000	.110	7.63	2.04	.0000	.110	7.72

	B (S.E.)	Sig.	R	Exp(B)	B (S.E.)	Sig.	R	Exp(B)
Convicted of Household Burglary	−.11 (.2160)	.4138	.000	.90	−.09 (.2161)	.4720	.000	.91
Convicted of Supplying Drugs	.96 (.1309)	.0000	.055	2.62	.88 (.1310)	.0000	.049	2.41
Convicted of Reckless Driving	.28 (.1975)	.1588	.000	1.33	.30 (.2022)	.1382	.005	1.35
Convicted of Other Offence	−2.61 (.2016)	.0000	−.054	.07	−2.64 (.2016)	.0000	−.054	.07
Convicted of Burglary/Theft	−.53 (.5478)	.0000	−.053	.59	−.52 (.5485)	.0000	−.051	.59
Convicted of Fraud/Receiving	−.88 (.1133)	.0000	−.074	.41	−.87 (.1134)	.0000	−.073	.42
Convicted of Minor Violent Offence	−.99 (.1365)	.0000	−.094	.37	−.98 (.1366)	.0000	−.083	.38
Convicted of Section 20 GBH	−.18 (.1363)	.2669	.000	.83	−.17 (.1367)	.3018	.000	.84
Convicted of Public Order Offence	.17 (.1629)	.1438	.004	1.19	.19 (.1634)	.1018	.011	1.21
Value of Property Stolen		.0000	.123			.0000	.125	
£0–£499	−.69 (.1180)	.0000	−.107	.50	−.70 (.1186)	.0000	−.107	.50
£500–£999	−.30 (.0760)	.0051	−.029	.74	−.30 (.0761)	.0051	−.029	.74
£1,000–£9,999	−.12 (.1083)	.1465	−.004	.89	−.12 (.1084)	.1335	−.006	.88
Over £10,000	1.12 (.1244)	.0000	.105	3.05	1.13 (.1245)	.0000	.123	3.08
Violence was due to a dispute	−.56 (.0814)	.0000	−.054	.57	−.56 (.0815)	.0000	−.054	.57

	(.1167)				(.1171)			
Appeared in Court for Trial – Pleaded Not Guilty	.51 (.1049)	.0000	.055	1.67	.50 (.1056)	.0000	.053	1.65
Not Triable Either-Way Case	.32 (.0958)	.0010	.035	1.37	.32 (.0963)	.0009	.035	1.38
Vulnerable Victim¹	.33 (.1049)	.0017	.033	1.39	.33 (.1050)	.0018	.033	1.39
Evidence of Continuing Impairment	.74 (.1763)	.0000	.047	2.09	.74 (.1766)	.0000	.046	2.09
Injuries Caused to Victim		.0000	.082			.0000	.082	
No Harm	-.62 (.1139)	.0000	-.062	.54	-.62 (.1141)	.0000	-.062	.54
Bruises	.17 (.0873)	.0571	.015	1.18	.16 (.0874)	.0702	.013	1.17
Stitches	.58 (.1070)	.0000	.061	1.78	.58 (.1072)	.0000	.062	1.78
Fracture/Internal Injuries	.33 (.1266)	.0095	.026	1.39	.33 (.1266)	.0085	.026	1.40
Black Offender	*****	****	****	****	.17 (.0977)	.0795	.012	1.19
Asian Offender	*****	****	****	****	-.13 (.1203)	.2911	.000	.88

¹ The victims were either female, children under 16 years of age or elderly people.

Appendix 8

TABLE 1B

LOGISTIC REGRESSION MODEL CONTROLLING BY TPCS, RACE AND
COURT[2]

Discriminant power 75% (74% non custody, 76% custody)

VARIABLE	Coeff. (Standard Error)	Wald Sig	R Statistic	Odds Multiplier
Constant	−2.55 (.0785)	.0000		
TPCS[3]	.05 (.0014)	.0000	.422	1.05
Black Offender at Birmingham	−.19 (.1116)	.0890	−.011	.83
Black Offender at the Dudley Courts	.74 (.1667)	.0000	.049	2.09
Black Offender at Coventry	.48 (.4096)	.2367	.000	1.62
Black Offender at Warwick	.62 (.5498)	.2569	.000	1.87
Black Offender at Stafford	1.63 (.8177)	.0466	.017	5.09
Asian Offender at Birmingham	−.26 (.1477)	.0753	−.013	.77
Asian Offender at the Dudley Courts	.05 (.2037)	.8142	.000	1.05
Asian Offender at Coventry	.74 (.4906)	.1333	.006	2.09
Asian Offender at Warwick	−.16 (.4091)	.6881	.000	.85
Asian Offender at Stafford	−.37 (1.5571)	.8113	.000	.69

[2] The default category against which black and Asian offenders are compared is all the whites in all courts, for whom the odds multiplier is 1.0.

[3] Expressed in percentage points.

TABLE 1C

LOGISTIC REGRESSION MODEL CONTROLLING BY TPCS, RACE AND COURT[4]

Discriminant power 75% (73% non custody, 77% custody)

VARIABLE	Coeff. (Standard Error)	Wald Sig	R Statistic	Odds Multiplier
Constant	−2.75 (.0921)	.0000		
TPCS[5]	.05 (.0014)	.0000	.421	1.05
Black Offender at Birmingham	.00 (.1194)	.9917	.000	1.00
Black Offender at the Dudley Courts	.93 (.1725)	.0000	.061	2.53
Black Offender at Coventry	.68 (.4123)	.1000	.010	1.97
Black Offender at Warwick	.82 (.5521)	.1393	.005	2.26
Black Offender at Stafford	1.82 (.8192)	.0264	.020	6.17
Asian Offender at Birmingham	−.07 (.1540)	.6493	.000	.93
Asian Offender at the Dudley Courts	.24 (.2086)	.2468	.000	1.27
Asian Offender at Coventry	.93 (.4930)	.0591	.015	2.54
Asian Offender at Warwick	.03 (.4117)	.9472	.000	1.03
Asian Offender at Stafford	−.18 (1.5602)	.9065	.000	.83
White Offender at the Dudley Courts	.26 (.0917)	.0044	.029	1.30
White Offender at Coventry	.81 (.1364)	.0000	.068	2.26

[4] The default category in this Table is white offenders at Birmingham, for whom the odds multiplier is 1.0.

[5] Expressed in percentage points.

VARIABLE	Coeff. (Standard Error)	Wald Sig	R Statistic	Odds Multiplier
White Offender at Warwick	.21 (.1547)	.1785	.000	1.23
White Offender at Stafford	.18 (.2523)	.4735	.000	1.20

TABLE 2

TOTAL PROBABILITY OF CUSTODY SCORE FOR MALE SAMPLE
EXCLUDING REMAND STATUS AS EXPLANATORY VARIABLE (TPCS(RC))

Outcome Variable: Custody

5185   Weighted Observations
2650   non custody = 0
2535   custody = 1

Discriminant power 74% (77% non custody, 71% custody)

VARIABLE	ORIGINAL				ADDING RACE			
	Coeff. (Standard Error)	Wald Sig	R Statistic	Odds Multiplier	Coeff. (Standard Error)	Wald Sig	R Statistic	Odds Multiplier
Constant	1.11 (.1670)	.0000			1.07 (.1678)	.0000		
No Breach of Court Order	-.53 (.1293)	.0000	-.045	.59	-.53 (.1293)	.0000	-.046	.59
Breach of SS/CSO/Other Combination	.75 (.1970)	.0001	.042	2.12	.73 (.1971)	.0002	.040	2.07
No. & Type of Offences Found Guilty		.0000	.172			.0000	.173	
One Charge	-.73 (.0582)	.0000	-.147	.48	-.74 (.0584)	.0000	-.148	.48

	ORIGINAL				ADDING RACE			
VARIABLE	Coeff. (Standard Error)	Wald Sig	R Statistic	Odds Multiplier	Coeff. (Standard Error)	Wald Sig	R Statistic	Odds Multiplier
2 Same Type	-.42 (.0796)	.0000	-.060	.66	-.42 (.0797)	.0000	-.061	.65
2 Mixed type/3 Same Type	-.09 (.0826)	.2882	.000	.92	-.09 (.0826)	.2803	.000	.91
3 Mixed Type/4 Same Type	.42 (.0984)	.0000	.048	1.52	.42 (.0985)	.0000	.047	1.52
4 Mixed Type +	.82 (.0907)	.0000	.105	2.27	.83 (.0908)	.0000	.106	2.29
Total No. of Previous Proved Offences		.0000	.100			.0000	.096	
None	-.59 (.0718)	.0000	-.096	.55	-.57 (.0726)	.0000	-.092	.56
1–3	-.07 (.0690)	.2787	.000	.93	-.07 (.0691)	.2798	.000	.93
4–5	.04 (.0969)	.6952	.000	1.04	.04 (.0971)	.7136	.000	1.04
6–10	.33 (.0718)	.0000	.051	1.39	.32 (.0721)	.0000	.050	1.38
11 +	.30 (.0761)	.0001	.044	1.35	.29 (.0766)	.0001	.042	1.34
Previously Served a Custodial Sentence for the same type of Offence	.70 (.0990)	.0000	.082	2.01	.71 (.0992)	.0000	.082	2.03
Previously Served & Breached C.S.O.	.23 (.1165)	.0514	.016	1.25	.23 (.1166)	.0501	.016	1.26

Convicted Offence Type (12 Groups)	Coef. (SE)	Sig.	Change	Exp(B)	Coef. (SE)	Sig.	Change	Exp(B)
Convicted Offence Type (12 Groups)		.0000	.220			.0000	.216	
Convicted of Sex Offence	.48 (.1764)	.0063	.028	1.62	.51 (.1772)	.0041	.029	1.66
Convicted of Blackmail/Robbery/Kidnap	1.40 (.1642)	.0000	.099	4.05	1.38 (.1648)	.0000	.098	3.98
Convicted of Violent/Serious Crime	2.26 (.2110)	.0000	.125	9.56	2.28 (.2113)	.0000	.126	9.76
Convicted of Household Burglary	-.01 (.1271)	.9184	.000	.99	.00 (.1272)	.9762	.000	1.00
Convicted of Supplying Drugs	.91 (.1957)	.0000	.052	2.49	.80 (.2005)	.0001	.044	2.22
Convicted of Reckless Driving	.34 (.1979)	.0859	.012	1.40	.36 (.1980)	.0710	.013	1.43
Convicted of Other Offence	-2.82 (.5489)	.0000	-.058	.06	-2.86 (.5499)	.0000	-.059	.06
Convicted of Burglary/Theft	-.60 (.1113)	.0000	-.062	.55	-.59 (.1115)	.0000	-.060	.56
Convicted of Fraud/Receiving	-1.01 (.1346)	.0000	-.087	.36	-1.00 (.1347)	.0000	-.086	.37
Convicted of Minor Violent Offence	-.93 (.1341)	.0000	-.080	.39	-.92 (.1345)	.0000	-.079	.40
Convicted of Section 20 GBH	-.18 (.1607)	.2709	.000	.84	-.16 (.1613)	.3300	.000	.85
Convicted of Public Order Offence	.16 (.1168)	.1625	.000	1.18	.19 (.1172)	.1050	.009	1.21
Value of Property Stolen		.0000	.126			.0000	.127	
£0–£499	-.71 (.0744)	.0000	-.111	.49	-.71 (.0744)	.0000	-.112	.49

VARIABLE	ORIGINAL				ADDING RACE			
	Coeff. (Standard Error)	Wald Sig	R Statistic	Odds Multiplier	Coeff. (Standard Error)	Wald Sig	R Statistic	Odds Multiplier
£500–£999	-.29 (.1057)	.0064	-.028	.75	-.29 (.1058)	.0063	-.028	.75
£1,000–£9,999	-.10 (.0797)	.2115	.000	.91	-.11 (.0798)	.1842	.000	.90
Over £10,000	1.09 (.1238)	.0000	.103	2.99	1.11 (.1240)	.0000	.104	3.03
Violence was due to a dispute	-.59 (.1152)	.0000	-.059	.55	-.60 (.1157)	.0000	-.059	.55
Appeared in Court for Trial – Pleaded Not Guilty	.55 (.1036)	.0000	.061	1.74	.53 (.1044)	.0000	.058	1.70
Not Triable Either–Way Case	.39 (.0941)	.0000	.046	1.48	.39 (.0946)	.0000	.046	1.48
Vulnerable Victim[6]	.37 (.1027)	.0004	.039	1.44	.36 (.1028)	.0004	.038	1.44
Evidence of Continuing Impairment	.70 (.1746)	.0001	.044	2.01	.70 (.1750)	.0001	.044	2.02
Injuries Caused to Victim		.0000	.080			.0000	.080	
No Harm	-.57 (.1117)	.0000	-.058	.57	-.58 (.1060)	.0000	-.059	.56
Bruises	.15	.0805	.012	1.16	.14	.0967	.010	1.15

[6] See *supra* footnote, note 1.

Stitches	.58	.0000	.063	1.79	.58	.0000	.063	1.79

	Coeff.				Coeff.			
Stitches	.58 (.0858)	.0000	.063	1.79	.58 (.0860)	.0000	.063	1.79
Fracture/Internal Injuries	.28 (.1057)	.0222	.021	1.33	.29 (.1060)	.0194	.022	1.34
	(.1244)				(.1245)			
Black Offender	*****	*****	*****	****	.24 (.0960)	.0124	.024	1.27
Asian Offender	*****	*****	*****	****	−.07 (.1176)	.5363	.000	.93

TABLE 3A

PROBABILITY OF CUSTODY SCORE BASED ON WHITE MALE SAMPLE (WPCS)

Outcome Variable: Custody

3745	Weighted Observations
1932	non custody =0
1813	custody = 1

Discriminant power for white offenders 75% (79% non custody, 70% custody)

VARIABLE	Coeff. (Standard Error)	Wald Sig	R Statistic	Odds Multiplier
Constant	.75 (.3354)	.0255		
Appeared for sentence in Custody	1.13 (.1196)	.0000	.130	3.10
No Breach of Court Order	−.74 (.1520)	.0000	−.064	.48
Breach of SS/CSO/Other Combination	.49 (.2328)	.0350	.022	1.63
No. & Type of Offences Found Guilty		.0000	.057	
One Charge	−.64 (.0703)	.0000	−.125	.53
2 Same Type	−.50 (.0956)	.0000	−.069	.61
2 Mixed type/3 Same Type	−.07 (.0977)	.4664	.000	.93
3 Mixed Type/4 Same Type	.48 (.1152)	.0000	.054	1.61
4 Mixed Type +	.73 (.1035)	.0000	.096	2.07
Total No. of Previous Proved Offences		.0002	.052	
None	−.30 (.0881)	.0006	−.044	.74
1–3	.07 (.0849)	.4199	.000	1.07
4–5	−.15 (.1220)	.2212	.000	.86

VARIABLE	Coeff. (Standard Error)	Wald Sig	R Statistic	Odds Multiplier
6–10	.30 (.0855)	.0005	.045	1.35
11 +	.08 (.0924)	.3614	.000	1.09
Previously Served a Custodial Sentence for the same type of Offence	.79 (.1188)	.0000	.090	2.20
Previously Served & Breached C.S.O.	.24 (.1351)	.0751	.015	1.27
Convicted Offence Type (12 Groups)		.0000	.167	
Convicted of Sex Offence	.59 (.3397)	.0809	.014	1.81
Convicted of Blackmail/Robbery/Kidnap	1.90 (.3647)	.0000	.070	6.66
Convicted of Violent/Serious Crime	1.87 (.3713)	.0000	.067	6.49
Convicted of Household Burglary	.17 (.3094)	.5838	.000	1.18
Convicted of Supplying Drugs	.89 (.4253)	.0361	.022	2.44
Convicted of Reckless Driving	.61 (.3567)	.0899	.013	1.83
Convicted of Other Offence	−5.12 (3.0332)	.0915	−.013	.01
Convicted of Burglary/Theft	−.10 (.3015)	.7383	.000	.90
Convicted of Fraud/Receiving	−.48 (.3142)	.1269	−.008	.62
Convicted of Minor Violent Offence	−.63 (.3143)	.0464	−.020	.53
Convicted of Section 20 GBH	−.25 (.3346)	.4564	.000	.78
Convicted of Public Order Offence	.55 (.3036)	.0709	.016	1.73
Value of Property Stolen		.0000	.123	
£0–£499	−.67 (.0853)	.0000	−.108	.51
£500–£999	−.25 (.1213)	.0379	−.021	.78

VARIABLE	Coeff. (Standard Error)	Wald Sig	R Statistic	Odds Multiplier
£1,000–£9,999	−.13 (.0913)	.1522	−.003	.88
Over £10,000	1.05 (.1382)	.0000	.104	2.87
Violence was due to a dispute	−.55 (.1397)	.0001	−.051	.57
Appeared in Court for Trial – Pleaded Not Guilty	.60 (.1360)	.0000	.058	1.82
Not Triable Either–Way Case	.54 (.1169)	.0000	.061	1.72
Vulnerable Victim[7]	.33 (.1282)	.0105	.030	1.39
Evidence of Continuing Impairment	.71 (.1995)	.0004	.045	2.03
Injuries Caused to Victim		.0000	.101	
No Harm	−.72 (.1450)	.0000	−.066	.49
Bruises	.21 (.1031)	.0441	.020	1.23
Stitches	.74 (.1292)	.0000	.077	2.09
Fracture/Internal Injuries	.42 (.1504)	.0054	.033	1.52

[7] See *supra* footnote, note 1.

TABLE 3B

LOGISTIC REGRESSION MODEL CONTROLLING BY THE WPCS AND RACE
Discriminant power for total sample 74% (78% non custody, 70% custody)

VARIABLE	Coeff. (Standard Error)	Wald Sig	R Statistic	Odds Multiplier
Constant	−2.45 (.0764)	.0000		
WPCS[8]	.05 (.0014)	.0000	.485	1.05
Black Offender	.17 (.0915)	.0686	.014	1.18
Asian Offender	−.25 (.1140)	.0310	−.019	.78

TABLE 4A

PROBABILITY OF CUSTODY SCORE BASED ON BLACK MALE SAMPLE (BPCS)

Outcome Variable: Custody

889	Weighted Observations
386	non custody =0
503	custody = 1

Discriminant power for black offenders 80% (76% non custody, 82% custody)

VARIABLE	Coeff. (Standard Error)	Wald Sig	R Statistic	Odds Multiplier
Constant	−4.97 (.8728)	.0000		
Convicted Offence Type (12 Groups)		.0000	.303	
Convicted of Sex Offence	1.58 (.5131)	.0021	.078	4.84
Convicted of Blackmail/Robbery/Kidnap	1.84 (.3215)	.0000	.159	6.32

[8] Expressed in percentage points.

VARIABLE	Coeff. (Standard Error)	Wald Sig	R Statistic	Odds Multiplier
Convicted of Violent/Serious Crime	2.96 (.4915)	.0000	.168	19.39
Convicted of Household Burglary	−.25 (.3470)	.4654	.000	.78
Convicted of Supplying Drugs	.72 (.2730)	.0080	.064	2.06
Convicted of Reckless Driving	.06 (.5831)	.9171	.000	1.06
Convicted of Other Offence	−3.68 (.9684)	.0001	−.101	.03
Convicted of Burglary/Theft	−1.25 (.2725)	.0000	−.125	.29
Convicted of Fraud/Receiving	−1.91 (.3692)	.0000	−.143	.15
Convicted of Minor Violent Offence	−1.24 (.2958)	.0000	−.113	.29
Convicted of Section 20 GBH	.89 (.3120)	.0044	.071	2.43
Convicted of Public Order Offence	.27 (.2847)	.3426	.000	1.31
Appeared for sentence in Custody	1.32 (.2489)	.0000	.146	3.74
Total No. of Previous Proved Offences[9]	.20 (.0492)	.0000	.112	1.23
Value of Property Stolen[10]	.61 (.1415)	.0000	.116	1.83
Breach of SS/CSO/Other Combination	1.48 (.3894)	.0001	.101	4.39
No. of Previous Offences of Similar Type[11]	.37 (.1085)	.0007	.089	1.45
Offender was not Provoked	.98 (.4012)	.0141	.058	2.68
No. of Incidents[12]	.59 (.2270)	.0092	.063	1.81

[9] Grouped in the following levels: None; One; 2; 3; 4–6; 7–10; 11 Plus.
[10] Grouped in the following levels: £0–499; £500–999; £1,000–9,999; Over £10,000.
[11] Grouped in the following levels: None; One; 2; 3 or more.
[12] Grouped in the following levels: None; One; 2 or more.

VARIABLE	Coeff. (Standard Error)	Wald Sig	R Statistic	Odds Multiplier
Minor Street Robbery	−1.49 (.5207)	.0043	−.071	.23
Appeared in Court for Trial – Pleaded Not Guilty	.53 (.2273)	.0197	.053	1.70
Violent Offence–No Harm Caused	−.62 (.2988)	.0394	−.043	.54
Previous CSO & Breached	.57 (.3286)	.0838	.029	1.77
Unemployed	.33 (.1987)	.0983	.025	1.39
Acting in a Group of Same Race	.41 (.2235)	.0634	.035	1.51

TABLE 4B

LOGISTIC REGRESSION MODEL CONTROLLING BY THE BPCS AND RACE

Discriminant power for total sample 72% (71% non custody, 74% custody)

VARIABLE	Coeff. (Standard Error)	Wald Sig	R Statistic	Odds Multiplier
Constant	−1.88 (.1003)	.0000		
BPCS[13]	.04 (.0012)	.0000	.443	1.04
White Offender	−.26 (.0871)	.0025	−.04	.77
Asian Offender	−.24 (.1302)	.0622	−.02	.78

[13] Expressed in percentage points.

Appendix 8

TABLE 5A

PROBABILITY OF CUSTODY SCORE BASED ON ASIAN MALE SAMPLE (APCS)

Outcome Variable: Custody

536	Weighted Observations
323	non custody =0
213	custody = 1

Discriminant power for white offenders 83% (87% non custody, 77% custody)

ORIGINAL VARIABLE	Coeff. (Standard Error)	Wald Sig	R Statistic	Odds Multiplier
Constant	−.35 (.6700)	.5990		
Convicted Offence Type (12 Groups)		.0000	.256	
Convicted of Sex Offence	1.00 (.7121)	.1603	.000	2.72
Convicted of Blackmail/Robbery/Kidnap	.73 (.3491)	.0354	.058	2.08
Convicted of Violent/Serious Crime	3.42 (.9679)	.0004	.121	30.70
Convicted of Household Burglary	1.00 (.5112)	.0516	.050	2.71
Convicted of Supplying Drugs	−.41 (.8984)	.6503	.000	.67
Convicted of Reckless Driving	.55 (.6372)	.3847	.000	1.74
Convicted of Other Offence	−.98 (1.1126)	.3808	.000	.38
Convicted of Burglary/Theft	−1.36 (.3503)	.0001	−.135	.26
Convicted of Fraud/Receiving	−1.12 (.3515)	.0014	−.107	.33
Convicted of Minor Violent Offence	−1.90 (.4877)	.0001	−.136	.15
Convicted of Section 20 GBH	.18 (.3648)	.6260	.000	1.19

ORIGINAL VARIABLE	Coeff. (Standard Error)	Wald Sig	R Statistic	Odds Multiplier
Convicted of Public Order Offence	−1.11 (.3751)	.0030	−.097	.33
Appeared for sentence in Custody	2.46 (.4432)	.0000	.200	11.72
Value of Property Stolen Over £10,000	1.69 (.4630)	.0003	.126	5.43
No. & Type of Offences Found Guilty		.0002	.136	
One Charge	−.76 (.1839)	.0000	−.145	.47
2 or 3 Same Type/3 Mixed Type	.12 (.1966)	.5553	.000	1.12
3 Mixed Type +	.65 (.2362)	.0062	.087	1.91
Total No. of Previous Convictions		.0249	.069	
None	−.44 (.1700)	.0097	−.081	.64
One	.10 (.1941)	.6035	.000	1.11
2 or more	.34 (.1864)	.0689	.043	1.40
Most Serious Charge Not Proceeded With	−.51 (.3077)	.0964	−.033	.60
2 or more Victims	.82 (.4817)	.0905	.035	2.26

Appendix 8

TABLE 5B

LOGISTIC REGRESSION MODEL CONTROLLING BY THE APCS AND RACE

Discriminant power for total sample 71% (72% non custody, 70% custody)

VARIABLE	Coeff. (Standard Error)	Wald Sig	R Statistic	Odds Multiplier
Constant	−1.85 (.1096)	.0000		
APCS[14]	.03 (.0011)	.0000	.418	1.04
Black Offender	.46 (.1265)	.0003	.044	1.59
White Offender	.17 (.1069)	.1080	.010	1.19

[14] Expressed in percentage points.

TABLE 6A

PROBABILITY OF CUSTODY SCORE BASED ON MALE SAMPLE FOR BIRMINGHAM CROWN COURT (BIRMPCS)

Outcome Variable: Custody

2642	Weighted Observations
1437	non custody = 0
1205	custody = 1

Discriminant power for Birmingham 77% (79% non custody, 75% custody)

VARIABLE	ORIGINAL				ADDING RACE			
	Coeff. (Standard Error)	Wald Sig	R Statistic	Odds Multiplier	Coeff. (Standard Error)	Wald Sig	R Statistic	Odds Multiplier
Constant	.59 (.2527)	.0195			.59 (.2539)	.0193		
Appeared for Sentence in Custody	1.39 (.1399)	.0000	.163	4.02	1.39 (.1405)	.0000	.162	4.01
No Breach of Court Order	-.42 (.1962)	.0313	-.027	.66	-.42 (.1963)	.0317	-.027	.66
Breach of SS/CSO/Other Combination	1.01 (.2731)	.0002	.057	2.75	1.01 (.2730)	.0002	.057	2.76
No. & Type of Offences Found Guilty		.0000	.159			.0000	.158	

VARIABLE	ORIGINAL				ADDING RACE			
	Coeff. (Standard Error)	Wald Sig	R Statistic	Odds Multiplier	Coeff. (Standard Error)	Wald Sig	R Statistic	Odds Multiplier
One Charge	−.68 (.0842)	.0000	−.132	.51	−.68 (.0845)	.0000	−.131	.51
2 Same Type	−.55 (.1224)	.0000	−.070	.58	−.55 (.1224)	.0000	−.070	.58
2 Mixed Type/3 Same Type	.26 (.1192)	.0313	.027	1.29	.26 (.1191)	.0313	.027	1.29
3 Mixed Type/4 Same Type	.24 (.1442)	.0947	.015	1.27	.24 (.1443)	.0986	.014	1.27
4 Mixed Type +	.73 (.1291)	.0000	.091	2.07	.73 (.1296)	.0000	.090	2.07
Total No. of Previous Proved Offences		.0000	.091			.0000	.087	
None	−.63 (.1074)	.0000	−.094	.53	−.62 (.1091)	.0000	−.091	.54
1–3	−.07 (.1037)	.4837	.000	.93	−.071 (.1039)	.4955	.000	.93
4–5	.17 (.1376)	.2065	.000	1.19	.17 (.1377)	.2038	.000	1.19
6–10	.15 (.1036)	.1441	.006	1.16	.15 (.1041)	.1625	.000	1.16
11 +	.37 (.1075)	.0005	.053	1.45	.37 (.1085)	.0007	.051	1.44

	Coefficient (SE)				Coefficient (SE)			
Previously Served a Custodial Sentence for the same type of Offence	.37 (.1415)	.0084	.037	1.45	.37 (.1416)	.0082	.037	1.45
Convicted Offence Type (12 Groups)		.0000	.191			.0000	.189	
Convicted of Sex Offence	.52 (.2726)	.0577	.021	1.68	.51 (.2731)	.0600	.021	1.67
Convicted of Blackmail/Robbery/Kidnap	1.29 (.2306)	.0000	.090	3.64	1.30 (.2324)	.0000	.090	3.66
Convicted of Violent/Serious Crime	2.22 (.3215)	.0000	.112	9.17	2.22 (.3216)	.0000	.112	9.23
Convicted of Household Burglary	-.16 (.1887)	.4095	.000	.86	-.16 (.1890)	.4052	.000	.85
Convicted of Supplying Drugs	.93 (.2472)	.0002	.058	2.53	.93 (.2558)	.0003	.055	2.52
Convicted of Reckless Driving	.15 (.2801)	.5807	.000	1.17	.16 (.2808)	.5767	.000	1.17
Convicted of Other Offence	-2.54 (.6759)	.0002	-.058	.08	-2.54 (.6761)	.0002	-.058	.08
Convicted of Burglary/Theft	-.66 (.1570)	.0000	-.066	.52	-.66 (.1571)	.0000	-.066	.52
Convicted of Fraud/Receiving	-1.02 (.1910)	.0000	-.085	.36	-1.01 (.1911)	.0000	-.085	.36
Convicted of Minor Violent Offence	-.67 (.1898)	.0004	-.054	.51	-.67 (.1901)	.0004	-.054	.51
Convicted of Section 20 GBH	-.15 (.2374)	.5377	.000	.86	-.15 (.2382)	.5273	.000	.86
Convicted of Public Order Offence	.08 (.1673)	.6200	.000	1.09	.08 (.1683)	.6282	.000	1.08

VARIABLE	ORIGINAL				ADDING RACE			
	Coeff. (Standard Error)	Wald Sig	R Statistic	Odds Multiplier	Coeff. (Standard Error)	Wald Sig	R Statistic	Odds Multiplier
Value of Property Stolen	.0000	.126	.0000	.126				
£0–£499	-.72 (.1178)	.0000	-.099	.48	-.72 (.1179)	.0000	-.099	.49
£500–£999	-.69 (.1738)	.0001	-.062	.50	-.69 (.1737)	.0001	-.062	.50
£1,000–£4,999	-.13 (.1390)	.3335	.000	.87	-.13 (.1392)	.3422	.000	.88
£5,000–£9,999	.26 (.2237)	.2459	.000	1.30	.26 (.2238)	.2532	.000	1.29
Over £10,000	1.29 (.2087)	.0000	.100	3.64	1.29 (.2089)	.0000	.100	3.64
Violence was due to a dispute	-.74 (.1704)	.0000	-.068	.48	-.74 (.1711)	.0000	-.067	.48
Appeared in Court for Trial – Pleaded Not Guilty	.57 (.1419)	.0001	.062	1.76	.57 (.1429)	.0001	.062	1.77
Not Triable Either-Way Case	.53 (.1326)	.0001	.062	1.70	.54 (.1333)	.0001	.063	1.71
Vulnerable Victim[15]	.40 (.1514)	.0089	.037	1.49	.40 (.1514)	.0088	.037	1.49

[15] See *supra* footnote, note 1.

	Coefficient (SE)				Coefficient (SE)			
Evidence of Continuing Impairment	.34 (.2787)	.2265	.000	1.40	.33 (.2796)	.2418	.000	1.39
Injuries caused to Victim		.0000	.098			.0000	.098	
No Harm	-.93 (.1708)	.0000	-.087	.40	-.93 (.1711)	.0000	-.087	.39
Bruises	.33 (.1335)	.0129	.034	1.39	.33 (.1339)	.0146	.033	1.39
Stitches	.66 (.1547)	.0000	.066	1.93	.66 (.1549)	.0000	.067	1.94
Fracture/Internal Injuries	.25 (.2036)	.2222	.000	1.28	.25 (.2037)	.2221	.000	1.28
Black Offender	*****	*****	*****	****	-.00 (.1347)	.9812	.000	1.00
Asian Offender	*****	*****	*****	****	-.10 (.1686)	.5720	.000	.91

Appendix 8

TABLE 6B

LOGISTIC REGRESSION MODEL CONTROLLING BY THE BIRMPCS, RACE AND COURT

Discriminant power for Total 75% (80% non custody, 70% custody)

VARIABLE	Coeff. (Standard Error)	Wald Sig	R Statistic	Odds Multiplier
Constant	−2.04 (.0836)	.0000		
BIRMPCS[16]	.05 (.0014)	.0000	.414	1.05
Black Offender	.21 (.0925)	.0213	.021	1.24
Asian Offender	−.08 (.1156)	.4721	.000	.92
Courts		.0000	.083	
Dudley Courts	.01 (.0750)	.8464	.000	1.01
Coventry	.43 (.1053)	.0000	.046	1.54
Warwick	−.08 (.1154)	.4898	.000	.92
Stafford	.02 (.1838)	.9242	.000	1.02

[16] Expressed in percentage points.

TABLE 7

PROBABILITY OF CUSTODY SCORE FOR WOMEN SAMPLE (FPCS)

Outcome Variable: Custody

433   Weighted Observations
329   not Custody = 0
104   Custody = 1

Discriminant power 83% (79% non custody, 87% custody)

VARIABLE	ORIGINAL				ADDING RACE[17]			
	Coeff. (Standard Error)	Wald Sig	R Statistic	Odds Multiplier	Coeff. (Standard Error)	Wald Sig	R Statistic	Odds Multiplier
Constant	-1.78 (.4515)	.0001			-1.72 (.4628)	.0002		
Appeared for sentence in Custody	2.49 (.5467)	.0000	.198	12.05	2.47 (.5662)	.0000	.240	11.79
2 or more Offences taken into consideration	1.24 (.4847)	.0106	.097	3.45	1.32 (.4918)	.0074	.132	3.73
Court Order Breached	1.09 (.4287)	.0111	.097	2.97	1.05 (.4332)	.0158	.114	2.84

[17] Excludes 14 Asian Observations.

VARIABLE	ORIGINAL				ADDING RACE			
	Coeff. (Standard Error)	Wald Sig	R Statistic	Odds Multiplier	Coeff. (Standard Error)	Wald Sig	R Statistic	Odds Multiplier
Found Guilty of 2 or more Offences of Same Type	.71 (.3325)	.0340	.072	2.02	.61 (.3436)	.0740	.064	1.85
Total No. of Previous Proved Offences								
None	−.73 (.2626)	.0054	−.110	.48	−.70 (.2698)	.0096	−.126	.50
1	−.61 (.3829)	.1138	−.032	.55	−.48 (.3862)	.2159	.000	.62
2–3	.64 (.3188)	.0444	.065	1.90	.42 (.3405)	.2145	.000	1.53
4 +	.69 (.2567)	.0068	.106	2.00	.75 (.2593)	.0036	.148	2.13
Resident in Private Rented House/Flat/Room or NFA	1.03 (.3842)	.0076	.104	2.79	.95 (.3948)	.0161	.113	2.59
Value of Property Stolen		.0011	.145			.0012	1.83	
£0–£499	−1.10 (.3272)	.0008	−.140	.33	−1.12 (.3354)	.0008	−.176	.33
£500–£4,999	−.69 (.3194)	.0316	−.074	.50	−.72 (.3301)	.0298	−.096	.49

£5,000–£9,999	.84 (.4381)	.0561	.059	2.31	.90 (.4427)	.0423	.085	2.46
Over £10,000	.95 (.4142)	.0219	.083	2.58	.94 (.4287)	.0283	.098	2.56
Weapon Used to Injure	1.17 (.5242)	.0255	.079	3.23	1.09 (.5276)	.0387	.088	2.98
Convicted Offence Type		.0000	.217			.0000	.283	
Convicted of Violent/Serious Crime	1.70 (.4433)	.0001	.163	5.48	1.76 (.4415)	.0001	.216	5.80
Convicted of Robbery	1.55 (.4540)	.0006	.143	4.73	1.72 (.4777)	.0003	.193	5.59
Convicted of Household Burglary	-.39 (.4076)	.3381	.000	.68	-.35 (.4152)	.4054	.000	.71
Convicted of Supplying Drugs	1.33 (.7368)	.0708	.052	3.79	1.32 (.7371)	.0728	.064	3.75
Convicted of Other Offence	-2.73 (.9909)	.0059	-.108	.07	-2.64 (.9947)	.0079	-.131	.07
Convicted of Fraud/Receiving	-.47 (.4444)	.2867	.000	.62	-.50 (.4590)	.2717	.000	.60
Convicted of Minor Violent Offence	-.97 (.5956)	.1045	-.037	.38	-.83 (.5972)	.1630	.000	.43
Convicted of Section 20 GBH	-.02 (.5610)	.9664	.000	.98	-.48 (.6470)	.4617	.000	.62
Black Offender	****	****	****	****	-.09 (.3865)	.8254	.000	.92

TABLE 8

PROBABILITY OF CUSTODY SCORE FOR TOTAL SAMPLE (MFPCS)

Outcome Variable: Custody

5619 Weighted Observations
2979 non custody = 0
2640 custody = 1

Discriminant power 75% (81% non custody, 69% custody)

VARIABLE	ORIGINAL				ADDING GENDER				ADDING GENDER AND RACE			
	Coeff. (Stand. Error)	Wald Sig	R Statistic	Odds Multiplier	Coeff. (Stand. Error)	Wald Sig	R Statistic	Odds Multiplier	Coeff. (Stand. Error)	Wald Sig	R Statistic	Odds Multiplier
Constant	.91 (.1618)	.0000			1.94 (.2270)	.0000			.97 (.1648)	.0000		
Appeared for sentence in Custody	1.30 (.0990)	.0000	.148	3.68	1.29 (.0995)	.0000	.171	3.63	1.28 (.0996)	.0000	.170	3.60
No Breach of Court Order	-.53 (.1251)	.0000	-.045	.59	-.58 (.1265)	.0000	-.058	.56	-.58 (.1267)	.0000	-.058	.56
Breach of SS/CSO/ Other Combination	.75 (.1914)	.0001	.041	2.12	.74 (.1930)	.0001	.047	2.09	.73 (.1933)	.0002	.047	2.07
No. & Type of Offences Found Guilty		.0000	.142			.0000	.170			.0000	.171	
One Charge	-.62 (.0574)	.0000	-.121	.54	-.63 (.0578)	.0000	-.144	.53	-.64 (.0579)	.0000	-.145	.53

2 Same Type	−.37 (.0785)	.0000	−.051	.69	−.38 (.0790)	.0000	−.060	.69	−.38 (.0791)	.0000	−.060	.69
2 Mixed type/3 Same Type	−.08 (.0816)	.3390	.000	.92	−.09 (.0821)	.2516	.000	.91	−.10 (.0821)	.2407	.000	.91
3 Mixed Type/4 Same Type	.38 (.0972)	.0001	.041	1.46	.39 (.0977)	.0001	.050	1.47	.39 (.0977)	.0001	.049	1.47
4 Mixed Type +	.68 (.0885)	.0000	.086	1.98	.71 (.0897)	.0000	.104	2.04	.72 (.0898)	.0000	.105	2.06
Total No. of Previous Proved Offences		.0000	.088			.0000	.093			.0000	.089	
None	−.54 (.0694)	.0000	−.086	.59	−.49 (.0700)	.0000	−.092	.61	−.48 (.0709)	.0000	−.088	.62
1–3	−.04 (.0672)	.5265	.000	.96	−.03 (.0676)	.6142	.000	.97	−.03 (.0677)	.6234	.000	.97
4–5	.03 (.0953)	.7272	.000	1.03	.04 (.0957)	.7074	.000	1.04	.04 (.0959)	.6951	.000	1.04
6–10	.31 (.0711)	.0000	.046	1.36	.28 (.0714)	.0001	.050	1.33	.28 (.0717)	.0001	.048	1.32
11 +	.24 (.0760)	.0017	.032	1.27	.21 (.0897)	.0067	.031	1.23	.20 (.0769)	.0099	.029	1.22
Previously Served a Custodial Sentence for the same type of Offence	.59 (.0990)	.0000	.066	1.81	.58 (.0994)	.0000	.075	1.79	.58 (.0995)	.0000	.076	1.79
Previously Served & Breached C.S.O.	.32 (.1187)	.0062	.027	1.38	.30 (.1189)	.0119	.028	1.35	.30 (.1190)	.0118	.028	1.35
Convicted Offence Type (12 Groups)		.0000	.205			.0000	.238			.0000	.235	
Convicted of Sex Offence	.56 (.1739)	.0012	.033	1.76	.49 (.1747)	.0052	.032	1.63	.50 (.1754)	.0041	.033	1.65

VARIABLE	ORIGINAL				ADDING GENDER				ADDING GENDER AND RACE			
	Coeff. (Stand. Error)	Wald Sig	R Statistic	Odds Multiplier	Coeff. (Stand. Error)	Wald Sig	R Statistic	Odds Multiplier	Coeff. (Stand. Error)	Wald Sig	R Statistic	Odds Multiplier
Convicted of Blackmail/Robbery/Kidnap	1.35 (.1597)	.0000	.094	3.84	1.34 (.1601)	.0000	.110	3.83	1.34 (.1610)	.0000	.109	3.83
Convicted of Violent/Serious Crime	1.84 (.1896)	.0000	.109	6.31	1.90 (.1916)	.0000	.130	6.66	1.91 (.1918)	.0000	.131	6.76
Convicted of Household Burglary	−.11 (.1264)	.3793	.000	.89	−.13 (.1267)	.2994	.000	.88	−.12 (.1268)	.3504	.000	.89
Convicted of Supplying Drugs	.96 (.1877)	.0000	.056	2.62	.97 (.1896)	.0000	.066	2.65	.90 (.1942)	.0000	.059	2.46
Convicted of Reckless Driving	.30 (.1982)	.1331	.006	1.35	.25 (.1983)	.2009	.000	1.29	.27 (.1983)	.1787	.000	1.31
Convicted of Other Offence	−2.47 (.4780)	.0000	−.056	.08	−2.41 (.4779)	.0000	−.064	.09	−2.44 (.4785)	.0000	−.065	.09
Convicted of Burglary/Theft	−.52 (.1077)	.0000	−.053	.59	−.53 (.1080)	.0000	−.062	.59	−.52 (.1081)	.0000	−.061	.60
Convicted of Fraud/Receiving	−.90 (.1278)	.0000	−.078	.41	−.83 (.1286)	.0000	−.084	.43	−.82 (.1287)	.0000	−.083	.44
Convicted of Minor Violent Offence	−1.00 (.1312)	.0000	−.085	.37	−1.00 (.1315)	.0000	−.100	.37	−.99 (.1319)	.0000	−.099	.37
Convicted of Section 20 GBH	−.16 (.1556)	.2991	.000	.85	−.17 (.1560)	.2816	.000	.85	−.16 (.1566)	.2943	.000	.85

Convicted of Public Order Offence	.15 (.1122)	.1831	.000	1.16	.12 (.1129)	.2865	.000	1.13	.14 (.1134)	.2258	.000	1.15
Value of Property Stolen		.0000	.128			.0000	.147			.0000	.148	
£0–£499	-.71 (.0732)	.0000	-.108	.49	-.69 (.0736)	.0000	-.124	.50	-.70 (.0737)	.0000	-.125	.50
£500–£999	-.33 (.1053)	.0020	-.031	.72	-.33 (.1058)	.0021	-.036	.72	-.32 (.1058)	.0022	-.036	.72
£1,000–£9,999	-.12 (.0780)	.1254	-.007	.89	-.11 (.0784)	.1666	.000	.89	-.11 (.0785)	.1508	-.003	.89
Over £10,000	1.15 (.1184)	.0000	.109	3.16	1.13 (.1188)	.0000	.125	3.09	1.13 (.1188)	.0000	.126	3.11
Violence was due to a dispute	-.60 (.1133)	.0000	-.058	.55	-.60 (.1136)	.0000	-.068	.55	-.60 (.1140)	.0000	-.068	.55
Appeared in Court for Trial – Pleaded Not Guilty	.50 (.1008)	.0000	.053	1.64	.49 (.1012)	.0000	.062	1.64	.48 (.1019)	.0000	.060	1.61
Not Triable Either – Way Case	.25 (.0928)	.0074	.026	1.28	.27 (.0932)	.0034	.034	1.28	.28 (.0936)	.0031	.035	1.32
Vulnerable Victim[18]	.24 (.0996)	.0145	.023	1.28	.29 (.1005)	.0034	.034	1.28	.29 (.1006)	.0036	.034	1.34
Evidence of Continuing Impairment	.66 (.1683)	.0001	.042	1.94	.68 (.1684)	.0001	.050	1.94	.68 (.1690)	.0001	.050	1.97
Injuries Caused to Victim		.0000	.085			.0000	.098			.0000	.098	
No Harm	-.58 (.1106)	.0000	-.057	.56	-.59 (.1110)	.0000	-.068	.56	-.60 (.1112)	.0000	-.069	.55

[18] See *supra* footnote, note 1.

VARIABLE	ORIGINAL				ADDING GENDER				ADDING GENDER AND RACE			
	Coeff. (Stand. Error)	Wald Sig	R Statistic	Odds Multiplier	Coeff. (Stand. Error)	Wald Sig	R Statistic	Odds Multiplier	Coeff. (Stand. Error)	Wald Sig	R Statistic	Odds Multiplier
Bruises	.20 (.0854)	.0186	.021	1.22	.20 (.0856)	.0222	.024	1.22	.19 (.0857)	.0275	.023	1.21
Stitches Needed	.58 (.1037)	.0000	.061	1.78	.58 (.1039)	.0000	.072	1.79	.59 (.1042)	.0000	.073	1.80
Fracture/Internal Injuries	.32 (.1217)	.0076	.026	1.38	.31 (.1220)	.0109	.028	1.36	.32 (.1221)	.0095	.029	1.37
Female Offender	******	*****	*****	****	-.94	.0000	-.085	.39	******	*****	*****	****
Black Male Offender	******	*****	*****	****	******	*****	*****	****	.17 (.0972)	.0794	.014	1.19
Asian Male Offender	******	*****	*****	****	******	*****	*****	****	-.11 (.1199)	.3780	.000	.90
Black Female Offender	******	*****	*****	****	******	*****	*****	****	-1.17 (.3245)	.0003	-.044	.31
White Female Offender	******	*****	*****	****	******	*****	*****	****	-.91 (.1639)	.0000	-.072	.40

APPENDIX 9

LOGISTIC MULTIPLE REGRESSION MODEL

ESTIMATED FOR THE REMAND STATUS

TABLE 1

PROBABILITY OF APPEARING FOR SENTENCE IN CUSTODY SCORE FOR MALE SAMPLE (PRCS)

Outcome Variable: remand status

5185	Weighted Observations
4105	bail = 0
1081	custody = 1

Discriminant power 81% (93% bail, 34% custody)

VARIABLE	ORIGINAL				ADDING RACE			
	Coeff. (Standard Error)	Wald Sig Error)	R Statistic	Odds Multiplier	Coeff. (Standard	Wald Sig	R Statistic	Odds Multiplier
Constant	-3.12 (.1628)	.0000			-3.24 (.1665)	.0000		
Type of Court Order Breached		.0099	.032			.0083	.037	
No Breach	-.14 (.0797)	.0850	-.014	.87	-.14 (.0797)	.0731	-.017	.87
Breach of Conditional Discharge	-.29 (.1626)	.0767	-.015	.75	-.29 (.1627)	.0764	-.016	.75
Breach of Probation Order	.23 (.1278)	.0773	.015	1.25	.25 (.1282)	.0502	.021	1.29
Breach of SS/CSO/Other Combination	.20 (.1184)	.0924	.013	1.22	.18 (.1187)	.1291	.008	1.20

	Coeff. (SE)	Sig.			Coeff. (SE)	Sig.		
Resident in Private Rented Room/Hostel/NFA	.72 (.1274)	.0000	.076	2.06	.73 (.1275)	.0000	.085	2.08
Total No. of Court Appearances Resulting in Custody		.0000	.196			.0000	.220	
None	-.26 (.0684)	.0001	-.050	.77	-.27 (.0685)	.0001	-.056	.76
One	.44 (.0749)	.0000	.078	1.55	.45 (.0754)	.0000	.088	1.57
2 or more	.80 (.0639)	.0000	.170	2.22	.83 (.0653)	.0000	.193	2.30
No Previous Convictions	-.97 (.1023)	.0000	-.129	.38	-1.01 (.1042)	.0000	-.146	.36
Appeared at Crown Court for Plea	.26 (.0891)	.0030	.036	1.30	.29 (.0895)	.0013	.044	1.33
Charged with Sex Offence	.74 (.2311)	.0014	.039	2.09	.77 (.2329)	.0009	.046	2.16
Charged with Blackmail/Robbery/Kidnap	1.36 (.1202)	.0000	.154	3.90	1.30 (.1216)	.0000	.162	3.67
Charged with Violent/Serious Crime	1.39 (.1168)	.0000	.163	4.03	1.39 (.1170)	.0000	.179	4.00
Charged with Household Burglary	.63 (.1135)	.0000	.074	1.89	.65 (.1140)	.0000	.084	1.92
Charged with Reckless Driving	.59 (.2427)	.0150	.027	1.80	.61 (.2431)	.0122	.032	1.84
Charged with Other Offence	-5.19 (4.5798)	.2571	.000	.01	-5.26 (4.5517)	.2474	.000	.01
Charged with Fraud/Receiving	-.68 (.2131)	.0014	-.039	.51	-.70 (.2141)	.0010	-.045	.50

VARIABLE	ORIGINAL Coeff. (Standard Error)	Wald Sig Error	R Statistic	Odds Multiplier	ADDING RACE Coeff. (Standard	Wald Sig	R Statistic	Odds Multiplier
Charged with Section 20 GBH	.36 (.2230)	.1060	.011	1.43	.37 (.2232)	.1000	.013	1.44
Unsettled Life Style	.69 (.0826)	.0000	.114	2.00	.72 (.0831)	.0000	.130	2.05
Regularly Unemployed	.76 (.1259)	.0000	.080	2.13	.75 (.1262)	.0000	.088	2.11
Black Offender	*****	****	****	****	.27 (.0999)	.0071	.035	1.31
Asian Offender	*****	****	****	****	.48 (.1394)	.0005	.048	1.62

APPENDIX 10

ORDINARY LEAST SQUARES MODELS

ESTIMATED FOR 'SEVERITY SCALE'

AND LENGTH OF CUSTODY

TABLE 1

SEVERITY SCALE FOR ADULT MALES

Outcome Variable: 'Severity Scale' for adult males in the following 17 levels:

1.	Other Sentence
2.	Fine & Compensation £1–100
3.	Fine & Compensation £101–249
4.	Fine & Compensation £250–499
5.	Fine & Compensation £500–999
6.	Fine & Compensation £1,000 or more
7.	Probability Length 1–18 months
8.	Probability Length 19 months or more
9.	CSO Length 1–125 hours
10.	CSO Length 126 hours or more
11.	Suspended Sentence Length 1–9 months
12.	Suspended Sentence Length 10 months or more
13.	Imprisonment Length 1–6 months
14.	Imprisonment Length 7–12 months
15.	Imprisonment Length 13–18 months
16.	Imprisonment Length 19–36 months
17.	Imprisonment Length 37 months or more

3385   Weighted Observations

VARIABLE	ORIGINAL Adj. R² = .40			ADDING RACE Adj. R² = .40		
	Coeff.	Beta	Sig T	Coeff.	Beta	Sig T
Constant	3.13		.0000	3.11		.0000
Appeared in Court for Trial–Pleaded Not Guilty	.48	.04	.0038	.44	.04	.0088
Appeared for sentence in Custody	1.14	.10	.0000	1.14	.10	.0000
Total No. of Offences Charged[19]	.24	.05	.0350	.25	.05	.0247
Most Serious Charge Not Proceeded with	-.74	-.07	.0000	-.74	-.07	.0000
Breached Court Order	.57	.05	.0014	.58	.05	.0010
No. of Offences taken into consideration[20]	.31	.04	.0085	.31	.04	.0071
No. & Type of Offences Found Guilty[21]	.18	.10	.0000	.20	.11	.0000
Drugs were confiscated	.89	.05	.0202	.76	.04	.0000
Violence was due to a dispute	-.56	-.05	.0044	-.61	-.06	.0021
Victim Required Stitches	.57	.05	.0096	.61	.05	.0055
Value of Property Stolen[22]	.54	.15	.0000	.55	.16	.0000
Offence was Planned/Premeditated	.92	.11	.0000	.93	.11	.0000
No. of Individual Victims[23]	.95	.05	.0006	.89	.05	.0014
Evidence of committing a crime since charged	.34	.03	.0483	***	***	****
Did not give evidence against other(s)	.40	.04	.0076	.41	.04	.0056
Did not Express Remorse/Regret	.28	.03	.0236	.30	.03	.0161
No evidence that Offender was provoked	.87	.06	.0002	.84	.06	.0003
No. of Previous Offences of Violent Disorder[24]	.99	.04	.0015	.96	.04	.0056
No. of Previous Offences of Criminal Damage[25]	***	***	****	.14	.04	.0313
No. of Previous Offences of Household Burglary	.09	.05	.0089	.08	.04	.0137
No. of Previous Offences of similar type[26]	.25	.05	.0146	.25	.05	.0164
Total No. of Previous Offences[27]	.20	.11	.0000	.17	.10	.0000

Total No. of months Prev. Sent. to Custody for Same Type[28]	.17	.06	.0016	.18	.07	.0011
Most serious previous sentence – C.S.O.	.98	.04	.0025	1.01	.04	.0020
Not Triable Either-Way Case	1.52	.16	.0000	1.49	.16	.0000
Magistrates Committed for Trial	1.10	.13	.0000	1.10	.13	.0000
Degrees of Violence[29]	.54	.13	.0000	.54	.12	.0000
Convicted of Sex against Female	2.24	.11	.0000	2.23	.11	.0000
Convicted of Blackmail/Robbery/Kidnap	2.99	.16	.0000	2.92	.15	.0000
Convicted of Severe Violence	4.35	.25	.0000	4.31	.24	.0000
Convicted of Household Burglary	1.48	.10	.0000	1.54	.10	.0000
Convicted of Drugs	2.66	.12	.0000	2.55	.12	.0000
Convicted of Reckless Driving	1.78	.07	.0000	1.80	.07	.0000
Convicted of Others	-2.74	-.09	.0000	-2.75	-.09	.0000
Convicted of Public Order	.88	.06	.0001	.86	.06	.0001
Convicted of Section 20 GBH	2.39	.15	.0000	2.35	.15	.0000
Victim was Asian	-1.18	-.06	.0001	-1.14	-.06	.0001
Black Offender	*****	***	****	.42	.04	.0094
Asian Offender	*****	***	****	-.22	-.01	.2694

[19] Grouped in the following levels: 1–2; 3; 4 or more.
[20] Grouped in the following levels: None; One; 2 or more.
[21] Grouped in the following levels: One Charge; 2 of Same Type; 2 of Mixed Type; 3 of Same Type; 3 of Mixed Type; 4 of Same Type; 4 of Mixed Type; 5 or more of Same Type; 5 or more of Mixed Type.
[22] Grouped in the following levels: £0–499; £500–999; £1,000–4,999; £5,000–9,999; Over £10,000.
[23] Grouped in the following levels: 0–2; 3 or more.
[24] Grouped in the following levels: None; One; 2 or more.
[25] Grouped in the following levels: None; One; 2; 3 or more.
[26] Grouped in the following levels: None; One; 2 or more.
[27] Grouped in the following levels: None; One; 2; 3; 4–5; 6–10; 11 or more.
[28] Grouped in the following levels: None; 1–6 months; 7–12 months; 13–24 months; 25 months or more.
[29] Weighted by injuries caused to the victims, type of weapon used and whether violence used in main and/or lesser offence.

TABLE 2

SEVERITY SCALE FOR MALES UNDER AGE 21

Outcome Variable: 'Severity Scale' for young adult males in the following 16 levels:

1. Other Sentence
2. Fine & Compensation £1–100
3. Fine & Compensation £101–249
4. Fine & Compensation £250–499
5. Fine & Compensation £500–999
6. Fine & Compensation £1,000 or more
7. Probability Length 1–18 months
8. Probability Length 19 months or more
9. CSO Length 1–125 hours
10. CSO Length 126 hours or more
11. Attendance Centre Order
12. Detention YOI 1–6 months
13. Detention YOI 7–12 months
14. Detention YOI 13–18 months
15. Detention YOI 19–36 months
16. Detention YOI 37 months or more

1798   Weighted Observations

VARIABLE	Adj. R² = .43 ORIGINAL			Adj. R² = .43 ADDING RACE		
	Coeff.	Beta	Sig T	Coeff.	Beta	Sig T
Constant	.78	.2117	.85	.1751		
Pros. Dropped Most Ser. Chg–Pleaded Guilty to Lesser Chg	-1.04	-.10	.0001	-1.04	-.10	.0001
Pleaded Guilty to Most Serious Charge	-.52	-.06	.0195	-.53	-.06	.0186
Appeared for sentence in Custody	1.11	.11	.0000	1.12	.11	.0000
Breached Court Order	1.10	.09	.0000	1.10	.09	.0000
No. & Type of Offences Found Guilty[30]	.21	.14	.0000	.21	.14	.0000
Sole Offender	1.25	.14	.0000	1.25	.14	.0000
Offender played Leading Role	1.43	.13	.0000	1.43	.13	.0000
Offender played Equal Role	1.18	.13	.0000	1.18	.14	.0000
Victim Required Stitches	.60	.06	.0201	.59	.05	.0230
Victim suffered Internal Injuries	2.99	.08	.0001	3.01	.08	.0000
Lesser Offence Involved Theft of Property	.73	.04	.0285	.73	.04	.0298
Stolen Property Cash/Household/Personal	.42	.05	.0221	.43	.05	.0203
Value of Property Stolen[31]	.72	.18	.0000	.72	.18	.0000
Offence was Planned/Premeditated	.49	.06	.0042	.50	.06	.0035
No. of Individual Victims[32]	.89	.06	.0023	.89	.06	.0023
Major Injured Party–Family	-1.37	-.04	.0198	-1.38	-.04	.0191
Major Injured Party–Stranger	.51	.06	.0061	.52	.06	.0055
Victim was Asian	-.58	-.04	.0420	-.53	-.03	.0726

[30] Grouped in the following levels: One Charge; 2 of Same Type; 2 of Mixed Type; 3 of Same Type; 3 of Mixed Type; 4 of Same Type; 4 of Mixed Type; 5 or more of Same Type; 5 or more of Mixed Type.

[31] Grouped in the following levels: £0–499; £500–999; £1,000–4,999; £5,000–9,999; Over £10,000.

[32] Grouped in the following levels: 0–2; 3 or more.

VARIABLE	Adj. R² = .43 ORIGINAL			Adj. R² = .43 ADDING RACE		
	Coeff.	Beta	Sig T	Coeff.	Beta	Sig T
No Children	.38	.04	.0355	.38	.04	.0349
No Evidence of Efforts to Reform	.63	.05	.0067	.62	.05	.0072
Did not Express Remorse/Regret	.61	.07	.0002	.60	.07	.0002
No evidence that Offender was provoked	1.14	.06	.0019	1.10	.06	.0031
Total No. of Previous Offences[33]	.23	.13	.0000	.22	.12	.0000
Prev. Sent. to Custody for Same Type of Offence	.73	.07	.0022	.73	.06	.0024
Regularly Unemployed	1.12	.11	.0000	1.14	.11	.0000
Seriousness of Drug Offence[34]	1.67	.06	.0006	1.68	.06	.0006
Convicted of Sex against Female	3.18	.11	.0000	3.17	.11	.0000
Convicted of Blackmail/Robbery/Kidnap	3.55	.29	.0000	3.57	.29	.0000
Convicted of Severe Violence	5.28	.25	.0000	5.30	.25	.0000
Convicted of Others	-3.28	-.05	.0064	-3.22	-.05	.0075
Convicted of Public Order	1.39	.12	.0000	1.38	.12	.0000
Convicted of Fraud/Reckless Driving	-1.43	-.08	.0001	-1.41	-.07	.0001
Convicted of Section 20 GBH	2.24	.15	.0000	2.23	.15	.0000
Black Offender	*****	****	*****	-.06	-.01	.7846
Asian Offender	*****	****	*****	-.20	-.02	.4201

[33] Grouped in the following levels: None; One; 2; 3; 4–5; 6–10; 11 or more.

[34] Weighted by small, medium or large scale of supplying drugs and whether in main and/or lesser offence.

TABLE 3

LENGTH OF IMPRISONMENT FOR ADULT MALE OFFENDERS (MONTHS)

Outcome Variable: length of imprisonment

1649   Weighted Observations

VARIABLE	ORIGINAL Adj. R² = .51			ADDING RACE Adj. R² = .51		
	Coeff.	Beta	Sig T	Coeff.	Beta	Sig T
Constant	-11.12		.0000	-11.56		.0000
Appeared in Court for Trial–Pleaded Not Guilty	3.11	-.04	.0116	-.08	.05	.0127
Appeared for sentence in Custody	11.20	.22	.0000	11.08	.21	.0000
Main Charge Not Proceeded with	-3.27	-.05	.0074	-3.28	-.05	.0070
No. of Offences taken into consideration[35]	2.14	.05	.0060	2.19	.05	.0048
No. & Type of Offences Found Guilty[36]	1.18	.13	.0000	1.18	.13	.0000
Sole Offender	-2.08	-.04	.0365	-2.00	-.04	.0442
Violence used in most and less serious offence	3.57	.06	.0092	3.48	.05	.0112
Violence was not due to a Dispute	10.42	.17	.0000	10.65	.17	.0000
Weapon used–Firearm/Knife	12.07	.16	.0000	12.11	.16	.0000
Weapon used to threaten	-3.82	-.04	.0332	-3.70	-.04	.0392
Violence caused Internal Injuries	14.10	.09	.0000	13.85	.09	.0000

[35] See *supra* footnote, note 16.
[36] See *supra* footnote, note 17.

VARIABLE	ORIGINAL			ADDING RACE		
	Coeff.	Beta	Sig T	Coeff.	Beta	Sig T
Evidence of Continuing Impairment	7.84	.09	.0000	8.08	.09	.0000
Value of Property Stolen[37]	2.31	.12	.0000	2.28	.12	.0000
Offence was Planned/Premeditated	3.76	.07	.0002	3.73	.07	.0002
Victim(s)—Female/Male&Female	5.18	.09	.0000	5.11	.08	.0000
No Social Inquiry Report	1.68	.03	.0973	1.69	.03	.0955
Did not give evidence against other(s)	2.46	.04	.0372	2.40	.04	.0419
No evidence that Offender was provoked	6.27	.07	.0005	6.36	.07	.0005
Previous Sex Offences	6.06	.05	.0030	6.15	.05	.0026
No. of Previous Offences of Dishonesty[38]	-2.29	-.08	.0003	-2.18	-.07	.0007
Total No. of months Prev. Sentenced to Prison[39]	1.42	.10	.0000	1.49	.10	.0000
Not Triable Either-Way Case	6.61	.13	.0000	6.67	.13	.0000
Seriousness of Drug Offence[40]	6.84	.20	.0000	6.90	.20	.0000
Convicted of Sex Offence	6.32	.06	.0101	6.22	.05	.0114
Convicted of Blackmail/Robbery/Kidnap	10.72	.13	.0000	10.59	.12	.0000
Convicted of Severe Violence	18.12	.23	.0000	17.75	.23	.0000
Convicted of Household Burglary	3.78	.05	.0078	3.75	.05	.0083
Asian Offender	******	****	*****	3.57	.04	.0414
Black Offender	******	****	*****	-.46	-.01	.6847

[37] See *supra* footnote, note 18.

[38] Grouped in the following levels: None; One; 2 or more.

[39] Grouped in the following levels: 1–6 months; 7–12 months; 13–24 months; 25–61 months.

[40] Weighted by small, medium or large scale of supplying drugs and whether in main and/or lesser offence.

TABLE 4

LENGTH OF CUSTODY FOR MALES UNDER AGE 21 (MONTHS)

Outcome Variable: length of custody (detention in a Young Offenders Institution)

859   Weighted Observations

VARIABLE	Adj. R² = .46 ORIGINAL			Adj R² = .46 ADDING RACE		
	Coeff.	Beta	Sig T	Coeff	Beta	Sig T
Constant	-6.04		.0519	-6.12		.0508
Age at time of sentence[41]	5.27	.10	.0003	5.27	.10	.0003
Appeared for sentence in Custody	2.89	.11	.0003	2.88	.11	.0003
Total No. of Offences Charged	1.84	.13	.0000	1.85	.13	.0000
Most Serious Charge Proceeded with	2.68	.10	.0010	2.69	.10	.0010
No. of Offences taken into consideration	1.69	.10	.0005	1.68	.10	.0006
Property was forfeited/confiscated/destroyed	2.53	.06	.0361	2.54	.06	.0356
Violence was due to a dispute	-4.88	-.13	.0000	-4.89	-.13	.0000
Weapon used-Firearm/Knife	3.00	.09	.0041	3.00	.09	.0046
Stolen Property was recovered	-2.67	-.10	.0009	-2.67	-.10	.0009
Value of Property Stolen	2.67	.23	.0000	2.69	.23	.0000
Major Injured Party-Family	6.29	.06	.0280	6.34	.06	.0276
Major Injured Party-Stranger	3.64	.13	.0000	3.62	.13	.0000
Married	-2.74	-.05	.0441	-2.75	-.05	.0444
History of Mental/Emotional illness	4.04	.06	.0262	4.08	.06	.0253

[41] Grouped in the following way: 14–16, 17–20.

VARIABLE	ORIGINAL			ADDING RACE		
	Coeff.	Beta	Sig T	Coeff	Beta	Sig T
Total No. of Previous Offences	1.41	.08	.0046	1.41	.08	.0061
No. of Previous Sex Offences	5.98	.08	.0038	5.91	.07	.0045
Previously served Borstal/YOI sentence	3.30	.11	.0001	3.30	.11	.0001
Offender elected for Trial	-6.20	-.11	.0004	-6.16	-.11	.0005
Magistrates Committed for Trial	-6.51	-.25	.0000	-6.50	-.25	.0000
Convicted of Sex Against Female	6.56	.08	.0060	6.57	.08	.0060
Convicted of Blackmail/Rob/Kidnap	2.17	.07	.0688	2.14	.07	.0750
Convicted of Severe Violence	13.16	.27	.0000	13.15	.27	.0000
Convicted of Burglary/theft	-4.30	-.13	.0000	-4.31	-.13	.0000
Convicted of Fraud/Receiving	-4.70	-.05	.0499	-4.71	-.05	.0502
Black Offender	*****	****	*****	.26	.007	.7867
Asian Offender	*****	****	*****	.15	.003	.8954

REFERENCES

ALIBHAI YASMIN, "How the Legal System Treats Blacks", *New Statesman and Society*, (8 July 1988), 34

ALLEN HILARY, *Justice Unbalanced: Gender, Psychiatry and Judicial Decisions*, (1987), Open University Press

ASHWORTH ANDREW, *Sentencing and Penal Policy*, (1983), Weidenfeld and Nicolson (new edition, *Sentencing and Criminal Justice*, 1992)

ASHWORTH ANDREW, GENDERS ELAINE, MANSFIELD GRAHAM, PEAY JILL and PLAYER ELAINE, *Sentencing in the Crown Court: Report of an Exploratory Study*, (1984), University of Oxford, Centre for Criminological Research, Occasional Paper No. 10

BALDUS DAVID C, WOODWORTH GEORGE W and PULASKI JR CHARLES A, *Equal Justice and the Death Penalty: A Legal and Empirical Analysis* (1989), NorthEastern University Press

BISHOP DONNA M and FRAZER CHARLES E, "The Difference of Race in Juvenile Justice Processing", *J Research in Crime and Delinq*, (1988), 25, 242–263

BOTTOMS A E, "Delinquency Among Immigrants", *Race*, (1967), 8, 357–83

CARLEN PAT, "Criminal Women and Criminal Justice: The Limits to, and the Potential of, Feminist and Left Realist Perspectives", in Roger Matthews and Jock Young (eds.), *Issues in Realist Criminology* (1992), 51–69, Sage Publications

CARLEN PAT, *Women, Crime and Poverty*, (1988), Open University Press

COMMISSION FOR RACIAL EQUALITY, *Ethnic Minorities in Britain: Statistical Information on the Pattern of Settlement*, (1985)

COMMISSION FOR RACIAL EQUALITY, *Response to the Home Office White Paper: Crime Justice, and Protecting the Public* (1989)

COMMISSION FOR RACIAL EQUALITY, *Review of the Race Relations Act*, [1991]

CROW IAN and COVE JILL, *Ethnic Minorities and the Courts*, Criminal Law Review (1984), 413–417

DALY KATHLEEN, "Neither Conflict Nor Labeling Nor Paternalism Will Suffice: Intersections of Race, Ethnicity, Gender and Family in Criminal Court Decisions" *Crime and Delinquency*, (1989), 35, 136–168

DAY MICHAEL, "Naught for our Comfort", *Black People and the Criminal Justice System*, Howard League, (May 1989), 5–8

EATON MARY, *Justice for Women? Family, Court and Social Control*, (1986), Open University Press

FARRINGTON DAVID and MORRIS ALLISON, "Sex, Sentencing and Reconviction", *Brit J Criminol*, (1983), **23**, 229–248

FITZGERALD MARIAN, *Ethnic Minorities and the Criminal Justice System in the UK: Research Issues*, Paper presented at the British Criminology Conference, York, (July 1991)

GARDNER JOHN, "Section 20 of the Race Relations Act 1976: 'Facilities' and 'Services'", *Modern Law Review*, (1987), 50, 345–353

GENDERS ELAINE and PLAYER ELAINE, *Race Relations in Prisons*, (1989), Oxford University Press

HARVARD LAW REVIEW, "Race and the Criminal Process", (1988), **101**, 1472–1641

HASKEY JOHN, "The Ethnic minority populations resident in private households – estimates by county and metropolitan district of England and Wales", *Population Trends*, (Spring 1991), No. **63**, 22–35

HEDDERMAN CAROL, "Custody Decisions for Property Offenders in the Crown Court", *Howard J*, (1991), **30**, 207–217

HEDDERMAN CAROL and MOXON DAVID, *Magistrates' Court or Crown Court? Mode of Trial Decisions and Sentencing*, (1992), Home Office Research Study No. **125**, H.M.S.O.

HEIDENSOHN FRANCES, "Women and Crime in Europe" in F Heidensohn and M Farrell (eds.), *Crime in Europe*, (1991), 55–71, Routledge

HOLMES MALCOLM D, DAUDISTEL HOWARD C and FARRELL RONALD A, "Determinants of Charge Reductions and Final Dispositions in Cases of Burglary and Robbery", *J Research in Crime and Delinq*, (1987), **24**, 233–254

HOME OFFICE, *The Ethnic Origin of Prisoners: The Prison Population on June 30 1985 and Persons Received July 1984 – March 1985*, Statistical Bulletin 17/86 (1986)

HOOD ROGER and SPARKS RICHARD, *Key Issues in Criminology*, (1970), Weidenfeld and Nicolson, Chapter 5

HOOD ROGER, *Sentencing in Magistrates' Courts*, (1962), Stevens

HOOD ROGER, *Sentencing and Motoring Offender* (1972), Heinemann

Hood, Roger, *The Death Penalty: A World-Wide Perspective* Clarendon Press, Chapter 5

HUDSON BARBARA, "Discrimination and Disparity: The Influence of Race on Sentencing", *New Community*, (1989), **16**, 23-34

JEFFERSON TONY and WALKER MONICA, "Ethnic Minorities in the Criminal Justice System", *Criminal Law Review*, (1992), 83–95

JUDICIAL STUDIES BOARD, *Report for 1987–1991*, H.M.S.O., 1992

KATZ MARJORIE S, "Race, Ethnicity and Determinate Sentencing", *Criminology*, (1984), **22**, 147–171

KATZ MARJORIE S, "The Changing Forms of Racial/Ethnic Biases in Sentencing", *J Research in Crime and Delinq*, (1987), **24**, 69–92

KLEIN STEPHEN, PETERSILIA JOAN and TURNER SUSAN, "Race and Imprisonment Decisions in California", *Science*, (16 February 1990), **247**, 812–816

MADEN A, SWINTON M, and GUNN J, "The Ethnic Origin of Women Serving a Prison Sentence", *Brit J Criminol*, (1992), **32**, 218–221

MAIR GEORGE, "Ethnic Minorities, Probation and Magistrates' Courts", *Brit J Criminol*, (1986), **26**, 147–155

MAIR GEORGE (ed.), *Risk Prediction and Probation*, Research and Planning Unit Paper 56 (1989), Home Office

MCCONVILLE MICHAEL and BALDWIN JOHN, "The Influence of Race on Sentencing in England", *Criminal Law Review*, (1982), 652–658

MORRIS ALLISON, *Women, Crime and Criminal Justice*, (1987), Blackwell

MORRIS NORVAL, "Race and Crime: What Evidence is there that Race Influences Results in the Criminal Justice System?", *Judicature*, (Aug–Sept 1988), **72**, No. 2, 111–113

MOXON DAVID, *Sentencing Practice in the Crown Court*, 1988, Home Office Research Study No. 103, H.M.S.O.

MUIR KATE, "Black look at white justice", *The Times*, 15 May 1992

MYERS MARTHA A and TALARICO SUSETTE M, "The Social Contexts of Racial Discrimination in Sentencing", *Social Problems*, (1986), **33**, 236–251

NACRO, *A Fresh Start for Women Prisoners: The Implications of the Woolf Report for Women*, (1986)

NACRO, *Race and Criminal Justice: A Way Forward*, Conference Report, (3 March 1989)

NAGEL ILENE H, "Sex Differences in the Processing of Criminal Defendants" in A. Morris (ed.), *Women and Crime*, (1981), 104–124, Institute of Criminology, University of Cambridge

NAGEL ILENE H and HAGAN JOHN, "Gender and Crime: Offense Patterns and Criminal Court Sanctions" in M Tonry and N Morris (eds.), *Crime and Justice: An Annual Review of Research*, Vol 4 (1983), Univ. Chicago Press, 91–144

NAGEL STUART and NEEF MARIAN, "Racial Disparities that Supposedly do not Exist: Some Pitfalls in Analysis of Court Records", *Notre Dame Lawyer*, (1976), **52**, 87–94

ODUBEKUN LOLA, "A Structural Approach to Differential Gender Sentencing", *Criminal Justice Abstracts*, (June 1992), 343–360

PETERSILIA JOAN and TURNER SUSAN, *Guideline–Based Justice: The Implications for Racial Minorities*, (1985), Rand Corporation

PETERSILIA JOAN, *Racial Disparities in the Criminal justice System*, (1983), Rand Corporation

REINER ROBERT, "Race and Criminal Justice", *New Community*, (1989), **16**, 5–21

RILEY DAVID and VENNARD JULIE, *Triable-Either-Way Cases: Crown Court or Magistrates' Court*, 1988, Home Office Research Study No. 98, H.M.S.O.

ROBERTSHAW PAUL, *Rethinking Legal Need: The Case of Criminal Justice*, Dartmouth Books, Aldershot, (1991)

ROSE, DAVID, "Acts but no real faith", *The Guardian*, 13 June 1990

RUNNEYMEDE TRUST, *Racial Justice and Criminal Justice: A Submission to the Royal Commission on Criminal Justice*, (1992)

SEEAR N and PLAYER E, *Women in the Penal System*, (1986), Howard League for Penal Reform

SELLIN THORSTEN, *Culture Conflict and Crime*, (1938), New York, Social Science Research Council, Bulletin No. **41**

SHALICE, A and GORDON P, *Black People, White Justice?*, Runneymede Trust, (1990)

SKOGAN WESLEY, *The Police and Public in England and Wales: A British Crime Survey Report*, Home Office Research Study, No. **117**, H.M.S.O.

SMITH DAVID J and GRAY JEREMY, *Police and People in London*, The Policy Studies Institute Report, (1985), Gower

SMITH SUSAN, *The Politics of 'Race' and Residence*, (1989), Polity Press

SPOHN CASSIA, GRUHL JOHN and WELCH SUSAN, "The Effect of Race on Sentencing: A Re-Examination of an Unsettled Question", *Law & Society Review*, (1981–82), **16**, 71–88

STEVENS P and WILLIS C F, *Race, Crime and Arrests*, Home Office Research Study No. **58**, (1979), H.M.S.O.

TARLING ROGER, *Sentencing Practice in Magistrates' Courts*, Home Office Research Study, No. **56**, (1979)

THOMAS D A (ed.), *Current Sentencing Practice*, (1983, continuing), Sweet and Maxwell

UNNEVER JAMES D and HEMBROFF LARRY A, "The Prediction of Racial/Ethnic Sentencing Disparities: An Expectation States Approach", *J Research in Crime & Delinq.*, (1988), **25**, 53–82

VOAKES ROB and FOWLER QUENTIN, *Sentencing, Race and Social Enquiry Reports*, West Yorkshire Probation Service, (1989)

WALKER MONICA, "Interpreting Race and Crime Statistics", *J Royal Statistical Society Series A (General)*, (1982), **150** Part 1, 39–56

WALKER MONICA, "The Court Disposal and Remands of White, Afro-

Caribbean and South Asian Men (London 1983)", *Brit J Criminol*, (1983), **29**, 353–367

WALKER MONICA, JEFFERSON TONY and SENEVIRATNE MARY, *Race and Criminal Justice in the Inner City*, Report to the ESRC, (1990)

WALKER NIGEL, "Feminists' Extravaganzas", *Criminal Law Review*, (1981), 379–386

WASIK M and TAYLOR R D, *Blackstone's Guide to the Criminal Justice Act 1991*, (1991), Blackstone Press

WATERS ROBERT, "Race and the Criminal Justice Process", *Brit J Criminol*, (1988), **28**, 82–94

WATERS ROBERT, *Ethnic Minorities and the Criminal Justice System* (1990), Avebury

WELCH SUSAN, GRUHL JOHN, and SPOHN CASSIA, "Sentencing: The Influence of Alternative Measures of Prior Record", *Criminology*, (1984), **22**, 215–227

WEST MIDLANDS PROBATION SERVICE, *Report on the Birmingham Court Social Enquiry Monitoring Exercise* (February 1987)

WOLFGANG MARVIN E and COHEN BERNARD, *Crime and Race: Conceptions and Misconceptions* (1970), New York: Institute of Human Relations Press